Gallica

Volume 9

PHILIPPE DE VIGNEULLES AND THE ART OF PROSE TRANSLATION

Over fifty chansons de geste were reworked into prose between the fourteenth and sixteenth centuries for patrons and audiences who demanded updated, de-rhymed versions of heroic songs. While most prose translations were commissioned by noble patrons, Philippe de Vigneulles (1471–1527), a cloth merchant of Metz, operated outside the system of patronage, on self-imposed projects with a pronounced civic bias. His translation of the monumental Lorraine epic cycle into Middle French prose afforded him an opportunity to reconfigure the city's legendary past and validate the concerns of a prosperous merchant class.

The craft of *mise en prose* is examined in the context of the author's larger cultural agenda as he weaves the epic legend into his civic, personal and aesthetic preoccupations. This perspective illuminates a previously neglected sphere of medieval literary production, revealing fundamental assumptions about the epic tradition and the power of prose in urban culture.

CATHERINE M. JONES is Associate Professor of French and Provençal at the University of Georgia.

Gallica

ISSN 1749–091X

General Editor: Sarah Kay

Gallica aims to provide a forum for the best current work in medieval French studies. Literary studies are particularly welcome and preference is given to works written in English, although publication in French is not excluded.

Proposals or queries should be sent in the first instance to the editor, or to the publisher, at the addresses given below; all submissions receive prompt and informed consideration.

Professor Sarah Kay, Department of French and Italian, Princeton University, 303 East Pyne, Princeton, NJ 08544, USA
The Managing Editor, Gallica, Boydell & Brewer Ltd., PO Box 9, Woodbridge, Suffolk IP12 3DF, UK

Already Published
1. *Postcolonial Fictions in the 'Roman de Perceforest': Cultural Identities and Hybridities*, Sylvia Huot
2. *A Discourse for the Holy Grail in Old French Romance*, Ben Ramm
3. *Fashion in Medieval France*, Sarah-Grace Heller
4. *Christine de Pizan's Changing Opinion: A Quest for Certainty in the Midst of Chaos*, Douglas Kelly
5. *Cultural Performances in Medieval France: Essays in Honor of Nancy Freeman Regalado*, eds Eglal Doss-Quinby, Roberta L. Krueger, E. Jane Burns
6. *The Medieval Warrior Aristocracy: Gifts, Violence, Performance, and the Sacred*, Andrew Cowell
7. *Logic and Humour in the Fabliaux: An Essay in Applied Narratology*, Roy J. Pearcy
8. *Miraculous Rhymes: The Writing of Gautier de Coinci*, Tony Hunt

PHILIPPE DE VIGNEULLES
AND THE ART OF PROSE TRANSLATION

Catherine M. Jones

D. S. BREWER

First published 2008
D. S. Brewer, Cambridge

ISBN 978–1–84384–158–6

D. S. Brewer is an imprint of Boydell & Brewer Ltd
PO Box 9, Woodbridge, Suffolk IP12 3DF, UK
and of Boydell & Brewer Inc.
668 Mt Hope Avenue, Rochester, NY 14620, USA
website: www.boydellandbrewer.com

A catalogue record for this title is available
from the British Library

This publication is printed on acid-free paper

Printed in Great Britain by
Antony Rowe Ltd, Chippenham, Wiltshire

CONTENTS

For my parents,
Ron and Mary Beth Jones

ACKNOWLEDGEMENTS

This project could not have been completed without strong institutional support from the University of Georgia. A grant from the University of Georgia Research Foundation supported travel to collections in Brussels and Paris, and the Willson Center for Humanities and Arts provided a book subvention grant. I am indebted to the following libraries for the opportunity to consult manuscript and print sources: the Bibliothèque Nationale de France, the Bibliothèque de l'Arsenal, the Koninklijke Bibliotheek/Bibliothèque Royale de Belgique in Brussels, the Library of Congress, and the Libraries of the University of Georgia and the University of Wisconsin. I particularly wish to thank Ms. Gill Cannell of the Parker Library, Corpus Christi College, Cambridge, for her invaluable assistance in the consultation of the only surviving manuscript of Philippe de Vigneulles's prose epic, currently on loan through the generosity of the James E. and Elizabeth J. Ferrell Collection.

I am grateful to Peggy McCracken and Cathy Sanok for inviting me to present my work on Philippe de Vigneulles at the University of Michigan Medieval Seminar in the fall of 2005. The questions arising from these challenging discussions allowed me to clarify my thinking on the *mise en prose* and its accompanying authorial interventions. Norris Lacy tirelessly provided guidance and wisdom, especially during the final stages of the project. Other medievalists have been generous in responding to my requests for information: Keith Busby, Bernard Guidot, Jean-Charles Herbin, Maureen Boulton, Sophie Marnette, William Kibler, Leslie Zarker Morgan, and most of all Douglas Kelly, who cheerfully continues to mentor his students long after the statute of limitations has expired.

It has truly been a pleasure to work with Boydell & Brewer. I thank Sarah Kay, Editor of the Gallica Series, for her tact and expertise in resolving thorny problems during the revision process. I am deeply grateful to the anonymous evaluator, whose meticulous report led to numerous corrections and improvements. Every author should be fortunate enough to collaborate with a Managing Editor like Ellie Ferguson, whose efficiency and kindness are unparalleled.

My colleagues at the University of Georgia are an unending source of moral and scholarly support. Space does not allow me to thank all of them here, but I do wish to acknowledge Diana Ranson, Jan Pendergrass, Francis

Assaf, Noel Fallows, Doris Kadish, Jean-Pierre Piriou, Betty Jean Craige, Elizabeth Wright, Joel Walz, Nina Hellerstein, Sarah Spence, and Debbie Bell. I am particularly indebted to Jonathan Krell, who read and critiqued portions of the study, and Jerry Daniel and Jeff Clippard, who offered crucial technical assistance. I benefited greatly from discussions with my students, who tackled difficult readings in Middle French and came to share my enthusiasm for Philippe de Vigneulles. My daughter Sophie provided unfailing inspiration and a sense of comic perspective. It is impossible to express my gratitude to my husband Richard, a rigorous but most gentle reader and listener. Finally, I thank my parents, Ron and Mary Beth Jones, for their enduring confidence in all of my endeavors. This book is dedicated to them.

1

Introduction:
Philippe de Vigneulles and
the Late Medieval *mise en prose*

By his own account, Philippe de Vigneulles was born on a Friday in June, around Pentecost, in the year 1471.[1] He was a native of the hamlet of Vigneulles, situated approximately thirty-five kilometers from Metz. Much of our information about his life comes from his *Journal*, in which he relates his humble origins, his youthful *errances*, his eventual establishment as a cloth merchant in Metz, and his participation in the rich economic and cultural life of that thriving city.[2] Philippe's formal education was apparently sketchy and intermittent. He learned to read and write at the village school, but regrets that his parents did not send him away for further instruction, an omission he attributes to their fond attachment to him. He briefly attended several other monastic and village schools, and as an adolescent was placed in Metz with an *aman* (an official charged with preserving parish contracts) to learn "le stille," but this arrangement was abruptly terminated owing to the master's cruelty (*Journal* 12–13).[3]

At the age of fifteen, against his father's wishes, Philippe began a five-year odyssey to broaden his knowledge of the world. Traveling on foot with little money to his name, he went first to Geneva, where he spent a year in

---

[1]   Pentecost fell on June 2 in 1471, which suggests that Philippe was likely born on the following Friday, June 7.

[2]   *Gedenkbuch des Metzer Bürgers Philippe von Vigneulles aus den Jahren 1471 bis 1522*, ed. Heinrich Michelant (1852; Amsterdam: Rodopi, 1968). Philippe himself did not provide a title for this work, and it is difficult to classify, as it combines elements of the journal, the memoir, and the chronicle. For the sake of simplicity, I adopt the solution chosen by most modern scholars, who refer to the text as the *Journal*. See also the recent translation into German, *Das Journal des Philippe de Vigneulles: Aufzeichnungen eines Metzer Bürgers (1471–1522)*, trans. Waltraud and Eduard Schuh (Saarbrücken: Conte Verlag, 2005).

[3]   On Philippe's education and professional training, see Pierre Demarolle, "La Place des apprentissages dans la littérature et dans la vie d'après l'oeuvre de Philippe de Vigneulles," *La Transmission du savoir dans l'Europe des XVIe et XVIIe siècles*, ed. Marie Roig Miranda (Paris: Champion, 2000), 13–26.

the service of a canon. Philippe claims that this master encouraged him to develop his budding artistic talents. Impressed with the boy's paintings and other subtle works of art, the canon offered to establish him as a silversmith or other sort of craftsman, but Philippe was impatient to continue his travels (*Journal* 19). After a brief visit to Rome, he proceeded to Naples, where he worked as a valet over a period of three and a half years. While serving a number of different masters, the youth journeyed across southern Italy. He learned to play the rebec during a week-long wedding feast:

> la firent molt grant chière une semaine tout entiere, car son maistre juoit des instruments avec ceulx du roy et apernoit le dit Phelippe à jower du rebecque et les faixoit luy meisme, dont son maistre l'amoit bien pour sa subtilité et aussy luy faixoit biaulcop d'avantaiges. (*Journal* 28)[4]

> [there they celebrated merrily for an entire week, for his master played instruments with the king's men, and Philippe learned to play the rebec and made them himself, for which his master liked him well, appreciating his skill, and he also gave him special treatment.][5]

After returning to Metz, Philippe was apprenticed to a cloth merchant. His initial training was, however, interrupted by grave misfortune. Metz was at the time embroiled in conflict with the duchy of Lorraine, which conducted periodic raids in the hopes of annexing the city to its domain. Caught in the crossfire, Philippe and his father were abducted by bandits associated with the duke of Lorraine and held for ransom under the harshest of conditions. The crime is recounted in detail in Philippe's *Journal*, and corroborated by archival evidence.[6] During his fourteen-month captivity, Philippe claims to have scavenged enough paper and coal to compose two poems lamenting his

----

[4] Although much of the *Journal* is written in the first person, this portion depicts the author's adventures in the third person. This is a problem to which we shall return in Chapter 4.

[5] All translations from Old and Middle French are my own. In order to highlight certain stylistic features of the medieval texts, the translations are fairly literal, retaining such traits as the historic present and synonymic doubling. The resulting passages are thus somewhat "foreignizing," but are intended only to facilitate access to the originals.

[6] The document, identified in a modern hand as "Déposition comment Jean Gérard, maire de Vigneulle, et Philippe son fils, ont été nuitamment enlevés de leur maison, et livrés aux Lorrains. 1490," is part of the *Collection Emmery sur l'histoire de Metz* (II: 1451–1500), BnF nouv. acq. fr. 22660, fol. 153r. See Charles Bruneau, *La Chronique de Philippe de Vigneulles* (Metz: Société d'histoire et d'archéologie de la Lorraine, 1927), Introduction, I: v, note 1. The text is given by Michelant in the appendices to Philippe's *Journal*, 377–79. On Philippe's account of his experience as a hostage, see Philippe Contamine, "Autobiographie d'un prisonnier-otage: Philippe de Vigneulles au Château de Chauvency," *Les Prisonniers de guerre dans l'Histoire: Contacts entre peuples et cultures*, ed. Sylvie Caucanas, Rémy Cazals and Pascal Payen (Toulouse: Privat, 2003), 39–46.

plight as well as three religious pieces or "oresons," one to the Virgin Mary, one to Saint Nicholas, and one to Saint Barbara (*Journal* 75).[7]

This difficult period was followed by a time of relative calm and prosperity, as Philippe settled into family life and established himself in the textile trade. He specialized in the fabrication of *chausses*, or men's garments worn below the waist.[8] He traveled frequently to fairs, particularly the celebrated Lendit fair in Saint-Denis, and undertook various pilgrimages. Philippe eventually became one of the wealthiest merchants in Metz, and devoted his leisure time to artistic, theatrical and literary pursuits. In 1507, he produced an elaborate mosaic fabric, accompanied by texts in verse and prose, which he displayed in front of the cathedral on St. Mark's feast day.[9] He continued to play the rebec, financed and participated in dramatic presentations, and is credited with a number of drawings.[10]

In light of his active role as merchant and citizen, Philippe's literary production is nothing short of astonishing. While he occasionally dabbled in poetry, his preferred medium was prose, as demonstrated by his four major narrative works:

1. The *Chronique de Metz, de Lorraine et de France*, a chronicle of events from the beginning of the world through 1525, focusing primarily on the author's beloved city of Metz. The text occupies four volumes in Charles Bruneau's modern edition. Bruneau's base manuscript, Metz 838–840, perished in the 1944 fire that destroyed forty per cent of the manuscripts held by the Bibliothèque Municipale de Metz. Four manuscripts are extant:

---

[7] The two *complaintes* are reproduced in the *Journal* (70–75, 132–34) and the *Chronique* (III: 215–20; III: 250–52). The *Journal* specifies that the second was composed partly in prison, partly in Metz (134). Both the *complaintes* and the *oraisons* are found in BnF nouv. acqu. fr. 3374, and the latter have been edited by V.-L. Saulnier: "Philippe de Vigneulles rimeur de fêtes, de saints et de prisons (avec ses poésies inédites, 1491)," *Mélanges d'histoire littéraire, de linguistique et de philologie romanes offertes à Charles Rostaing*, ed. Jacques de Caluwe et al. (Liège: Association des Romanistes de l'U de Liège, 1974), II, 965–91.

[8] See Pierre Demarolle, *La Chronique de Philippe de Vigneulles et la mémoire de Metz* (Caen: Paradigme, 1993), 11.

[9] Philippe inserted the verse compositions into his *Journal*, 154–55.

[10] Philippe included in his *Journal* (201) and his *Chronique* (IV: 106) the text of two quatrains he composed for a dramatic presentation during the Carnival season in 1512. The drawings attributed to Philippe are reproduced in the *Chronique*: I, frontispiece; I: 78 bis; II: 420 bis. One of the drawings, which depicts Philippe at his writer's desk with the city of Metz in the background, is also reproduced by Charles Livingston as the frontispiece of his edition of Philippe's *Cent Nouvelles Nouvelles* (Travaux d'Humanisme et Renaissance 120, Geneva: Droz, 1972). See Jean-Charles Herbin, "Notice du manuscrit *h* de la Prose des Loherains par Philippe de Vigneulles," *Romania* 117 (1999): 218–244, for a brief comparison of these drawings with the miniatures that adorn MS h of the *mise en prose* (esp. 236–237).

Archives départementales de la Moselle 2 F 1, Épinal 139–141 (formerly 34), BnF nouv. acq. fr. 3374, and BnF nouv. acq. fr. 6687.[11]

2. A *Journal* of his life, which Heinrich Michelant published in 1852 under the title *Gedenkbuch des Metzer Bürgers Philippe von Vigneulles aus den Jahren 1471 bis 1522*. The *Journal* relates not only the author's own experiences, but also events of broader historical significance (such as the wars in Italy) as well as various *faits divers* occurring in and around Metz. Much of this historical and autobiographical material is reproduced in the *Chronique*. The *Journal* survives in one manuscript, BnF nouv. acq. fr. 6720, generally considered to be written in Philippe's own hand.[12]

3. *Cent Nouvelles Nouvelles*, a collection of novellas in the manner of (but distinct from) the mid fifteenth-century Burgundian work. In the Prologue, Philippe says that he began the book in 1505, during a lengthy and debilitating illness:

> car de mes membres ne me povoie encor bien aidier pour ouvrer ne besongner, je me mis lors à escrire pluseurs adventures, advenues la pluspart tant à la noble cité de Mets comme au pays environ. (57)

> [because I could not yet use my limbs to labor or work, I began at that time to write several adventures, most of which had occurred in the noble city of Metz or in the surrounding area.]

According to the *Journal* and the *Chronique*, an initial collection of one hundred tales was completed in the summer of 1515 (*Journal* 283; *Chronique* IV: 198). The final version, however, contains evidence of 110 novellas, so it appears that ten were added after that date. Many of the novellas are mutilated or missing entirely in the sole surviving manuscript, Metz 1521, edited by Charles Livingston in 1972. The extant stories, many of which have their analogues in folklore, exempla, fabliaux, and the Italian novella, adapt traditional narrative motifs to the cityscape of Metz.[13]

---

[11] Bruneau, Introduction, xx–xxi; Pierre Demarolle, "A propos d'annotations de Philippe de Vigneulles: Comment travaillait le chroniqueur messin?" *Cahiers lorrains* 1 (1989): 3–10. Of the four manuscripts, only Epinal 34 is complete, and two of its three volumes are modern copies.

[12] Bruneau considered the *Journal* to be a partial draft of the *Chronique*. The *Journal*, as it appears in the sole extant manuscript, is poorly executed, contains numerous corrections, and stops abruptly in the year 1520, with a few lacunary notations for 1522. Bruneau's edition of the *Chronique* is based on manuscript Metz 838–840, which he considered to be a "mise au point définitive"; moreover, the *Chronique* relates events up to the beginning of 1526. See Bruneau, Introduction, xiii–xv. On the problem of autograph manuscripts, see Pierre Demarolle, "A propos d'annotations de Philippe de Vigneulles."

[13] On the sources and analogues of the *Cent Nouvelles Nouvelles*, see the excellent introduction by Charles Livingston, 31–51.

4. A prose translation of the Lorraine epic cycle, largely unedited to date, containing versions of all four branches of the monumental *geste*. The original verse texts are as follows, according to their conventional modern French titles.[14] *Garin le Lorrain*, the core of the cycle, was composed in the late twelfth century and relates the bitter conflict between two feudal houses, the worthy "Loherains" (led by Garin and Begon) and the treacherous "Bordelais." The first continuation (*Gerbert de Metz*, ca. 1200), recounts the perpetuation of the war by the sons of Garin and Begon. Another early thirteenth-century continuation, *Hervis de Metz*, extends the *geste* back in time to depict the early adventures of the Lorraine heroes' father, whose later exploits and death had been related in the first part of *Garin le Lorrain*. The fourth branch survives in two versions, the shorter *Vengeance Fromondin* (late thirteenth century) and the lengthier redaction *Anseÿs de Metz* or *Anseÿs de Gascogne* (late thirteenth century); there is evidence of a lost verse poem entitled *Yonnet de Metz*.[15] The Lorraine cycle enjoyed tremendous success throughout the Middle Ages. The verse epic is preserved in over fifty manuscripts and fragments, including a translation into Middle Dutch. The cycle was also the object of two other prose redactions, both dating from the mid-fifteenth century: the anonymous *Prose de l'Arsenal*, and the anonymous *Histoire de Charles Martel* copied by David Aubert.[16]

---

[14] These modern titles will be used for general references to the poems. Quotations and references from critical editions will follow the titles of these editions.

[15] *Garin le Loherenc*, ed. Anne Iker-Gittleman, 3 vols. (Paris: Champion, 1996); *Gerbert de Mez: Chanson de geste du XIIe siècle*, ed. Pauline Taylor, Bibliothèque de la Faculté de Philosophie et de Lettres de Namur 11 (Namur, Lille, Louvain: Nauwelaerts, 1953); *Hervis de Mes*, ed. Jean-Charles Herbin (Geneva: Droz, 1992); *La Vengeance Fromondin*, ed. Jean-Charles Herbin (Paris: S.A.T.F.; Abbeville: Paillart, 2005); *Anseÿs de Mes According to Ms. N (Bibliothèque de l'Arsenal 3143): Text, published for the first time in its entirety, with an Introduction*, ed. Herman J. Green (Paris: Les Presses modernes, 1939). Unless otherwise indicated, all references to and quotations from the cycle will be drawn from these editions. *Anseÿs* itself survives in two versions, the Green edition representing a shorter redaction. See Jean-Charles Herbin, "*Anseÿs de Gascogne* et la Flandre," *Picard d'hier et aujourd'hui*, *Bien dire et bien aprandre* 21 (Lille: Centre de Gestion et de l'Édition Scientifique, 2003), 207–228; Herbin proposes revising the conventional title *Anseÿs de Metz* with the more appropriate *Anseÿs de Gascogne*, since the hero never sets foot in Metz or in Lorraine. On the hypothetical *Yonnet de Metz*, see Jean-Charles Herbin, "*Yonnet de Metz*," *Les mises en prose*, Ateliers 35, UL3, année 2006 (Lille: CEGES, 2006), 31–45. For Herbin, this lost version, Philippe de Vigneulles's source, is the only "internal" conclusion to the cycle, the *Vengeance Fromondin* and *Anseÿs* having only tenuous links to the other poems. See his "L'Histoire otage des chansons de geste ou l'inverse – Le cas d'*Anseÿs de Gascogne* et de la *Vengeance Fromondin*," *Le Nord de la France entre épopée et chronique* (Arras: Artois Presses U, 2005), 239–65.

[16] The anonymous *Prose de l'Arsenal* has been edited: *La Mise en prose de la geste des Loherains dans le manuscrit Arsenal 3346*, ed. Jean-Charles Herbin (Valenciennes: PU de Valenciennes, 1995). *L'Histoire de Charles Martel et de ses successeurs*, KBR 6, 7, 8, and 9, is the object of a partial edition by Valérie Naudet: *Guerin le Loherain: Édition*

Philippe completed his *mise en prose* in 1515, the year in which he
finished the first version of his *Cent Nouvelles Nouvelles*.[17] Both the *Journal*
and the *Chronique* humbly record the double literary achievement among
other notable events of that summer, including poor fruit harvests, the fair
in Frankfurt, and the construction of windmills with tails along the Seille
river:

> Item, aussy en celle année, je, Phelippe, escripvains et facteurs de ces
> présente, translata et mis de anciennes rimes et rétoricque, c'on dit *chanson
> de geste*, en prose et par chapistre, le livre c'on dit *La belle Beaultris*, avec
> celluy du *Lorain Guérin et du duc Baigue de Bellin*, ces deux filz, et consé-
> quanment de toutte leur généalogie et dessandue. Et d'iceux en fis quaitre
> partie, comme chacun pourrait veoir à qui il plairait de les lire. Pareille-
> ment, en la meisme année, fis et composa ung aultre livre contenant cenc
> novelles ou contes joieulx. Lesquelles livres furent fait et eschevis en l'an
> dessus dis. Non pas que je die ou le mecte ycy estimant que ce soit chose
> digne de mémoire, ne de quoy l'on en doyve perler ne faire estime, mais
> seullement affin que en les lysant voustre plaisir soit de corrigier les faulte,
> quant aulcune en y trouvenrés. (*Chronique* IV: 198–99; cf. *Journal* 283)

> [Item, also in that year, I Philippe, writer and composer of the present work,
> translated and changed from ancient rhyme and verse, called *chanson de
> geste*, into prose, by chapters, the book called *La belle Beaultris*, along
> with the book of *Lorain Guerin and Duke Baigue de Bellin*, her two sons,
> and subsequently the story of their entire lineage and descendants. And I
> divided this material into four parts, as anyone who wishes to read them
> can see. Similarly, in the same year, I made and composed another book
> containing one hundred novellas or amusing tales. These books were made
> and completed in the year indicated above. I do not say or indicate this
> here because I think that it is a thing worth recalling or talking about or
> holding in high esteem, but only in order that in reading the books you
> might correct the errors, should you find any.]

*critique et commentaire par Valérie Naudet de la prose de David Aubert extraite des
Histoires de Charles Martel (manuscrit 7 de la Bibliothèque Royale de Belgique)* (Aix-en-
Provence: Publications de l'U de Provence, 2005). See Valérie Naudet, "Une Compilation
de David Aubert: *Les Histoires de Charles Martel*," *Les Manuscrits de David Aubert*, ed.
Danielle Quéruel, Cultures et civilisations médiévales 18 (Paris: CNRS-Paris IV, 1999),
69–79. Rubrics and excerpts from the manuscripts may be found in Richard E. F. Straub,
David Aubert, escripvain et clerc, Faux Titre 96 (Amsterdam & Atlanta: Rodopi, 1996),
51–59, 198–242. The work's title is misleading: MS 6 and the first fifty folios of MS 7
are devoted to a *mise en prose* of *Girart de Roussillon*, and the Lorraine epic occupies
the remaining volumes.

[17] He may have written *Yonnet* after this date. In the prologue to this last branch,
Philippe claims to have searched high and low for manuscripts providing the end of the
story (fol. 306r).

Two manuscripts of the *mise en prose* dating from Philippe's lifetime survived into the twentieth century. Metz 847 (*v*) burned in the 1944 fire. This document, which contained 325 folios, nonetheless survives in a microfilm produced by the MLA.[18] Although there is evidence of at least two different hands, *v* is considered an autograph manuscript.[19] A second version, known as the Hunolstein manuscript (*h*), is more elaborate and adorned with miniatures that were likely executed by Philippe himself. It has always been held in private collections and remained largely inaccessible to scholars during the last century. Now part of the James E. and Elizabeth J. Ferrell Collection, it is on temporary loan to the Parker Library, Corpus Christi College, Cambridge (Ferrell MS 6). Excerpts from this manuscript, including text of the rubrics and reproductions of the seven miniatures, were published in 1901 by Maurice de Pange.[20] Jean-Charles Herbin has convincingly demonstrated that *h* represents a revised version of *v*. Nonetheless, neither document represents the definitive text that Philippe clearly intended to produce, judging from the numerous corrections present in *h* that appear to be in the author's own hand.[21]

Philippe died in 1527 or 1528.[22] In succeeding centuries, he was known principally as a chronicler, and was cited most often in works devoted to the history of Metz and Lorraine.[23] Scholars generally classify him as a late medieval author, as his literary production appears untouched by Renaissance

[18] MLA 430F. See the *Catalogue des manuscrits relatifs à l'histoire de Metz et de la Lorraine* (Metz: F. Blanc, 1856), 75–76 and Jean-Charles Herbin, "La 'Translation en prose' de la Geste des Loherains, par Philippe de Vigneulles: Une (Re)trouvaille," *Romania* 109 (1988): 562–65. A partial transcription of Metz 847 executed by Edmund Stengel may be found in the "Collection Stengel" at the Université Catholique de Louvain. See Herbin, "La 'Translation,'" 563–64, note 7.

[19] Jean-Charles Herbin, "Approches de la mise en prose de la *geste des Loherains* par Philippe de Vigneulles," *Romania* 113 (1992–95): 470, note 12. This does not include folios 314r–325r, which were copied in a modern hand.

[20] *La Chanson de Garin le Loherain mise en prose par Philippe de Vigneulles de Metz, Table des chapitres avec les reproductions des miniatures d'après le manuscrit appartenant à M. le comte d'Hunolstein* (Paris: Leclerc, 1901). Although published anonymously, the book can be attributed without doubt to de Pange. See Herbin, "Notice du manuscrit *h*," 219, note 3. One of the seven miniatures reproduced in the 1901 edition is now missing from the manuscript.

[21] See Herbin, "Notice du manuscrit *h*," esp. 224.

[22] His name appears in a legal document in November 1527, and his wife is listed as a widow in 1528. See Marie Dorner, "Philippe de Vigneulles: un chroniqueur messin des XVe et XVIe siècles," *Mémoires de l'Académie de Metz* (1913–1914): 45–110, at p. 71.

[23] See Augustin Calmet, *Bibliothèque lorraine; ou Histoire des hommes illustres qui ont fleuri en Lorraine, dans les trois Évêchés, dans l'archevêché de Trèves, dans le duché de Luxembourg*, etc. (1751; Geneva: Slatkine Reprints, 1971), 1012–1013; Auguste Prost, *Études sur l'histoire de Metz: les légendes* (1865; Brionne: G. Monfort, diffusion le Portulan, 1972), 343, 399–400, 490, 499. Modern histories of the region continue to rely on Philippe's chronicle: see *Histoire de Metz*, ed. François-Yves Le Moigne, Univers de la France et des pays francophones (Toulouse: Privat, 1986), 197, 200, 212, 214.

humanism and the technology of printing.[24] Lacking the rhetorical training
and sophistication of clerkly writers, the autodidact of peasant ancestry has
not always fared well with commentators. In 1848, Théodore Joseph Boudet,
comte de Puymaigre, published a volume commemorating poets and "romanciers" from the Lorraine region. Drawing analogies between the political
history of Metz and Florence in the Middle Ages, the Lorraine historian
regrets that no such comparison can be made between the literary figures
of the two cities:

> Metz n'eut pas ce que Florence eut tant, elle fut privée de ces écrivains
> éminents dont le génie illumine le passé, poétise d'un vif reflet les événe-
> ments des temps anciens [...] Au lieu de Boccace et de Villani, elle a seule-
> ment Philippe de Vigneulle [...] Chez lui point d'étude, point d'art [...] il ne
> fait pas une oeuvre vraiment littéraire, il n'est pas un grand prosateur.[25]

Fortunately, Philippe's literary reputation has been somewhat rehabilitated
in recent decades. In particular, studies by Pierre Demarolle and Armine Kotin
have illuminated the writer's craft as chronicler and storyteller.[26] Only one
scholar has attempted a more comprehensive analysis of Philippe's corpus:
Jean-Pierre Mas's unpublished French dissertation situates the *Journal*, the

---

24 See Armine Kotin, *The Narrative Imagination: Comic Tales by Philippe de
Vigneulles* (Lexington: UP of Kentucky, 1977), 104; Jens Rasmussen, *La Prose narrative
française du XVe siècle, Étude esthétique et stylistique* (Copenhagen: Munksgaard, 1958),
15; and Demarolle, "Philippe de Vigneulles chroniqueur, Une manière d'écrire l'histoire,"
Revue des langues romanes 97 (1993): 57–73, at p. 58.

25 Théodore Joseph Boudet, comte de Puymaigre, *Poètes et romanciers de la Lorraine*
(Metz: Pallez et Rousseau, 1848), 315. Puymaigre does find limited merit in Philippe's
work, namely his accurate description of Metz as it existed in the Middle Ages (315–
16).

26 On the *Chronique*, see Pierre Demarolle, *La Chronique de Philippe de Vigneulles
et la mémoire de Metz*, and the following articles: "A propos d'annotations" and "Philippe
de Vigneulles Chroniqueur," cited above; "A la recherche des sources de Philippe de
Vigneulles. A propos d'un passage de sa *Chronique*: La découverte de Terre-Neuve," *Le
Moyen Âge* 100 (1994): 263–69; "La Mort dans l'univers mental de Philippe de Vigneulles
d'après le livre V de la *Chronique* (1500–1526)," in *La Mort en toutes lettres*, ed. Gilles
Ernst and Louis-Vincent Thomas (Nancy: PU de Nancy, 1983), 25–32; "Philippe de
Vigneulles et les tombeaux de la cathédrale de Metz," in *Regards sur le passé dans
l'Europe des XVIe et XVIIe siècles*, ed. Francine Wild (Berlin: Peter Lang, 1997), 173–81;
"Philippe de Vigneulles et le terroir messin," in *Provinces, régions, terroirs au moyen
âge: De la réalité à l'imaginaire*, ed. Bernard Guidot (Nancy: PU de Nancy, 1993),
143–51; "Tourments et inquiétudes dans le dernier livre de la Chronique de Philippe de
Vigneulles (1500–1526)," in *Tourments, doutes et ruptures dans l'Europe des XVIe et
XVIIe siècles*, ed. Claude Arnould and Pierre Demarolle (Paris: Champion, 1995), 21–30.
On the *Cent Nouvelles Nouvelles*, see Armine Kotin (now Armine Kotin Mortimer), *The
Narrative Imagination*. A recent volume on the novella contains a chapter on Philippe:
David LaGuardia, *The Iconography of Power: The French Nouvelle at the End of the
Middle Ages* (Newark: U of Delaware Press; London: Associated UP, 1999).

Chronique and the novellas in the social, material and ideological context of late fifteenth- and early sixteenth-century Metz.[27] The *mise en prose*, however, has received comparatively little critical attention. This neglect may be attributed to two factors: first, the marginalization of prose reworkings in general, and second, Philippe's peripheral status among late medieval prosifiers.

Until very recently, the *mises en prose* were largely overlooked by most medievalists, and most scholars who did examine the works summarily excluded them from the literary canon. Léon Gautier, who devoted sixty pages to the prose epic, nonetheless considered the texts decadent and mediocre, scarcely worthy of being edited.[28] Georges Doutrepont, who produced an invaluable catalogue and preliminary study of the *mises en prose*, is only slightly more forgiving. Doutrepont concedes that the reworkings played a role in the germination of the grand tradition of French prose. He finds them especially useful as historical documents that illuminate the social, intellectual, and moral climate of the waning Middle Ages as well as the content of lost epic poems. As literary works, however, they are said to have little value, as Doutrepont emphasizes in a section entitled "Le mal qu'il faut dire des proses considérées en tant qu'oeuvres littéraires":

> esthétiquement parlant, nous avons montré qu'à recevoir le lot, qu'on sait, de chansons de geste et de narrations romanesques remaniées, la France intellectuelle ne s'est pas enrichie de façon visible [....] Il eût fallu des "acteurs" d'une autre taille [...] pour engager le genre épique dans des voies nouvelles et le lancer à la reconquête de ses lauriers de jadis.[29]

In assessing both medieval and modern adaptations of the *chansons de geste*, scholars have tended to reserve their highest praise for echoes of epic tone and flavor, since strict lexical and narrative accuracy cannot faithfully reproduce early medieval poetic practice. One always senses a marked nostalgia for the original, an unspoken regret that the new audience cannot be

---

[27] Jean-Pierre Mas, "Une Étude de l'oeuvre de Vigneulles: *Journal*, tomes III et IV de la *Chronique et recueil de contes*," Diss. Université Blaise Pascal Clermont II, 1989. Abstract in *Réforme, Humanisme, Renaissance* 28 (June 1989), 63–67. For an interesting comparison between the *Chronique* and the *Cent Nouvelles Nouvelles*, see Marie-Thérèse Noiset, "La Fonction parodique des *Cent Nouvelles Nouvelles* de Philippe de Vigneulles," *Études françaises* 27 (1992): 107–16.

[28] Léon Gautier, *Les Épopées françaises: Étude sur les origines et l'histoire de la littérature nationale*, 4 vols. (1878–97; Osnabrück: Zeller, 1966), II, 600: "Quand on aura achevé de publier le texte antique de nos vieilles chansons dont un si grand nombre, hélas! sont encore inédites; quand on aura enfin édité des oeuvres telles que les *Lorrains* et le *Moniage Guillaume*, il conviendra de donner une édition critique de cette méchante prose qui est parfois si instructive."

[29] Georges Doutrepont, *Les Mises en prose des épopées et des romans chevaleresques du XIVe au XVIe siècle* (1939; Geneva: Slatkine Reprints, 1969), 653–71, at p. 653.

trained to understand and appreciate the genuine article.[30] Similarly, today's scholarly translators often present their works by admitting that a translation into comprehensible modern prose can never truly succeed in recreating the aesthetics of the *chanson de geste*.[31]

The authors of the late medieval *mises en prose* made no such apologies. Their patrons and audiences clearly did not share the modern disdain for prosification, as evidenced by the large number of prose adaptations, both epic and romance, produced during the period. Doutrepont estimates that half the extant *chansons de geste* (of which there are roughly one hundred and twenty) were derhymed and reworked, many of them in multiple versions, between the fourteenth and sixteenth centuries.[32] According to their prologues, patrons and audiences were not particularly interested in the musicality of the genre.[33] Rather, they sought to revive the content or *istoire* of a tradition whose language and form were perceived to be outmoded. Since the thirteenth century, prose had been gaining ground as the medium of choice for narrative works; its supposed claims to greater veracity and authority are well known.[34] By the fifteenth century, however, authors were framing their choice of prose in terms of aesthetic appreciation. The prologue to the *Roman de Guillaume d'Orange* highlights the shift in this horizon of expectations:

> comment Aimery de Beaulande conquist par sa proesce la cité de Nerbonne, que Sarrasins octupoient et tenoient en leur pocession, et avoient de tout temps ancienement tenue et possedee avecques tout le païs qu'on nomme presentement Languedoch ou Terre Basse, que depuis tint Guillaume son filz, comme l'istoire, qui n'est mie messongiere, devisera en ce livre, se Dieu donne par sa grace que je le puisse translater de *vielle rime* en telle prose. Car *plus volentiers s'i esbat l'en maintenant qu'on ne souloit, et plus est le laingage plaisant prose que rime, ce dient ceulx aux quieulx il plaist et qui ainsi le veulent avoir.*[35]

---

[30] Recent prose translations of the Lorraine cycle have met with mixed praise: see Norris J. Lacy's review of *Hervis de Metz*, tr. Philippe Walter, *Olifant* 11 (1986): 260–63, and my own review of *Gerbert*, tr. Bernard Guidot, *Olifant* 14 (1989): 212–16.

[31] See, for example, Philippe Walter's "postface" to his modern prose translation of *Hervis de Metz* (Nancy: PU de Nancy; Metz: Editions Serpenoise, 1984), 202.

[32] Doutrepont, *Les Mises en prose*, 8. See also François Suard, "L'Épopée," *Grundriss der romanischen Literaturen des Mittelalters*, VIII/1: *La Littérature française aux XIVe et XVe siècles* (Heidelberg: Winter, 1988), 161–77.

[33] See Edward Heinemann on the "musicality" of the *chansons de geste*, which he analyzes in terms of laisse structure and echo: *L'Art métrique de la chanson de geste: Essai sur la musicalité du récit* (Geneva: Droz, 1993).

[34] See Wlad Godzich and Jeffrey Kittay, *The Emergence of Prose: An Essay in Prosaics* (Minneapolis: University of Minnesota Press, 1987); Gabrielle Spiegel, *Romancing the Past: The Rise of Vernacular Prose Historiography in Thirteenth-Century France* (Berkeley, Los Angeles, Oxford: U of California P, 1993).

[35] *Le Roman de Guillaume d'Orange*, ed. Madeleine Tyssens, Nadine Henrard, Louis Gemenne (Paris: Champion, 2000), I,1; my emphasis.

[how Aimery de Beaulande conquered by means of his bravery the city of Narbonne, which Saracens occupied and held in their possession, and had always since ancient times held and possessed along with the entire country that is now called Languedoc or Terre Basse, and which since that time was held by Aimery's son Guillaume, as the story, which does not lie at all, will show in this book, if God grants me by His grace the ability to translate it from *old verse* into such prose. For *people take more pleasure now than before in prose, and the language of prose is more pleasing than verse, according to those who prefer it and wish to have it thus.*]

Similarly, Philippe de Vigneulles suggests in his general prologue that the language and style of the old songs are impediments to readerly comprehension and pleasure:

je Phelippe de Vignuelle le marchamps, a l'honneur de Dieu et de la cité, ay heu deliberé de mettre ladite histoire de ancienne rime ou chansson de geste en prose, et au plus brief que j'é peu ne sceu. Et la cause pourquoy que l'istoire est de grande excellance et merveilleux faitz d'armes, laquelle se lessoit du tout au lire et n'estoit quasy plus memoire d'icelle, par ce que moult de gens *n'antendoient pas bien le langage* de quoy l'on souloit huser, ne *ne prenoient plaisir a le lire, pour l'anciennetey d'icelluy*, et weullent les gens de maintenant avoir choses abregee et plaisante.

(fols. 1r–1v, my emphasis)[36]

[I Philippe de Vigneulles the merchant, in honor of God and the city, decided to change the story from ancient verse or chanson de geste into prose, and as briefly as I could or knew how to do so. And this is because the story is about great excellence and marvelous feats of arms, but it was no longer being read and there was hardly any memory of it, because many people *did not understand well the language* that was used in the past, and they *did not take pleasure in reading it because of its antiquity*, and people nowadays want to have short and pleasing things.]

Philippe thus frames his project as a multi-layered *translatio* of a time-honored *istoire*. In addition to the transmodal shift from verse to prose, he refers to the language change that has rendered the old texts unintelligible to his contemporaries. Like other prosifiers, he privileges brevity as well as narrative content and accessibility, as his audience dismisses the lyrical virtuosity of the *chansons de geste* as inflated and obsolete.

---

[36] Unless otherwise indicated, quotations from Philippe's *mise en prose* are taken from the microfilm of MS *v*. This is the only manuscript fully accessible to scholars at this time. However, MS *h* is now available for limited consultation thanks to the generosity of the Ferrell Collection and the Parker Library. I have examined the document for variants and revisions to the passages quoted in this study, and will cite these where pertinent, particularly in Chapter 4. Quotations from *v* are indicated by folio number, while those from *h* refer to the modern page numbers provided in that manuscript.

Although specialists of oral-formulaic style have ample reason to take issue with this approach, it is perhaps time to shed our critical disdain and judge the adaptations on their own merits. Such was the aim of François Suard's seminal study of the *Guillaume en prose*, published in 1979.[37] It is unfortunate that this exemplary work did not generate a flurry of research devoted to the other major prose epic cycles. The sheer length of the texts in question as well as the relative paucity of critical editions have undoubtedly contributed to the halting progress of scholarship in this area. The latter obstacle is being addressed, as the last several years have seen the appearance of a few first-rate editions, and others are in preparation.[38] Nonetheless, the epic *mise en prose* stands as one of the last frontiers in medieval studies, and each individual work deserves scrutiny as scholars attempt to determine the generic specificity of this brand of rewriting. Indeed, in his plenary address to the Société Internationale Rencesvals in 1997, Bernard Guidot urged scholars to reread the avatars of medieval epic in a new light: "Il est temps d'ouvrir de nouveaux chantiers!"[39]

Rather than focusing on what is "lost" in the rendering of Old French verse into Middle French prose, we might do well to consider the *mise en prose* as a "surplus de sens," an illuminating supplement to the original text. Luce Guillerm emphasizes the inherently dual and fissured nature of translation: as a site of both reading and writing, respect for the original and desire for authorial liberty, the translated text constitutes "un carrefour d'enjeux, où repérer les relations de l'écrit au champ historique."[40] In the fissures between original and adaptation we may choose to read not the insufficiency of a derivative discourse, but rather the traces of the aesthetic, social, and geopolitical preoccupations shared by the translator and his implied audience.

Philippe de Vigneulles and his fellow prosifiers fostered a veritable renaissance of Romance epic narrative. In some respects, however, Philippe's translation project was exceptional. Most of the *mises en prose* were commissioned by noble patrons, the most prominent of whom was Philippe le Bon, Duke of

[37] François Suard, *Guillaume d'Orange: Étude du roman en prose* (Paris: Champion, 1979).

[38] See, for example, *Histoire de la Reine Berthe et du Roy Pepin, mise en prose d'une chanson de geste*, ed. Piotr Tylus (Geneva: Droz, 2001); Jehan Wauquelin, *La Belle Hélène de Constantinople: Mise en prose d'une chanson de geste*, ed. Marie-Claude de Crécy, Textes littéraires français 547 (Geneva: Droz, 2002); and Valérie Naudet's edition of *Guerin le Loherain*. Jean-Charles Herbin is currently preparing a critical edition of Philippe's *prose des Loherains*.

[39] Bernard Guidot, "Formes tardives de l'épopée médiévale," *L'Épopée romane au moyen âge et aux temps modernes*, ed. Salvatore Luongo (Naples: Fridericiana Editrice Universitaria, 2001), II, 579–610, at p. 610.

[40] Luce Guillerm, "L'Intertextualité démontée: le Discours sur la traduction," *Littérature* 55 (1984): 54–63, at p. 60.

Burgundy from 1419 to 1467.[41] This princely bibliophile enriched his library with numerous manuscripts, many of them luxuriously illustrated.[42] Philippe le Bon ordered a number of prose adaptations of earlier *chansons de geste*. Under his patronage, Jehan Wauquelin reworked *Girart de Roussillon* and *La Belle Hélène de Constantinople*, and David Aubert copied (and perhaps authored) *L'Histoire de Charles Martel et de ses successeurs*, a four-volume compilation comprising over 2000 folios, of which 1400 are devoted to the aforementioned prose version of the Lorraine cycle.[43] These authors were learned men whose talents served the interests of a particular dynasty. By resurrecting and appropriating heroic figures of the past, the Burgundian court sought to legitimize its politics of expansion.[44]

Philippe de Vigneulles, on the other hand, did not work within the system of patronage and had no clerkly pretensions. No known manuscript of his prose translation of the Lorraine cycle rivals the material and stylistic elegance of the version produced for the Duke of Burgundy. Rather, Philippe lived and worked on the margins of the space occupied by professional writers and illuminators. Although his genre choices paralleled those of the Burgundian court (i.e. chronicle, novella, and epic), his projects were self-imposed and reflect a pronounced civic bias. He demonstrates in his *mise en prose*, as in all of his works, a desire to "aggrandize the importance of his dearly beloved and 'noble' city of Metz."[45] The Lorraine epic afforded him an opportunity to reconfigure the city's legendary past in order to validate the concerns and aspirations of the present. At the turn of the sixteenth century, Metz was a free municipality within the German empire, governed by five *parages* or elites as well as a "parage du commun."[46] As Philippe makes clear in his *Chronique de Metz* and his *Journal*, nobility and commoners were united in their opposition to the dukes of Lorraine, whose periodic attacks on the

41 The prose *Guillaume* was not composed for a specific patron, but was produced in the literary sphere of the Burgundian court by a man of letters. See Suard, *Guillaume d'Orange*, 601–2.

42 On the literature of the Burgundian court, see Danielle Quéruel, "Des mises en prose aux romans de chevalerie dans les collections bourguignonnes," *Rhétorique et mise en prose au XVe siècle*, ed. Sergio Cigada and Anne Slerca (Milan: Vita e Pensiero, 1991), 173–93; *Les Manuscrits de David Aubert*, ed. Danielle Quéruel; Hans-Erich Keller, "The *Mises en prose* and the Court of Burgundy," *Fifteenth-Century Studies* 10 (1984): 91–105; Georges Doutrepont, *La Littérature française à la cour des ducs de Bourgogne: Philippe le Hardi, Jean sans Peur, Philippe le Bon, Charles le Téméraire* (1909; Geneva: Slatkine Reprints, 1970).

43 Wauquelin's reworking of *Girart de Roussillon* appears in *Cronicques des faiz de feurent monseigneur Girart de Rossillon*, ed. Léonce de Montille (Paris: Champion, 1880).

44 Straub, *David Aubert, escripvain et clerc*, 12.

45 Kotin, *The Narrative Imagination*, 3.

46 On the geographical and political history of Metz during the Middle Ages, see Pierre Demarolle, *La Chronique de Philippe de Vigneulles et la mémoire de Metz*.

city represented a constant political and economic threat.[47] Similarly, the population of Metz was wary of imperial power, particularly when it threatened to diminish the fortunes of local nobles and merchants. We shall see that Philippe's desire to assert and maintain the privileged status of Metz is evident not only in his historical writing, but also in the interstices of his *mise en prose*.

This is not to suggest that Philippe effected a radical transformation of his source material. Prose translations of the period have traditionally been classified according to degrees of adaptation, from basic derhyming to large-scale reworking. Hans-Erich Keller distinguishes the *dérimeur*, who generally identifies with the message of the original, from the *remanieur*, who imbues the text with a fundamentally new meaning.[48] Within this continuum, Philippe's prose is situated closer to the *dérimage*. Unlike many of his contemporaries, he does not transform the fierce and bloodthirsty warriors of the *chansons de geste* into heroes of courtly romance, nor does he consistently amplify his material by adducing moral commentary.

Yet I cannot agree with Jean-Charles Herbin that Philippe's work represents the "degree zero" of prose adaptation.[49] As Rupert Pickens has demonstrated with regard to Marie de France's *Fables*, faithfulness to one's source does not preclude the dynamic process of "discovery, renewal, and modernization" inherent in the "poetics of *translatio*."[50] This process is also at work in what might be called the late medieval "prosaics" of *translatio*.[51] Through his choice of material, paratextual explanations, and textual composition, Philippe de Vigneulles reveals fundamental assumptions about the function of prose, the role of the legendary past, and shifting modes of signification in the epic tradition. These problems form the basis of my inquiry into the theory and practice of *dérimage* in the "merchant's tale" of the Lorraine saga.

The present study does not seek to establish an exhaustive textual comparison between the verse epics of the Lorraine cycle and Philippe's *mise en prose*. In preparation for his projected critical edition, Jean-Charles Herbin has already undertaken a rigorous examination of the extant verse manuscripts and their relationship to Philippe's text. He has determined quite convincingly that none of the surviving manuscripts served as Philippe's

---

[47] In his *Journal*, Philippe relates, for example, Nicolas of Lorraine's invasion of Metz as well as the citizens' resistance (3–6).

[48] Hans-Erich Keller, "La Chanson de geste au XVe siècle: Bilan," *Le Moyen Français* 44–45 (1999): 297–307, at p. 303.

[49] Herbin, "Approches," 499.

[50] Rupert T. Pickens, "Marie de France Translatrix," *Le Cygne* n.s.1 (2002): 7–24, at p. 7.

[51] The term is inspired by Godzich and Kittay, *The Emergence of Prose: An Essay in Prosaics*.

models.[52] The verse versions may certainly serve as points of reference, particularly those manuscripts deemed by Herbin as approximating Philippe's sources.[53] However, I believe that this particular *dérimage* must be examined in a broader context that includes the author's other works as well as the prose epic tradition that framed his translation of the Lorraine cycle. Within Philippe's corpus, the following selections will be most pertinent to my analysis: the *Chronique*, Book I, which integrates the Lorraine epic material into the history of Metz, and Book V (volume IV of Bruneau's edition), which relates the events of Philippe's lifetime; the *Cent Nouvelles Nouvelles*, particularly those novellas that deal explicitly with language and translation; and the *Journal*, which, in addition to providing an historical and biographical context, offers valuable insights into Philippe's conception of verse and prose. Among the *mises en prose*, special consideration will be given to the two other prose renderings of the Lorraine cycle (which Philippe likely did not know): the court-commissioned *Histoire de Charles Martel* (generally referred to here as the "Burgundian prose") and the much abbreviated *Prose de l'Arsenal*.

I have organized this study to a great extent around the major principles and textual operations outlined by Philippe in his general prologue and reiterated in subsequent commentaries to the reader. These passages reveal first of all an intense preoccupation with modes of signification and authority involved in the transfer from Old to Middle French and from verse to prose. Chapter 2, "Truth, Translation and the Medium of Prose," considers the art of prose translation as Philippe himself conceived of it. I explore here not only statements recorded in the author's numerous prologues and epilogues, but also the ways in which his *mise en prose* intersects with narratives of language and communication in the corpus as a whole. This chapter demonstrates that far from being an incidental composition, the derhymed epic is part of a coherent literary project.

The value of the Lorraine cycle as story and history is another overarching concern. Chapter 3, "Excellent Stories, Marvelous Deeds and the Prosaics of Crisis," examines Philippe's particular treatment of the Lorraine material. In justifying his choice of subject matter, Philippe consistently invokes the characters' ancestral ties to Metz, with special emphasis on the feminine ancestors of the lineage. His prose also foregrounds the Lorraine heroes' sensational deaths, suggesting interesting parallels between heroic legend and the local crime stories that he records in the *Journal* and the *Chronique*. This chapter is a highly selective study of Philippe's narrative choices, examined in the context of gender, regional politics, and the culture of worry that dominates his writing.

---

52 Herbin, "Approches," 491.

53 For *Hervis*, BnF fr. 19160 (which corresponds to Herbin's edition); for *Garin* and *Gerbert*, the "groupe lorrain" (BnF fr. 19160, BnF fr. 1622, BnF fr. 1442), especially after line 10,152; for *Yonnet*, Arsenal 3143.

Finally, the voice of the translator intervenes rather frequently to explain the "nuts and bolts" of his work. Most often, he signals a decision to abridge the source: "en l'ancienne histoire y ait de grant procès de parolles lesquelles j'ay lessié pour eviter prolixitez" (fol. 1v; in the ancient story there is a great abundance of words that I have left out in order to avoid prolixity). Chapter 4, "The Craft of *dérimage*," considers not only abridgement, but other compositional and discursive practices involved in the shift from oral-formulaic verse to written prose. Such practices were by no means uniform among the prosifiers: Philippe's approach to derhyming, while conservative in its adherence to basic content, reveals distinctive patterns of authorial intervention.

In addition to its historical and philological interest, Philippe's prose epic offers a unique perspective on one of the most popular genres of the late Middle Ages. Although the writer worked within established literary traditions, his status outside the dominant modes of production and patronage fostered a distinctive authorial voice that resonates throughout his works. By placing the Lorraine heroes and their exploits in the service of civic glory, this text attests to the diverse and enduring appeal of epic in the late medieval negotiations between past and present.

2

Truth, Translation and the Medium of Prose

The art of the *mise en prose* was never elucidated by rhetorical manuals or treatises during the Middle Ages. In the absence of formal theoretical reflection, translators' prologues and epilogues furnish valuable insight into the principles and attitudes governing the adaptation of "ancienne rime" into prose. Philippe de Vigneulles is a particularly important source of information on late medieval prosaics. Like many of his contemporaries, he fills the paratextual spaces of his works with abundant commentary on sources, modes of adaptation, and audience reception. In addition, however, his literary legacy includes a substantial number of narratives related to the very tasks involved in reinventing the language of the *chansons de geste*. The *Journal* and the *Cent Nouvelles Nouvelles* frequently stage scenes of bilingualism and mediation, while the *Chronique de Metz* and the *Journal* depict the relative functions of verse and prose in Philippe's personal and civic productions. These authorial interventions and metanarratives reveal the conceptual underpinnings of a work composed outside the sphere of the courtly, erudite culture that sponsored the vast majority of prose translations. While he was clearly familiar with the practices established by generations of professional prosifiers, Philippe adapts the genre to his own interests and to those of a specific urban population called upon to celebrate and preserve its cultural heritage.

Whether they are anonymous or signed, the *mises en prose* are generally prefaced and concluded by an authorial voice whose discourse mediates between source, translation, and an implied audience. The length of such passages and the translator's engagement with the material vary widely from one text to another. The highly abridged version of the Lorraine epic contained in the anonymous *Prose de l'Arsenal* contains virtually no prologue, and the epilogue simply asks readers to pray "pour celui qui le roman fit, et pour celuy qui le translata" (148; for the one who composed the romance, and for the one who translated it). At the other end of the spectrum, the lengthier version of the same cycle included in the *Histoire de Charles Martel* frames each book with prologues and epilogues composed by the copyist, David Aubert, and separate prologues attributed to the anonymous author. Jehan Wauquelin names himself and his patron in *La Belle Hélène de Constanti-*

nople, while the identity of translator and patron are effaced in the *Roman de Guillaume d'Orange*.

The more developed authorial interventions typically display a combination of the following topoi, which are common to all forms of late medieval translation:[1] truth of the source material; excellence and moral value of the tale; summary of content; *envoi* to the princely patron; circumstances of composition; reasons for the undertaking; justification of prose as a medium; obscurity of the language used in the source; difficulty of the task; insufficiency of the translator; invitation to correct errors; place and date of composition. Of these commonplaces, only the first three appear in both verse epics and prose translations, and their manner of presentation is quite different. Indeed, the modulation of narrative voice is one of the more radical transformations involved in derhyming. In the case of the *chansons de geste*, this stems not only from the reworking of verse into prose, but also the shift from oral performance to written book.

To be sure, the written *chansons* that have come down to us in manuscript form may not have been orally composed or even orally delivered, at least in their entirety. Andrew Taylor has convincingly argued that the surviving verse epics are products of nostalgia, incorporating fictions of live performance to recapture "lost origins and a simpler and nobler time."[2] Regardless of their status as oral/aural artifacts, however, the *chansons de geste* consciously bear the traces of and commemorate the performance of a jongleur whose voice and gestures embody truth. Jean-Pierre Martin has described the jongleur's prologue as a ceremonial discourse implicating singer and audience. Encompassing past, present, and future, the intonations of the epic prologue inscribe the content of the *chanson de geste* in an infinitely renewable mythic time and space.[3] The prose translator does not participate in the ritual function associated with the jongleur's prologue. As Wlad Godzich and Jeffrey Kittay have written, "Prose operates in a space of its own making, a purely textual space, rather than one of performance."[4] This does not preclude the possibility of recitation and aural reception. As we shall see, references to listening and hearing are frequent in the *mises en prose*. However, the clerkly redactor does not seek to recreate the immediacy or the complicity of the jongleur's voice.

---

[1] See François Bérier, "La Traduction en français," *Grundriss der romanischen Literaturen des Mittelalters*, VIII/1: *La Littérature française aux XIVe et XVe siècles* (Heidelberg: Winter, 1988), 219–65 and Claude Buridant, "*Translatio medievalis*: Théorie et pratique de la traduction médiévale," *Travaux de linguistique et de littérature* 21 (1983): 81–136.

[2] Andrew Taylor, "Was There a Song of Roland?" *Speculum* 76 (2001): 28–65, at p. 64.

[3] Jean-Pierre Martin, "Sur les prologues des chansons de geste: Structures rhétoriques et fonctions discursives," *Le Moyen âge* 93 (1987): 185–201, esp. 191 and 201. See also Suard, *Guillaume d'Orange*, 167–71.

[4] Godzich and Kittay, *Emergence of Prose*, 34.

While still engaged in preserving the memory of past deeds, the prosifier circumscribes his own activity within precisely drawn boundaries of textual transmission. He presents himself as being at least twice removed from the memorable feats of his forebears, for the stories have already been recorded in texts now perceived as archaic. Rather than effecting a poetic return to the epic moment, he seeks to resurrect and restate exemplary stories for the historical and moral edification of his reading public.[5]

In the preambles and epilogues that frame the five sections[6] of his *mise en prose*, Philippe de Vigneulles incorporates many of the conventions characteristic of clerkly exordia. I will focus here on his treatment of three fundamental concepts that appear in the general prologue to the work and resurface in his other writings: truth and authority; the task of the translator; and the medium of prose.

Truth and Authority

Philippe's general prologue begins with an assertion that the seemingly unbelievable events he is about to relate are nonetheless true:

> Les choses anciennement advenues sanble a aulcunes personnes bien estrainges et quasi incredibles par ce qu'ilz ne pensent point a la fondacion d'icelles et de la cause comment icelles choses peullent estre faictes et advenues. Et quant du fait des anciens ilz oient pairler il disent que se sont fables ou trowés. (fol. 1r)

> [Things that occurred in the distant past seem to some people very strange and nearly unbelievable because they do not think about their underlying cause and about the reason why these things were done and came to pass. And when they hear about the deeds of the ancients, they say that these are untrue or made up.]

The anonymous version of the Lorraine epic composed for Philippe le Bon, the *Histoire de Charles Martel*, also acknowledges that readers might have difficulty believing the story. However, the two translators authenticate their subject matter in very different ways. The anonymous author of the Burgundian version swiftly absolves himself of all responsibility by deferring to his source:

> Et pour ce que moi quy ay prins le loisir de ce faire en passant le temps ne

5   See Suard, "L'Épopée," 173–74.
6   In the *Chronique*, Philippe claims to have divided the work into four parts (IV: 198). However, he distinguishes five sections in the *mise en prose*: the book of "la belle Beaultris" (fol. 306r); the book of the *Lourain Guerin*, which he subdivides into three "livres" (145r; 189r); and *Yonnet*.

me puis mie retrouver en la presence de tous ceulx quy ceste histoire lirront ou orront lire ou racompter, leur requiers que se ilz y treuvent aucunes choses fortes a croire, ilz ne s'i voeullent arrester ne y empeschier leur imagination ou entendement, car a la verité le mien n'est pas a ce pour y rien gloser, retrenchier ou adjouster, sinon de moy y conduire tellement que ma conscience n'en soit chargé, et tout ainsi que oudit volume rymé l'ay trouvé sur lequel j'ay ceste besongne encommencee [...].[7]

[And because I, who took the trouble to complete this project by spending time on it, cannot be present in person with all of those who will read this story or hear it read or told, I ask that if they find anything there that is difficult to believe, they might not dwell on it or let their imagination or understanding linger on it, for in truth I have not applied my own [understanding] to it in order to gloss, omit or add anything, but only to lead me through it in such a way that my conscience not be burdened, and such as I found it in the verse text that serves as the basis for the work I have begun.]

Philippe de Vigneulles, on the other hand, appears to have a great deal more invested in the truth value of his material, as he defends it at some length, and with a variety of arguments. In an initial bid to counter the reader's anticipated incredulity (for the legendary wars between "Loherains" and "Bordelais" are indeed spectacularly violent and longlasting), he introduces comparative evidence from the terrible wars that plague the contemporary world:

Mais je dis moy que en ce present livre n'y ait guerre de chose tant soit estrainge et difficile a croire que encor aujourd'uy ne ce faicent bien chose plus mervilleuse selon le temps qui court et selon la maniere de faire que nous avons a ceste heure tant en guerre comme aultrement au resgart de la maniere de faire qu'il avoient ancie[nne]ment. Et encor daventaige je dis que *s'il eust esté possible qu'en celuy temps anciens et paissés l'on eust troweis par escript une cronicque des guerres et battailles que maintenant se font et des grandes tueries c'on y fait, tant en artilleries comme aultrement, il n'y eust heu homme pour l'heure qui l'eust vollu croire* et qui n'eust dit que c'estoit menterie. (fol. 1r, my emphasis)[8]

---

[7] KBR 6, fol. 1v. Quotations from the *Histoire de Charles Martel* other than those cited from the edited MS 7 (Naudet, *Guerin le Loherain*) will subsequently be indicated after the text by the manuscript number (KBR 6, 8, or 9). Quotations from Naudet's edition will be identified as *Guerin le Loherain*.

[8] By the early sixteenth century, it had become commonplace to evoke modern artillery as a destructive force that would have amazed the ancients. In his *Epistre du Roy à Hector*, Jean Lemaire de Belges has the king declare to Hector:

Ha, prince Hector, pensez-y bien et juge!
Tu ne viz onc si horrible deluge;
Car de ton temps, les guerres et victoires,

[But I say for my part that in the present book there is nothing, however strange or difficult to believe, that is not surpassed by the marvelous things of today, bearing in mind the present epoch and our modern customs, in war and in other matters, in comparison with the ways of the ancients. And in addition, I declare that *if it had been possible that people in ancient times had found a written chronicle of the wars and battles that are waged right now, and the great slaughters that go on, by artillery and otherwise, there would not have been anyone at that time who would have believed it* and would not have said that these were lies.]

There is no question but that Philippe firmly believed that the Lorraine epic was the stuff of chronicle: he includes a summary of the story in his *Chronique de Metz*, and he often refers to his source as "vraye istoire" and "vraye chronique." For him, however, the truth of historical events is demonstrated not only by written sources from the past, but also by parallel happenings in the present. Imagining a sort of time warp in which men of old come across chronicles of the early 1500s, Philippe attributes to them a similar skepticism – a skepticism invalidated by the self-evident truth of events that his contemporaries have experienced personally or heard about from reliable witnesses.

This is not only a sound argument in favor of the veracity of his sources. It is also an interesting scenario of exchange between readers and writers of different historical periods. For the virtual chronicle of current events that Philippe transports back to the time of the ancients surely refers to his own *Chronique de Metz*, the fifth book of which relates events occurring in the author's own lifetime. The prologues and epilogues of the *Chronique* describe its contents in terms that echo the matter of the Lorraine cycle: "merveilles et chose digne de mémoire, estrange et admirative à raconter" (II: 191; marvels and things worth remembering, strange and wondrous to tell); "merveilleuse guerre et grant tuerie" (IV: 2; marvelous war and great slaughter). The chronicler cites three kinds of sources: written documents, the testimony of credible eye witnesses and his own experience (I: 1–2). In the prologue to the fifth book of the *Chronique*, the obligatory humility topos includes a nod to future historiographers who might one day incorporate his writings into their own works:

je prye à tous les lyseur et audicteur que mon fait vueulle tenir pour escusés; et les faulte qu'il y trouvanront vueulle corrigier et amender: car je ne l'ay fait sinon pour advertir ceulx qui après moy vanront, affin

On les faisoit en braz fulminatoires
Tant seullement; mais nostre artillerie,
Sans point de faulte, est une deablerie.
Epistre du Roy à Hector et autres pièces de circonstances (1511–1513), ed. Adrian Armstrong and Jennifer Britnell (Paris: Société des Textes Français Modernes, 2000), vv. 215–20.

que, se en cestuy mien livre aulcune chose de bon y est trouvés, qu'il le
praigne pour joindre avec le leur, et que par eulx soit le mien amendés et
méliorés. (IV: 2)

[I beg all readers and listeners to excuse my work and to correct and modify
the errors that they find there, for I have undertaken this only to inform
those who will come after me, so that if they find anything good in my
book, they might join it to their own, and thus by them my book might be
corrected and improved.]

According to custom, Philippe declares and often reiterates his lack of technical artistry, both in his chronicle and his *mise en prose*. At the same time,
however, he envisions past and future audiences alike reading his memorable
accounts of war and destruction so astonishing that they strain credulity.
This free-flowing *translatio* transcends chronological time and succeeds in
establishing a solid and reflexive authority for the *mise en prose*, as Philippe's
own corpus authenticates the new work at hand.

The authenticity of the Lorraine epic seems to require extensive documen-
tary evidence, as the general prologue pursues its truth assertions even further.
Could Beatrice, princess of Tyre and future mother of Garin le Lorrain, really
have been kidnapped from her father's garden, as he is about to relate? For
this adventure, further authority must be sought in venerated books, such
as the stories of the Trojan War, Livy's History of Rome, and Ovid's *Meta-
morphoses*, all of which recount similar events. And in case readers might
consider these stories apocryphal (although he does not), Philippe turns to
Holy Scripture and the abduction of Dinah, daughter of Jacob and Leah, a
crime that led to the sort of "cruelle vangeance" that permeates the tale of
Beatrice and her lineage (fol. 1r).

Finally, textual proof is corroborated by concrete, visual reminders that
serve as supreme indices of authenticity:

Oultre plus de ceste presante cronicque moult de choses s'en moustrent
encor aujourd'uy, tant de la sepulture a duc Hervy, lequel gist au portal
de l'esglise et monastere de Sainct Arnoult devant Mets avec plusieurs
aultres de leur lignies, et de la sepulture de la belle Beautrix qui est au
cloistre d'ung monastere, comme aussi du Lhorains Guerin que gist au
grant moustier de Mets toutte enthier elleveis en hault en ung sercus de
piere et le peult en veoir, comme cy aprés serait dit. Pareillement voit on
encor le gerdin et le lieu anciennement fabricqué, fors que du nuef owraige
que l'en y ait nowellement reffait, la ou fut prinse ladicte Beautrix, lequel
gerdin est pres de Nostre Dame aux Champs devant ladicte cité de Metz.
(fol. 1r)

[In addition to the present chronicle, many things from it can still be
seen today, such as Duke Hervis's sepulchre, which lies in the church
and monastery of St. Arnoult in Metz, along with many others from their

lineage, and the sepulchre of the fair Beatrice that is in the cloister of a monastery; also, the tomb of Garin le Lorrain which lies intact in Metz cathedral raised on high in a stone coffin, and one can see it, as will be told afterward. Similarly, one can still see the garden and the place constructed long ago (except for the new construction that was recently repaired) where Beatrice was kidnapped. This garden is near Nostre Dame aux Champs in the city of Metz.]

Indeed, the legend that placed Garin's remains in the great cathedral was common throughout the later Middle Ages. Visiting dignitaries were taken to the site to see Garin's tomb as well as the "cloche Garin le Loherain."[9] By incorporating the local tradition into his translation, Philippe invests the material with truth. In return, these sites, in the manner of Roncevaux, could be invested with new meaning by their association with a textual monument to the community's past.[10]

For Philippe, then, the truth of the Lorraine epic as history and story is not limited to the excellence of the source. Rather, the general content of the work (i.e. tales of horrific bloodshed) is authenticated by recent history as Philippe himself has recorded it. Specific incidents are supported by analogues from classical and Biblical texts. Above all, artifacts preserved in the urban space occupied by the author and his intended audience anchor the heroes and their surroundings in familiar territory.[11] Philippe takes care to situate his writing endeavor in this same space when he attaches his name to the work:

> lesquelles guerre et baitaille je Philippe de Vignuelle mairchampz de draps demourant a Mets derrier l'esglise collegialle de Sainct Salveur sus le tour de la rue dez Bons Affants [...] ait estrait cest presante cronicque et istoire de ancienne rime et chanson de geste en prose. (fol. 305r, cf. fol. 59r)

> [the wars and battles that I, Philippe de Vigneulles, cloth merchant residing in Metz behind the collegiate church of St. Sauveur above the place where the Rue des Bons Enfants turns {...} translated the present chronicle and history from ancient rime and chanson de geste into prose.]

The translator thus identifes himself by his principal trade and his precise spatial coordinates in the city that produced the heroes of his tale.

---

⁹ Doutrepont, *Les Mises en prose*, 400–02. Jehan Aubrion, a bourgeois chronicler of the preceding generation, mentions this bell in his Journal: *Journal de Jehan Aubrion, bourgeois de Metz, avec sa continuation par Pierre Aubrion, 1465–1512*, ed. Lorédan Larchey (Metz: F. Blanc, 1857), 40–41.

¹⁰ Cf. Stephen G. Nichols, *Romanesque Signs* (New Haven and London: Yale University Press, 1983), 148–203.

¹¹ See Catherine M. Jones, "Modernizing the Epic: Philippe de Vigneulles," *Echoes of the Epic*, eds. David and Mary Jane Schenck (Birmingham: Summa, 1998), 115–32; and Herbin, "Approches," 494.

Toponyms often appear in the prologues of the other *mises en prose*, but they generally designate and celebrate the lands held by the princely patron who commissioned the work. The prologue of the *Histoire de Charles Martel* is typical of the genre, as the copyist David Aubert enumerates in customary fashion the titles of his powerful benefactor, Philippe le Bon:

> par le commandement et ordonnance de treshault, tresexcellent et trespuissant prince, et mon tresredoubté et souverain seigneur tryumphant en gloire et en paix, Phelippe, par la grace de Dieu duc de Bourgoingne, de Lothrijk, de Brabant et de Lembourg, conte de Flandres, d'Artois et de Bourgoingne, palatin de Haynnau, de Hollande, de Zeellande et de Namur, marquis du saint empire, seigneur de Frise, de Salins et de Malines.
>
> (KBR 6, fol. 1v)

> [by the command and order of the most exalted, most excellent and most powerful prince and my most revered and sovereign lord, who triumphs in glory and in peace, Philippe, by the grace of God Duke of Burgundy, of Lorraine, of Brabant and of Limburg; Count of Flanders, of Artois and of Burgundy; Palatine of Hainaut, of Holland, of Zealand and of Namur, marquis of the Holy Empire, lord of Frisia, of Salins and of Mechelen.]

Neither the copyist nor the anonymous "acteur" draws any explicit connection between the patron's domains and the geographical setting of the story itself, although such connections do exist.[12]

Philippe de Vigneulles, on the other hand, bonds his audience to the diegetic space of Garin le Lorrain, his ancestors and his descendants. The general prologue pointedly dedicates the *mise en prose* to God and to the city of Metz (fol. 1r). The translator's stated reasons for unearthing the old story are intimately linked to the city that he shares with his readers and characters:

> Non pais que mon intancion soit de escripre l'istoire tout du loing ne a la moitiet, car elle est grande merveilleusement et autant ou plus que la destruction de Troyes. Mais touteffois *pour ce que les dessusdis furent de la nacion et estrais d'icelle noble cité de Mets*, j'en direis et raconterés aulcune chose et pairtie de leur vie et fais d'airme qu'il ont fait en leur temps, aucy de la ligne que d'iceulx sont saillis et dessandus et des aventures qui leur sont advenues et les cause pourquoy.
>
> (fol. 59v, my emphasis; cf. fol. 305r)

> [Not that I intend to write the entire story or even half of it, for it is marvelously long, as much or more so than the destruction of Troy. Nonetheless, *because the aforesaid {heroes} were from this region, and born in this noble city of Metz,* I will tell and relate some things and portions of their

---

12 In particular, Brabant and Flanders.

life and feats of arms that they accomplished in their lives, as well as the lineage that sprang and descended from them, and the adventures that befell them, and the reasons why.]

While acknowledging the temporal distance and seeming otherness of his tale, Philippe actively seeks to integrate its heroes and their deeds into local history. In fact, he rather overstates the connection between the Lorraine epic cycle and Metz, as only the song of *Hervis* and a smattering of episodes from the other verse texts actually take place in that city.

It will be evident from the passages quoted above that the voice and style of Philippe's interventions represent a significant departure from the intonations of a jongleur's prologue. The translator employs what Jens Rasmussen calls the emphatic and diffuse style of late medieval prose, with its mannerisms and lengthy sentences articulated by subordinate clauses.[13] His somewhat belabored assertions of truth contrast markedly with the incantatory invitation issued in the prologue of *Garin le Lorrain*:

> Vielle chançon voire volez oïr,
> de grant estoire et de merveilleus pris,
> si com li Woandre vindrent en cest païs?
> [...]
> Huimés comence la chançon a venir,
> et la merveille qui la porroit oïr!
>
> (*Garin le Loherenc* vv. 1–3, 12–13)

[Do you wish to hear an old song, about a great story of wondrous worth, about how the Vandals came to this country? {...} Now begins the song, and its marvels, for those able to hear it!]

Nonetheless, Philippe's attitude toward his material is close in spirit to that of the jongleur. Like the epic narrator, he takes care to establish an affective bond between story and audience. Both the jongleur and his prose successor use demonstratives ("cest païs" and "icelle noble cité") to transport past events into the present surroundings of the listener or reader. To a far greater extent than professional translators, then, he implicates himself and his public in the time and space of the ancestral heroes. Narrator and audience alike have a stake in the *istoire*.

The Task of the Translator

The *translatio* of epic material also involved "translation" as we understand it today, that is the transposition of signs from one language to another.

---

[13] Rasmussen, *La Prose narrative française du XVe siècle*, 32–43.

Most scholarly work on medieval translation has focused on the interlingual variety, principally the vulgarization of Latin texts by clerical writers. Over the past twenty years, a number of monographs and collections have been devoted to literary, philosophical, and scientific translations as well as the intellectual formation of those who produced them.[14] The context of translation as it was practiced in the *mises en prose*, on the other hand, merits further exploration. Intralingual and diachronic, this operation required significantly less linguistic intervention on the part of the translator, who had merely to account for variations in French occurring over a period of two to four hundred years. However, the same terminology was consistently used for both forms of translation: the verbs *translater, metre* and *reduire* all designate the mediation between older and newer forms of French as well as between Latin and the vernacular. As Claude Buridant has pointed out, a complete history of medieval translation will not be complete without serious study of intralingual adaptation, including the "mental architectonics" of those engaged in this particular activity.[15]

Modern linguists do not agree on the precise temporal boundary between "Old" and "Middle" French. Several factors make it difficult to date the advent of a new stage in the development of the language: the slow process of linguistic change, the unreliability of written texts as indicators of actual usage, and the diversity of "French" (or "romanz") in the Middle Ages. Christiane Marchello-Nizia situates the shift toward the beginning of the fourteenth century, and judiciously bases her periodization on both linguistic considerations and broader historical circumstances.[16] Significant language changes include the definitive reduction of diphthongs and hiatus, the disappearance of the two-case system, the Latinization of vocabulary, and the replacement of verb-subject with subject-verb word order. These developments coincided with the profound political, economic, and demographic crisis that began in the early fourteenth century. Marchello-Nizia also cites cultural trends, including the rapid rise of the vernacular chronicle and the emergence of glosses, commentaries, and debates with respect to literary texts composed in French. These two "reflexive" movements attest to a new perception of

---

[14] In addition to Bérier, "La Traduction" and Buridant, "*Translatio medievalis*," see Jeanette Beer, ed., *Translation Theory and Practice in the Middle Ages* (Kalamazoo, Mich.: Medieval Institute Publications, Western Michigan U, 1997); Fiona Somerset and Nicholas Watson, ed., *The Vulgar Tongue: Medieval and Postmedieval Vernacularity* (University Park: The Pennsylvania State UP, 2003); Geneviève Contamine, ed., *Traduction et traducteurs au moyen âge* (Paris: Editions du CNRS, 1989); Peter Andersen, ed., *Pratiques de traduction au moyen âge / Medieval Translation Practices* (Copenhagen: Museum Tusculanum Press, U of Copenhagen, 2004).

[15] Buridant, "*Translatio medievalis*," 87–88, 93, 96–99.

[16] Christiane Marchello-Nizia, *La Langue française aux XIVe et XVe siècles* (Paris: Nathan, 1997), 4–5.

national identity, as *clercs* and their powerful patrons sought to make sense of and capitalize on their own history and literature.[17]

The evidence of a dividing line between distinct stages of French is not limited to linguistic features alone, but is accompanied by the testimony of native informants. A small number of texts from the fifteenth and sixteenth centuries suggest that speakers (or more precisely, readers) perceived a marked difference between their language and that of earlier centuries. An oft-cited example is François Villon's "Ballade en vieil langage françoys," which adopts the old declension system (often erroneously) for ludic effect.[18] Further evidence may be gleaned from the *mises en prose*, at least two of which state unequivocally that earlier vernacular texts required interpretation. An early sixteenth-century prologue to the fifteenth-century prose *Mabrien* claims that the old language of the source was defective: "Et a esté ce present livre nouvellement reduict de vieil langaige corrompu: en bon vulgaire françois" (And the present work has been newly translated from old corrupt language into good vernacular French).[19]

More insistently than other prosifiers, Philippe de Vigneulles evokes a linguistic barrier that rendered the texts of earlier centuries obscure to modern audiences; as we have seen, he cites this barrier in the general prologue as part of his motivation for adapting the Lorraine cycle ("moult de gens n'antendoient pas bien le langaige de quoy l'on souloit user," fol. 1r; many people did not understand well the language that was used in the past). A later epilogue underscores the author's intense desire to decipher the language of documents that might otherwise fall into oblivion:

> je Philippe de Vignuelle [...] desirant et appettant que cest ystoire et cronicque fut weue et congneuez, laquellez aparavent pour ancienneteis du langaige et la difficulteis d'icelluy ce laissoit du tout a lire, et n'en estoit plus causy memoire. (fol. 305r)

> [I, Philippe de Vigneulles {...} desirous and eager for this {hi}story and chronicle to be seen and known, which previously, owing to the antiquity and difficulty of its language, was totally neglected by readers, and there was hardly any memory of it.]

The obscure language of Old French verse was certainly a less formidable obstacle for Philippe's audience than, say, a rhetorical treatise in classical

---

[17] Marchello-Nizia, *La Langue française aux XIVe et XVe siècles*, 5. Marchello-Nizia posits another break at the beginning of the sixteenth century, while others extend the period of Middle French to 1600 or to the end of the Wars of Religion (4–7).

[18] This is one of the three "ballads of yesteryear" in the *Testament*. See *Villon: Oeuvres*, ed. and trans. André Lanly (Paris: Champion, 1993), vv. 385–412.

[19] *Mabrien: Roman de chevalerie en prose du XVe siècle*, ed. Philippe Verelst, Romanica Gandensia XXVIII (Geneva: Droz, 1998), Introduction, 42. Also qtd. in Doutrepont, *Les Mises en prose*, 390–391.

Latin. Early sixteenth-century readers had difficulty with the old texts, and preferred easy access. In this respect, the motivation to produce an intralingual *mise en prose* was similar to that of Latin-to-vernacular translators working for patrons who knew some Latin, but were not immersed in the language. Jean de Meun, in the preface of *Li livres de confort de Philosophie*, graciously acknowledges the proper education received by Philippe le Bel, to whom he dedicates his translation: "Ja soit ce que tu entendes bien le latin, mais toutevois est de moult plus legiers a entendre le françois que le latin" [Although you know Latin well, French is nonetheless much easier to understand than Latin].[20] Christine de Pizan similarly praises her royal patron's knowledge of Latin in *Le Livre des fais et bonnes moeurs du sage roy Charles V*, but concedes that his successors might not be as fluent.[21] Allowing for a respectable dose of flattery in these cases, it is reasonable to assume that the French kings and their entourage had only limited proficiency and interest in reading Latin texts, and found the vernacular less burdensome. Likewise, the French reading public of the later Middle Ages enthusiastically welcomed interpreters willing to tackle the labor-intensive monuments of their own emerging language.

In analyzing the technical and stylistic transformations involved in the *mises en prose*, modern editors and scholars generally posit two discrete sets of operations: those concerned strictly with linguistic updating and those related to derhyming.[22] These processes will be discussed in greater detail in Chapter 4. Prosifiers' own descriptions of their work suggest that they themselves considered modernization and prosification to be inextricably linked. In Philippe's commentary, the "langaige" to be translated designates at once the rhythmic chant of epic verse and the antiquated usage of yesteryear ("vielle chanson de geste et rime ensiennes," fol. 59v; old *chanson de geste* and old verse). What is certain is that Philippe and his professional counterparts present their role in terms of linguistic mediation, making no qualitative distinction between what modern linguists consider intralingual and interlingual translation. Proficient in an endangered language, the prosifiers seek to render their material in "cler françois."[23] In order to accomplish their task, they typically claim to bring to the texts a certain *entendement*, that is, a capacity for understanding that is often linked in the prologues with *engin* and *imagination*.[24]

---

20 Qtd. in Serge Lusignan, *Parler vulgairement: Les intellectuels et la langue française aux XIIIe et XIVe siècles*, 2nd edition (Paris: Vrin; Montréal: PU de Montréal, 1987), 149.

21 Lusignan, *Parler vulgairement,* 149. See also Bérier, "La Traduction," 231.

22 See Tylus, *Histoire de la Reine Berthe*, Introduction, 51; and Bernard Cerquiglini, *La Parole médiévale: Discours, syntaxe, texte* (Paris: Éditions de Minuit, 1981), 38.

23 *Histoire de Charles Martel*, translator's prologue: KBR 6, fol. 1v.

24 See *Histoire de Charles Martel*, translator's prologue, KBR 6, fol. 1v; and Bérier, "La Traduction en français," 231.

One might well ask how an unschooled cloth merchant managed to comprehend texts that his contemporaries considered difficult and archaic. Philippe seems to anticipate this objection in the *captatio benevolentiae* that closes the general prologue. Begging the reader to excuse his ignorance, he asserts that he is neither wise nor educated enough to undertake such a lofty work ("je ne suis pas assés saige ne lestrés pour cy haulte owre entreprandre," fol. 1v). The conventional self-deprecating stance, however, is at odds with Philippe's well-documented intellectual curiosity and extensive reading. Both the *Chronique* and the *mise en prose* demonstrate that he had access to and consulted numerous manuscripts from official, ecclesiastical and private libraries.[25] And as we shall see, the *Journal* suggests that he had a knack for learning languages.

In fact, Philippe's corpus as a whole manifests a singular preoccupation with language and intercomprehension. His rich and varied literary production, comprising historiographical, autobiographical, epic and comic narratives, affords a valuable glimpse into the "mental architectonics" of lay vernacular translation, fleshing out the evidence found in his prologues and epilogues and those of other prosifiers. For a better understanding of the assumptions underlying Philippe's translation project, then, it is useful to consider the numerous passages in his works that foreground the difficulties and potential rewards involved in communicating across languages. The cloth merchant-translator figure that emerges from the *mise en prose* is more than just a bourgeois imitator of clerkly practices. He also participates in a network of clever polyglots appearing in the *Journal*, the *Chronique*, the *Cent Nouvelles Nouvelles*, and the *mise en prose* itself. These narratives serve to elucidate a conception of *translatio* rooted in the social realities and vernacular traditions of late medieval Europe.

The practical advantages of second language acquisition are dramatized in the early pages of the *Journal*. Philippe's journey to Italy was clearly a watershed event. His account of the Italian years is marked by a shift from first to third person narration, as the wandering hero "Phelippe" negotiates daily life and work in foreign territory (21). Language is first mentioned as an obstacle, when the narrator recounts his arrival in Naples and his initial frustration as a newcomer: "tant luy ennuioit que merveille pour la langue qu'il n'entendoit mye bien" (21; he was extraordinarily bothered because he didn't understand the language at all well).[26] However, we may suppose that he acquired some proficiency during his three-year sojourn, as he asserts that he eventually left Naples with unspecified books in Italian (32). Indeed, the *Cent Nouvelles Nouvelles* contain many analogues to Italian novellas,

---

25 Bruneau, *Chronique*, Introduction, XVI. Demarolle's research suggests that Philippe collaborated with a *clerc* on the *Chronique*: See his "A propos d'annotations."

26 Philippe uses the third person when referring to himself in this part of the *Journal*.

particularly those of Poggio, as well as two explicit references to Boccaccio's *Decameron*.[27]

The *Journal* also depicts Philippe using language as a survival tool on his return voyage from Italy. As the weary traveler approaches the region of Metz, he learns that the city is at war, and that any man from Metz attempting to enter the city is subject to attack. He twice conceals his identity, and each time employs linguistic disguise: "il olt grant pavoir et ne savoit quel conseil prendre [...] Touteffois il se pensa qu'il passeroit et qu'il contreferoit sa langue, par quoy il ne seroit point congnu" (31; he was very afraid and did not know what to do ... Nevertheless he decided he would get through, and that he would disguise his language so that he wouldn't be recognized). Initially, he pretends to be a "fol," but later, when questioned, claims to be from Geneva "et print a parler savoien" (32; and he began to speak the Savoy dialect). While this is perhaps an accurate account of Philippe's journey, it is also strongly reminiscent of an epic motif. Indeed, the figure of the fluent trickster is found the Lorraine epic itself, as the *chanson de geste* frequently mobilizes multilingual spies in the service of territorial conflict.[28] It is surely no accident that Philippe's prose version amplifies the polyglot motif as it appears in the branch of the Lorraine cycle devoted to Hervis and his conquest of Beatrice, Princess of Tyre. When Beatrice's brother Floire, King of Hungary, dispatches two servants to Metz to spy on the hero, the extant verse texts specify that the spies know all languages, mentioning English, Flemish and German.[29] Philippe's prose expands the list: "scevent yceulx parler de tous langaiges // de crestienté comme flansois [*sic*], anglois, allemant, espaignoille et flamans, ytailliens et plussieur aultre" (fols. 17r–17v; they knew how to speak all Christian languages, such as French, English, German, Spanish, Flemish, Italian, and several others). Like Philippe, the spies deceive would-be captors and penetrate enemy lines by passing as native speakers of another language.

Metz was a culturally diverse city, at the crossroads between the German empire, to which it belonged politically, and France, with which it shared its language. Philippe apparently had only the most rudimentary knowledge of Latin and German.[30] Yet his travels as merchant and pilgrim exposed him to

---

[27] Livingston, *Cent Nouvelles Nouvelles*, Introduction, 38. Livingston does not assume, however, that Philippe had direct knowledge of these texts, as many of the motifs circulated widely in oral tales.

[28] See Catherine M. Jones, "Polyglots in the *chansons de geste*," *"De sens rassis": Essays in Honor of Rupert T. Pickens*, ed. Keith Busby, Bernard Guidot, and Logan Whalen (Amsterdam & Atlanta: Rodopi, 2004), 281–91.

[29] *Hervis de Mes* vv. 3907–08. Mss. NT substitute "brebençon" for "alemans" at v. 3908.

[30] Livingston claims that Philippe had no knowledge of Latin (*Cent Nouvelles Nouvelles*, Introduction, 15). Word play in the *Cent Nouvelles Nouvelles* and translations of Latin inscriptions in the *Chronique* suggest that he had some limited proficiency, although

the multilingual culture of the empire, to which he frequently refers. During a pilgrimage in 1510 that took him to Aachen and Cologne, Philippe reports visiting the church of Nostre Dame d'Ervercluze: "et fumes au cloistre de la dite église qui est vairnés et est bien belle église et y lus en ung taubleau qui est en latin, en allemand et en roman, la manière comment la dite église fut faicte et fondée" (*Journal* 183; and we were in the cloister of the church, which is decorated with stained-glass windows and is a very beautiful church, and I read there on a tablet that is in Latin, German and French, the manner in which the church was built and founded). He obligingly informs the reader of German phrases he picks up along the way: "et nomme l'on ces chevailiers ycy duche herre" (174; and here they call knights *duche herre*). His *Journal* also mentions imperial correspondence and other public announcements made accessible to the public of Metz in both German and French (315, 319).

Philippe's autobiographical writing thus demonstrates that he was acutely aware of the practical, historical and political exigencies of a multilingual society. The early pages of the *Journal* are concerned primarily with foreign language proficiency as a tool for travelers, a skill to be mastered by the savvy adventurer. However, the narrator becomes progressively interested in translation as a means of educating a growing reading public about its past (the history of churches) and present (proclamations of war). This interest is reflected in the *Chronique* as well, where Philippe frequently reproduces the Latin inscriptions found in local monuments along with their French translation as part of the cultural heritage of Metz.[31] Interlingual and intralingual translation would seem, then, to have similar functions in Philippe's vast project of civic preservation.

The *Cent Nouvelles Nouvelles*, composed concurrently with the *mise en prose*, offer further evidence of Philippe's preoccupation with encoding and decoding languages. A substantial number of novellas extol the virtues of "subtilité," a mental attribute related to *engin*, and thus designating the insight possessed by authors and their most ingenious characters.[32] Philippe's tales often adapt the traditional motif of the *finesse*, or trick, to the culturally diverse setting of Metz. The fictions grant privileged status to those characters who possess a mastery of two or more languages, and who use this form of "subtilité" in the service of laughter and desire. On the other hand, the misadventures of less fluent characters demonstrate the perils of incomplete or faulty language acquisition. The novellas that employ foreign

---

Bruneau claims that Philippe had others translate the inscriptions for him (*Chronique*, Introduction, XVI).

31 See, for example, *Chronique* I: 334–35. Bruneau notes frequent errors in the Latin.

32 See Douglas Kelly, *The Art of Medieval French Romance* (Madison: U of Wisconsin Press, 1992), 124–25.

language as a plot device thus correspond rather neatly to the two structural models described by Armine Kotin in her study of Philippe's *Narrative
Imagination*. Although she allows for numerous variations from one tale to
another, Kotin divides the entire collection into "cleverness" and "foolish-
ness" sequences.[33]

More recent studies have focused on verbal play and power structures
in Philippe's novellas. While acknowledging the usefulness of structuralist
narratology in the analysis of Philippe's tales, Mary J. Baker finds that the
stories are concerned primarily with the success or failure of communicative
acts, those occurring between narrator and reader as well as those performed
by characters.[34] David LaGuardia, in his comparative analysis of fifteenth-
and sixteenth-century novellas, demonstrates the ways in which Philippe's
novellas subvert existing social hierarchies, granting wealth and power to
clever individuals of all social groups.[35] These studies are especially pertinent
to the sub-group of novellas that champion successful linguistic mediators.
Philippe's ingenious polyglots are male and female, bourgeois and noble,
clerical and lay. Like Philippe's authorial and autobiogaphical persona, they
use their skills to procure pleasure and knowledge. In these tales, I believe,
the linguistic ability of the local merchant-translator is further validated as
it is transposed into the comic register. At the same time, written translation is integrated into a larger communicative context in which *subtilité* and
entendement are deployed in daily human transactions.

Novella 38 deploys the familiar schema of a suitor covertly replacing
another man in the bed of an unsuspecting woman. Philippe's version shares
with similar tales the eavesdropping stratagem: a man overhears a woman
arranging a tryst, intercepts the time, place, and/or secret signal, and substitutes for the designated lover in a darkened bedroom. However, as he does
in most of his novellas, Philippe situates the action in a historically and
geographically specific context: Metz, 1490, during the war between Duke
René II of Lorraine and the city, when men of arms from various regions
could be found milling about ("gens d'armes [...] de beaucop de nacion et de
diverses sortes" 177). One of these men, a Frenchman, becomes enamored
of a female cloth merchant. While lingering in her boutique on the pretense
of buying textiles, he pretends to understand no French and speaks only
German to the woman. In his presence (for she believes the conversation
to be secure), the woman speaks French with her lover, another soldier, and
arranges a meeting for that very evening when her husband will be away. The

---

[33] Kotin, *The Narrative Imagination*, 38.

[34] Mary J. Baker, "Narrative Communication in Philippe de Vigneulles' *Cent Nouvelles nouvelles*," *Orbis litterarum: International Review of Literary Studies* 53 (1998):
73–82.

[35] David LaGuardia, *Iconography of Power*, 110–111.

bilingual spy, using the signal agreed upon by the lovers, arrives on the scene first, takes advantage of the darkness, and silently makes love to the woman, which gives much pleasure to both. Naturally, the designated lover eventually surfaces and takes his turn. The woman knows she has been deceived, but when the crafty substitute returns to buy more cloth, he succeeds in winning her love: "et ainsi par sa subtilité conquesta une dame par amour" (178; and thus owing to his subtlety he conquered a woman in love).

Foreign language as a tool of seduction is also apparent in Novella 99, which is likely based on tale 41 of Masuccio's *Novelino* and was later reworked by Rabelais in chapter 24 of *Pantagruel*.[36] It is one of the few novellas featuring characters drawn from the nobility. A lady, neglected by her lover, a gentleman of Lorraine, concocts a subtle scheme ("chose subtille et merveilleuse" 401). She sends him by messenger a false diamond along with a letter containing a single word in Hebrew (*lamazanbathani*) . The gentleman cannot decipher the message, but his curiosity renews his interest in the lady. He is eager to learn the meaning of her communication ("plus desirant et ardant que devant de savoir la signifficacion" 401). It is only Duke Nicholas of Lorraine who is able to interpret both the word and the object: *lamazanbathani* signifies "why have you abandoned me?" and the expression "false diamond" ("dyamant faulx") is a word play in French, signifying also a reproach to a false lover: "dis, amant faulx" (401). All present are impressed by the "subtillité" of both the lady and the princely translator (402), and the gentleman hastens to his lady's side to renew their liaison. In this novella, then, both the foreign utterance and its successful translation are employed in the service of desire.

Other novellas draw comic effects from dull-witted characters' lack of finesse in foreign languages. These tales, while mocking the ignorance of their scapegoats, nonetheless establish a firm complicity between narrator and reader, both of whom possess enough knowledge of Latin, French, and Metz/Lorraine dialect to appreciate the simpletons' errors.

Novella 4 generates its humor from an interlingual misunderstanding ("mal entendre" 69). The victim is a simple parish priest, rich in livestock but lacking any knowledge of Latin: "il ne sçavoit ne n'entendoit comme point de latin" (69). Among his most cherished possessions is a donkey named Modicum, which performs countless essential tasks in the running of his household. Because he is well off, the priest is chosen to host a meal for some visiting dignitaries. In his directive, the pretentious archpriest speci-fies that the guests should be served "*modicum et bonum*" (70). Stricken but obedient, the Latin-challenged priest has his donkey Modicum slaughtered

36 See Livingston's introduction to the novella, 397. The chapter number in *Pantagruel* refers to the 1542 edition, ed. Floyd Gray: Édition critique basée sur l'édition publiée à Lyon en 1542 par François Juste (Paris: Champion; diffusion Geneva: Slatkine, 1997).

and fed to the visitors, who do not find the odd-tasting meat to their liking. At this point, the bemused archpriest apologizes to the guests, repeating his initial order but glossing the Latin words in French: "*modicum et bonum, qui est à dire ung petit de bon et de legier*" (71; *modicum et bonum*, which is to say something light and tasty). When questioned, the priest explains that they are eating the donkey Modicum, as the archpriest requested. The consequences of this misunderstanding are relatively minor, as the donkey entree provokes only laughter and indigestion. It is not clear whether the unfortunate priest ever learns the nature of his interpretive failure. As Mary J. Baker has demonstrated, however, this failure is to be blamed equally on the archpriest, who miscalculated the language proficiency of his interlocutor and obscured his own intentions.[37] If the French gloss had been provided in timely fashion, both beast and diners would have been spared.

Novella 82, probably inspired by local oral sources, is loosely constructed around a series of miscommunications that arise from a combination of poor memory and dialectal interference. All of the protagonists, natives of Metz, fail to locate the people, places, and objects they seek because they engage in faulty word association. The anecdotes, most of which presuppose knowledge of the local Metz dialect, are difficult to retell, and thus I will summarize only the last one. A simple valet accompanies his master to Paris; charged with purchasing "mackerel" from a fishmonger, he forgets the name of the fish he is supposed to buy. Because the French word for "mackerel" (*maquereau*) also designates a pimp, the befuddled valet retrieves the word for "pimp" in his local dialect ("richou" 325). He asks countless Parisian fishmongers for a *richou*, but no one can interpret the word, and the valet returns empty-handed. His blunder provokes peals of laughter from his fellow-citizens of Metz, who instantly pinpoint the interdialectal error. It is worth noting that this novella links interpretive problems to short-term memory loss. The narrator characterizes all of the protagonists of the novella as "gens simples d'entendement lesquelles ne scevent retenir sen qu'on leur dist" (325; simple-minded people who don't know how to remember what they're told). Indeed, the story itself is ironically framed as the product of a memory gap, as the narrator playfully presents the tale as a sort of "filler" offered to the reader in a moment of forgetfulness: "En attendant que une aultre nouvelle me veingne en la memoire, je ferés passer ceste petite joyeuseté" (322; While waiting for another novella to come to mind, I will include this little pleasantry). This move is typical of Philippe's narratorial style, portraying the author figure at once as an artless man of the people and the clever interpreter of that people's culture.

A "photographic" memory does not suffice, however, to produce successful communication. Novella 60, which has analogues in exempla and numerous

---

[37] Baker, "Narrative Communication," 75.

oral tales throughout Europe, is an adventure in poor language method-ology. While the languages and nationalities of the protagonists vary widely, Philippe's version depicts three Germans who go to France for an immersion experience. They are exceptionally earnest in their desire to learn French ("tant grande voulenté de l'aprendre que mervoille" 252), to the extent that whenever they overhear a new utterance, they repeat it a hundred times to store it properly in memory. However, having no earthly idea of the meaning of these phrases, they soon find themselves in a serious predicament. In the course of their travels, they find a dead body and dutifully bring it to the local authorities. When questioned, they trot out their memorized responses. When asked who is responsible for the murder, the first German eagerly replies, "three Germans" ("trois Allemans" 252); when asked why the crime was perpetrated, the second German produces his phrase, "a large purse of money" ("une grosse bourse d'argent" 252); and finally, when it is decided that they will be hanged, the third German exclaims "that's fair" ("c'est raison" 253). The three simpletons are saved by the joint appearance of an interpreter (who interrogates the suspects) and the real murderers (who confess to the crime). When they are set free, the Germans return in haste to their native land without learning any more French, for what they had learned of the language had proved to be dangerous (254).

The *Cent Nouvelles Nouvelles* are by no means realistic depictions of life in late medieval Metz. The plots and actors are highly stylized and are drawn from time-honored traditions of short narrative. They do, however, highlight the essential function of fluent linguistic mediators in the context of everyday social exchange. Philippe's corpus consistently valorizes this form of knowledge and thus implicitly forges links between the merchant-translator of the *mise en prose* and other astute communicators endowed with subtlety and finesse. His rich panoply of polyglots suggests that Philippe's translation project was conceived as a natural outgrowth of his interest in and daily exposure to the languages of other people and other epochs.

The Medium of Prose

By the time Philippe set about to render the Lorraine epic songs into clear, modern French prose, the status of vernacular prose as a signifying practice was well established. Gabrielle Spiegel has admirably traced the ideological imperatives behind the rise of the vernacular prose narrative in thirteenth-century France. Turning to history as a means of legitimizing their role in a changing social order, the Flemish aristocracy in particular appropriated prose as a truthful, authoritative medium. Verse texts were deemed menda-cious, founded as they were upon the unreliable oral discourse of jongleurs. As Nicolas de Senlis proclaims in the prologue to the *Pseudo-Turpin*: "Tot est mencongie co qu'il en dient car il n'en sievent rienz fors quant par oïr dire" (Everything they say is a lie, because they know nothing except through hearsay.)[38] As verse epic and romance became the objects of prosification in the fourteenth and fifteenth centuries, the superior truth value of prose was already a given. As we have seen, prologues and epilogues of these *mises en prose* tend rather to underscore the aesthetic preferences of their patrons. The translator of the anonymous Burgundian version of the Lorraine epic attributes his choice of prose to the changing tastes of the aristocracy, who objected to the distortions wrought by verse in the interest of form: "au jour d'huy les grans princes et autres seigneurs appetent plus la prose que la ryme pour le langaige quy est plus entier et n'est mie constraint" (KBR 6, fol. 1r; Today, great princes and other lords take more pleasure in prose than in verse because the language of prose is more complete and not at all constrained). Similarly, Jehan Wauquelin, in the prologue to his *La Manekine*, claims to undertake "l'embellissement d'icelle [histoire], affin que plus patentement elle fust congnulte, et pour hoster la constrainte de la rhetorique" (the embellishment of the story, so that it might be apprehended more obviously, and in order to remove the constraints of verse).[39] Liberated from the bonds of versification, the translator may convey his material with the fullness and adornment it deserves.

Some prosifiers explicitly link this unfettered prose to brevity, another quality said to be appreciated by modern audiences. In the prologue to his prose *Belle Hélène de Constantinople*, Jehan Wauquelin declares that the prose version of the story will "retrenchier et sincoper les prolongacions et motz inutiles qui souvent sont mis et boutez en telles rimes" (14; cut and abbreviate the lengthy passages and useless words that are often put into such verse). Philippe de Vigneulles repeatedly associates prosification and abridgement with the locution "mettre en prose et au plus brief" and also professes his intention to eliminate "parolles inutille" in the interest of avoiding "prolixitey."[40] Brevity is not the word that comes to mind when one sets out to read the 400-page edition of Wauquelin's *Belle Hélène* or the 650-page manuscript of Philippe's prose epic. In fact, both prosifiers are prone to amplification as well as abbreviation. Nonetheless, they clearly censure the verse epic for its verbal excess, and locate a greater utilitarian value in the medium of prose. The kinds of "useless words" and "lengthy passages" omitted in translation are unique to each prosifier. Generally speaking, however, most translators tend to strip the *chansons de geste* of the repetitions that modulate the epic *laisse*. Anticipatory passages and recapitulations, consecutive echoes and certain lyrical motifs (such as prayers and speeches) are often deemed to be nonessential material.[41] In both

---

[38] Spiegel, *Romancing the Past*, 55; see also Godzich and Kittay, *Emergence of Prose*, xiii–xiv.

[39] Qtd. in Doutrepont, *Les Mises en prose*, 389.

[40] General Prologue, fol. 1r; "inutille" is added in MS *h*, p. 6. Similar statements are made in later prologues and epilogues: fols. 59r, 59v, 305r.

[41] Doutrepont, *Les Mises en prose*, 560–600; *Belle Hélène*, Introduction, xvi; Jones,

authorial interventions and actual practice, the prose translators privilege narrative progression over the lyric pause.

None of the prosifiers dwells at length on the relative merits of verse and prose in storytelling. Once again, however, Philippe de Vigneulles's other works provide indirect commentary on the author's conceptual framework with respect to signifying practices. Philippe was no stranger to versification, as he composed a number of lyric poems that are mentioned or included as insertions in his prose compositions. Most enlightening in this respect is the *Journal*, which records three major encounters between verse and prose associated with three key moments in the author's narrative of the self: his surreptitious departure for Italy at the age of fifteen; his imprisonment at the hands of Jean de Harcourt, "capitaine de Chavency," in 1490–91; and his rise to success as a cloth merchant, culminating in the lavish artistic and literary composition he offered to his fellow citizens in 1507.

Philippe relates in some detail his furtive preparations for the voyage to Italy, which his father had actively opposed. Torn between wanderlust and his attachment to his father, Philippe did not leave Metz until he had devised a rather elaborate message for his family:

> je mis touttes mes choses en ordonnance et fis et escrips une lestre aissez bien faicte et bien dictée, tout *par rime et par vers*, en laquelle je rescripvois tout mon despair, et avec ce y avoit *pourtraiture* de plusieurs sortes tant de mon père, de ma suer, de son mairi et de plusieurs aultres et de nous, qui estoit en celle peinture, monstrant que nous perniens congié. Car celle fueille de papier estoit paper de Troye, et grand voullume, auquel y avoit encor *une lestre au dessoubz de celle pointure escripte en proise*, en laquelle estoit escript toutte ma voullunté et les escuses et recomendacions que je faisois devers mon père; et estoit celle lestre piteusement faicte et dictée, parquoy ledit mon père en plourait aissez.
>
> (*Journal* 13, my emphasis)

> [I put all of my things in order and made and wrote a letter, rather well written and well composed, all in *rhyme and verse*, in which I recounted everything about my departure, and with this there were several *portraits*: of my father, my sister, her husband, and several others, and the picture showed that we were taking leave of each other. For this piece of paper was paper from Troyes, of considerable proportions, on which there was also *a letter below the picture written in prose*, in which were written my intentions and the excuses and recommendations that I made to my father; and this letter was made and composed in a pathetic tone, which made my father cry a great deal.]

"Modernizing," 7–9. On echo, see Edward Heinemann, *L'Art métrique de la chanson de geste*.

While the letter itself is not included in Philippe's account, it is significant that he proposes here a three-layered process of communication. Thanks in part to the dimensions of the paper, the message is composed first in verse, then in pictorial images, and finally in prose. The three modes appear to fulfill distinct functions: the well-crafted verse letter provides a narrative account of his departure; the drawing depicts the family's physical separation; and the prose letter serves to explain, justify, and arouse the reader's emotions.

The *Journal* devotes over sixty-five pages to the home invasion and subsequent captivity that Philippe and his father endured shortly after the young man returned from Italy. It is during this period that the narrator reports a second surge of lyrical invention. His father having been successfully ransomed and liberated, Philippe suffers the physical and emotional hardships of solitary confinement. He claims to have found scraps of paper (which had previously served as window coverings in the prison cell) and bits of coal in order to compose two poems of captivity and three religious "oresons." Philippe reproduces the religious poetry in a separate manuscript, as it does not directly pertain to his plight (75). However, the captivity laments are included as lyric insertions in both the *Journal* and the *Chronique*.[42] The first of these poems contains twenty-four stanzas, all ending with a form of the refrain "Mauldicte soit trayson" (Accursed be treachery). Alternately plaintive and vituperative, the poetic voice issues a warning to fellow citizens of Metz, and complains bitterly about his captors as he proceeds to recapitulate the circumstances of his abduction. The second poem, which the narrator characterizes as "vers coppés," contains six heterometric stanzas, and was completed in Metz after Philippe's release (*Journal* 134). The poem proceeds in three general movements. Initially, the poet reproaches Jean de Harcourt, "capitaine de Chavancy," for the distress inflicted upon the hapless prisoner: "Tu m'as fait mectre en unne tour, / Dont j'en puis bien avoir doilleur / Plain de pleur" (*Journal* 132; You had me placed in a tower, which causes me much suffering, full of weeping). He then relates his alternating moments of hope and despair, referring specifically to the "Mauldicte soit trayson" poem he composed earlier: "N'estoit-ce pas bonne chanson?" (*Journal* 133; wasn't it a good song?") Finally, evoking Biblical miracles such as Jonah's release from the whale's belly, he praises God for his eventual deliverance, vowing never to forget his his ordeal: "Tous les jours arais l'istoire / En mémoire" (*Journal* 134; I will keep the story in my memory forever).

The lyric insertion device, as Maureen Boulton has ably demonstrated, constitutes both a disruptive and a unifying force within the surrounding narrative.[43] Philippe's captivity laments are set off from the whole not only by their verse structure, but also by the use of the first person, which the narrator

---

[42] See Chapter 1, note 7.

[43] Maureen Barry McCann Boulton, *The Song in the Story: Lyric Insertions in French Narrative Fiction* (Philadelphia: U of Pennsylvania Press, 1993), esp. 284–289.

had temporarily abandoned for this portion of the *Journal*. The poems were ostensibly composed (at least in part) during the very period that the narrator attempts to reconstruct in his later prose account, and thus lend authenticity to the narrative of suffering. Verse and prose overlap to some extent, as both recall the circumstances of the crime as well as the victim's physical and psychological torment. The laments, however, are clearly intended to convey the subjective experience more forcefully, as the repeated accusations of "traÿson" structure the first poem, and the perpetrator's name and title echo throughout the second. The prose is much lengthier, providing a minute-by-minute report of the violence inflicted upon father and son.

The third juncture of verse and prose in the *Journal* is a veritable multimedia event that Philippe orchestrated for the city of Metz on St. Mark's feast day in 1507. The narrator proudly recalls how he fabricated an intricate "patchwork quilt" composed of 9,000 pieces of cloth and depicting various religious and political figures.[44] In addition to a brief prayer to the Virgin contained within the cloth, the production featured a tablet with a poem (six octosyllabic *huitains*), followed by a long prose letter. The entire installation was displayed in front of Metz cathedral throughout the feast day (*Journal* 154–56).

The poem opens with a prayer to the Trinity, asking God to protect the city and its inhabitants from the dangers that menace all humanity. However, the clothmaker-poet soon turns to his primary concern, which is denouncing slanderous rivals and daring them to produce a mosaic fabric of the same quality, wagering ten *escus* that no such artist will come forward: ("Contre eulx je y mestrai x escus" *Journal* 155). He would gladly have himself cut to pieces if his work were outdone, but vows by St. Germain that he can survive any challenge. The final stanza playfully introduces the prose letter to follow:

> Car il est temps que me repouze
> En délaissant ma retouricque;
> Je n'y entans teste ne glouze
> Fors ainsy que je m'aplicque.
> Aussy n'est-ce pas ma praticque;
> Pour ce vault mieux qu'acripve en prouze. (*Journal* 156)

[For it is time for me to rest, setting aside my poetry; I intend by it no text or gloss other than the one I apply myself to giving. Furthermore, this is not my usual practice; thus it is best that I write in prose.]

Immediately following this lyric insertion is a summary of the prose letter:

---

44 See Janine Janniere, "Filling in Quilt History: A Sixteenth-Century French Patchwork Banner," *Quilt Journal* 3 (1994): 1–6.

Item, dessoubz ces dits vers huictains et on dit taubliaux meisme y avoit une grande lestre en prose, où estoient plusieurs parolles en déclairant la manière et pourquoy ce dit draps avoit esté fait, et entre lesquelles parolles y avoit que je Phillippe dessus nommé me offrois et présantois à mectre x escus d'or en l'encontre de ung à tous ceulx qui ouseroient entreprendre de en faire ung pareil draps ou à moitié tant seulement. Et y avoit en la dite lettre que sans voulloir personne blaimer je me offrois à mectre la dite somme encontre tous ceulx de la cité de Mets, de la duchié de Bair et de Loraine. (156)

[Item, below these *huitains* and on the same tablet there was a long letter in prose, where there were many words declaring the manner in which this cloth had been made, and why; and among these declarations it was indicated that I Philippe, the aforementioned, offered and proposed to wager ten *escus* in gold against one to all those who would dare attempt to produce such a cloth or even one half as good. And the letter said that without blaming anyone, I offered to wager this sum to anyone in the city of Metz, the duchy of Bar and the duchy of Lorraine.]

Like Philippe's youthful letter of departure, then, his later civic production mobilizes image, verse, and prose. Here, however, the mature narrator expresses a distinct inclination for the medium of prose, which he uses to fill in the attendant circumstances of the exhibition. Significantly, the prose letter is placed last on the tablet and appears to be, at least in part, a "translation" of the preceding verse, reiterating the wager but stripping the verse account of its internal repetitions and colorful oaths.

The juxtapositions of verse and prose mentioned and incorporated in the *Journal* are not blueprints for the prosification of verse epic. However, they do reveal some fundamental assumptions about the aesthetic and cultural values the author attached to each medium. While Philippe echoes the widespread preference for the practice of prose, he repeatedly deploys prose in conjunction with verse, with or without accompanying images. Furthermore, in the *Journal*, verse composition consistently precedes prose: physically, in the case of the departure letter and the tablet, and historically, in the case of the captivity narrative, as the poetry is said to pre-date the prose autobiography that encompasses it. This anteriority privileges verse as a primary though more obscure form of discourse: born of the moment, it requires subsequent interpretation and amplification in prose.[45] Both verse and prose are used as vehicles of narration and providers of circumstantial information, although prose predictably dominates this function. Both are capable of conveying and evoking emotion (it is the prose portion of the departure letter

---

[45] In this respect, Philippe's notions of prosaics diverge somewhat from the conventional view, dating from Aristotle's *Poetics*, that prose is anterior to verse, and is more "natural" than elaborate verse. See Godzich and Kittay, *Emergence of Prose*, xi.

that moves Philippe's father to tears). Most often, the two practices fulfill distinct but complementary functions: like the portraits, prose enhances the verse, but does not replace it.

In similar fashion, Philippe appears to have conceived of his epic *mise en prose* as a helpful supplement to the original verse epic, rather than a replacement. Just as he includes miniatures for pictorial support (in MS *h*), the translator offers his prose rendering as a sort of auxiliary tool. When he chooses to retell an episode in abridged form, for example, he cordially invites the more inquiring reader to consult the source for further details: "Et qui plus savoir en vouldrait cy lise le livre nommez le *Lorainz Guerins* et la trowairait le tout" (fol. 11v; And whoever wishes to know more should read the book called the *Lorainz Guerins* and there find the whole passage). Whereas the prose historiographers and romancers of earlier generations had sought to critique the inherent value of verse, Philippe's notion of prosaics is more inclusive. In imagining the ideal reception of the Lorraine epic, he envisages a reader similar to the spectator of his textile/textual masterpiece, a reader capable of moving freely through the language of image, verse, and prose.

Philippe's adaptation of the Lorraine cycle has typically been construed as an incidental composition, tied to his other works only by the common thread of civic pride. When collated with his other narrative (and lyrico-narrative) texts, however, the *mise en prose* proves to be consonant with the more general cultural concerns that preoccupied the author. More than any other translator-derhymer, Philippe demonstrates an intellectual and personal attachment to the material and the process of *translatio*.

3

Excellent Stories, Marvelous Deeds and the Prosaics of Crisis

This chapter will consider Philippe de Vigneulles' particular engagement with the matter of Lorraine, which he extols in the general prologue as a story of "grande excellance et merveilleux faitz d'armes" (fol. 1r; great excellence and marvelous feats of arms). Philippe's prose, as we have seen, faithfully reproduces the narrative content of all four branches of the Lorraine cycle. Rigorous comparison of verse and prose has thus led some to conclude that the rewriting is distinguished only by formal and stylistic modifications. Otto Böckel, in his analysis of the *Hervis* branch, declares that Philippe's work is essentially a linguistic modernization, without any change in meaning or narrative coherence.[1] It is my contention, however, that the content acquires supplementary meanings and functions in its *translatio* to early sixteenth-century Metz. The *istoire* reworked by this prolific author also forms new intertextual relationships as it joins a corpus conditioned by distinct historical and aesthetic forces. Implicit and explicit links between the *mise en prose* and Philippe's other works highlight specific aspects of the narrative, weaving the epic legend into the author's civic, personal and literary preoccupations. The excellence of the material proves to reside in its geopolitical resonance, its affinities with the author's own story of the self, and its affirmation of the culture of anxiety that permeates Philippe's writing.

The Burgundian Version: A Contrastive Model

By the fifteenth century, the Lorraine epic cycle was a virtual repository of narrative material susceptible of appropriation by diverse political and cultural interests. The story was renowned above all for its cyclical account of warfare between two clans. Indeed, the bitter feudal rivalry recounted in the Lorraine epics was so well known in the Middle Ages that lengthy conflicts

---

[1] Otto Böckel, *Phillipp de Vigneulles Bearbeitung des Hervis de Mes* (Marburg: C. L. Pfeil, 1883). Böckel affirms that "Vigneulles Bearbeitung wesentlich eine Erneuerung der Sprache, ohne irgend welche Aenderung an Sinn und Zusammenhang des Gedichtes ist" (39). See also Herbin's notion of "degree zero" in "Approches," 499.

in the real world were often said to be "as long as the wars fought by Garin le Lorrain."[2] The internecine hostilities in the poems are inextricably linked to power relations between king and vassal, as three generations of heroes on both sides fall victim to the whims of the seemingly immortal King Pepin. It is important to note, however, that this overall plot line applies only to *Garin le Lorrain* and the continuations devoted to succeeding generations (*Gerbert de Metz* and *Yon / Anseÿs*). The great feud between "Loherains" and "Bordelais" does not figure in the reverse sequel *Hervis de Metz*, which recounts the origins of Garin's lineage. This belated prologue to the *geste*, which reinvents the heroes as descendants of both royal and merchant ancestors, incorporates motifs from folklore and romance in its narration of the "enfances Hervis."[3]

In assessing Philippe's adaptation of this material, it is useful first to consider briefly an earlier prose redaction of the same cycle. (I shall set aside for the moment the highly abridged *Prose de l'Arsenal*, which reduces the verse texts to approximately one-seventh of their word content.[4]) We have seen that the Lorraine epic held considerable appeal for the Burgundian ducal court, owing principally to the cycle's depiction of valiant, powerful barons at odds with the weak, conniving Pepin. In the prosification commissioned by Philippe le Bon, three of the branches (*Garin, Gerbert*, and *Anseÿs*) are joined with *Girart de Roussillon* to form a compilation entitled (inappropriately) *L'Histoire de Charles Martel*.[5] Valérie Naudet suggests that the seemingly heterogeneous compilation responds in complex ways to the Duke's ambitious agenda.[6] Aligning himself at once with the royal ancestors of Charlemagne, of whom he claimed to be the descendant, and with the rebellious vassals, who struggle against inadequate kings, Philippe le Bon identified material that suited his political imagining. In his opening summary, the anonymous translator adroitly manages to convey the elevated status of Charlemagne's ancestors as well as their debt to great vassals:

---

2 Anne Iker Gittleman, *Le Style épique dans Garin le Loherain* (Geneva: Droz, 1967), 16–17.

3 See Catherine M. Jones, *The Noble Merchant: Problems of Genre and Lineage in Hervis de Mes*, North Carolina Studies in the Romance Languages and Literatures 241 (Chapel Hill: U.N.C. Dept. of Romance Languages, 1993).

4 See Jean-Charles Herbin, "Une Mise en prose de la *Geste des Loherains*: le manuscrit Arsenal 3346," *Traduction, transcription, adaptation au moyen âge*, Actes du Colloque du Centre d'études médiévales et dialectales de Lille III, septembre 1994, *Bien dire et bien aprandre* 13–14, 237–56, at p. 239.

5 After the death of Philippe le Bon, Charles le Téméraire continued to finance the project, ordering the illuminations. See Naudet, *Guerin le Loherain*, Introduction, 6–7; Naudet, "Une Compilation," 74, note 13; and Straub, *David Aubert, escripvain et clerc*, 195.

6 Naudet, *Guerin le Loherain*, Introduction, 10–11.

Il est a croire que Charles Martel fut roy de France en son temps non mie par vraye succession de droitte lignie, mais par la grace de Nostre Seigneur et par bonne fortune, quy ainsi luy aida. Et regna Pepin, son filz, aprés luy comme son filz et herittier par le moyen d'aucuns princes de France, mais non mie du consentement de tous, car la plus grant partie en fist reffus pour la petitesse de sa personne. Touttefois ung en y eut entre les autres quy, pour loyaulté soustenir, sachant qu'il estoit filz du roy Charles Martel, luy aida. (*Guerin le Loherain* 53)

[It should be believed that Charles Martel was King of France in his time, not by rightful succession, but by the grace of Our Lord and with the help of good fortune, which thus helped him. And Pepin his son reigned after him as his son and heir through the agency of some French nobles, but not with the consent of all, for the majority refused him because of his short stature. Nonetheless there was one among them who, to sustain loyalty, knowing that he was the son of Charles Martel, helped him.]

Indeed, the vassals in question figure the duke's real status as well as his desired one: Girart de Roussillon is Duke of Burgundy; Garin le Lorrain and his descendants hold claim to Lorraine, which the duchy had always aspired to possess as a means of joining the two parts of its bicephalous territory.[7]

Unlike Philippe de Vigneulles, the anonymous Burgundian translator frequently amplifies his sources, often in accordance with courtly conventions. The rearing of young Garin le Lorrain and his brother Begon is a case in point. The verse texts are content to inform us that the boys were raised by their uncle until they attained physical maturity:

> les enfanz garde que il velt porveïr
> tant que grant furent, parcreü et tehi.
> Plus beaux nen ot en .lx. païs. (*Garin le Loherenc* vv. 1018–19)

[he cares for the children, whom he wishes to protect, until they were tall, fully grown, and mature; there were none more handsome than they in sixty countries.]

The Burgundian prose version elaborates by furnishing the details of a proper aristocratic education:

> et tellement creurent en vertus et en puissance de corps et en toutes habilitez qu'en tout le paiis de Champaigne n'avoit ancoires deux aussi gentilz damoiseaulx ne ausquelz tous deduiz et tous esbattemens seissent mieulx. Certes ilz estoient endoctrinez et instruitz bien a merveilles en sçavoir estre entre les nobles, en parler, en respondre et en eulz sçavoir

---

[7] Naudet, "Une Compilation," 73–74. See also her introduction to *Guerin le Loherain*, 12.

en toutes joyeuses manieres conduire et maintenir en chasse, en gibier, en armes et en amours et autrement en toutes fachons, comme l'en eust sceu ou voulu souhaidier. (*Guerin le Loherain* 81)

[and they grew so much in virtue, in bodily strength and in all skills that in the entire region of Champagne there were no two young noblemen so courtly nor so adept in all elegant pastimes. Truly they were marvelously educated and accomplished in appropriate behavior in noble company, in speaking and responding, in knowing how to conduct themselves when observing all pleasant customs, in hunting beasts and birds, in arms and in love, and in all other respects, as much as anyone could know or wish for.]

Principally characterized in the verse by their fierce loyalty to lineage, Garin and Begon assume in addition the manners and comportment of courtly princes. Like the other works and spectacles commissioned by the dukes of Burgundy, the translation of the Lorraine epic served in part to preserve notions of chivalry that had lost their luster after centuries of failed Crusades.[8] It is thus no surprise that the translator later amplifies Garin le Lorrain's pious (though belated) repentance and desire to visit the Holy Land. While the verse devotes a few short lines to Garin's devout intentions, the Burgundian prose furnishes a lengthy enumeration of the warrior's past sins and an eloquent rendition of his contrition and promise to visit the Holy Sepulchre.[9] The following is but a short excerpt:

il se recordoit et en soy repentant faisoit si grande conscience en demenant ung doeul esmerveillable que il conclut en soy de faire raison a ceulx envers lesquelsz il povoit avoir mespris. Et ce fait il promist d'aler ou Saint // voyage de Jherusalem visitter le Sepulchre de Nostre Seigneur en penitance et amendrissement de ses pechiés. (KBR 8, fols. 4r–4v)

[He recalled {his sins}, and repenting, so deeply examined his conscience, lamenting marvelously, that he decided to make reparations toward those whom he might have wronged. He then promised to take the Holy pilgrimage to Jerusalem to visit the sepulchre of Our Lord in penitence and with a view to diminishing his sins.]

Thus the Burgundian translator fashioned his prose to respond to the cultural and moral climate of the ducal court. Nonetheless, he shares with all redactors – verse and prose alike – an overarching sense of wonder and horror at the long, endlessly renewable feud that destroyed generations of worthy knights:

---

8 Robert Guiette, "Chanson de geste, chronique et mise en prose," *Forme et Senefiance*, Études médiévales recueillies par Jean Dufournet, Marcel De Grève, and Herman Braet (Geneva: Droz, 1978), 135–62, esp. 39.

9 *Garin le Loherenc* vv. 15,945–47, 15,976–77; KBR 8, fols. 3v–4v.

l'istoire a parlé des peres, de leurs guerres et discordz, [voeul] parler des
enfans, de leurs fais, vaillances, entreprises et vangances, quy sont choses
moult merveilleuses a ouÿr racompter, car de pere en filz la paix ne se poult
oncques trouver que tousjours la guerre ne renouvellast, comme plus aplain
est contenu es croniques et livres anciens. (KBR 9, fol. 1v)

[the story has told of the fathers, of their wars and disputes, {I wish} to
speak of the children, their deeds, acts of valor, endeavors and acts of
vengeance, which are marvelous to hear and to recount, for from father to
son peace could never be found without the war always rekindling, as is
more fully stated in the old books and chronicles.]

Herein lies the tragic lesson of the Lorraine epic, a lesson that crosses
temporal and spatial boundaries.

This brief overview does not do justice to the *Histoire de Charles Martel*,
a literary monument worthy of being fully edited and examined in its own
right. However, the passages cited here are representative of the translation's
general orientation. Exemplars of chivalry and piety, the Lorraine heroes
prove terrible in their vengeance and worthy in their opposition to royal
injustice. For my purposes, the *Histoire* is of interest as a contrastive model,
composed for an aristocratic audience who sought in the prose adaptation a
reflection of its own chivalric ideals and aspirations.

Archeology and *Translatio*

As the self-appointed chronicler of an urban community, Philippe de
Vigneulles read these "political fictions" through a different grid of expectations.[10] It is true that, like his courtly counterpart, he highlights the value of
the story as a cautionary tale, going so far as to question the basis for the
conflict: "lesquelles deux lignees por bien peu d'occasion sont venues en
grant confusion et se sont mis l'ung l'autre a fin" (fol. 325r; two lineages
which, for very little reason, came to great destruction and caused each
other's end). He ends his translation by issuing a warning to contemporary
rulers: "avise a tous prince et seigneur que bien ce doit on garder de follie
entreprendre, car la fin est dangereuse et malvaise et n'en peult nul bien
venir" (fol. 325v; I warn all princes and lords that one should avoid foolish
endeavors, for the end result is dangerous and bad, and no good can come
of it).[11]

---

[10] The term is from Sarah Kay, *The Chansons de geste in the Age of Romance:
Political Fictions* (Oxford: Clarendon, 1995).

[11] For the quotations on fol. 325v, I have relied in part on the transcription in Karl
Jahn, *Philipp de Vigneulle's Yonnet de Mes und sein Verhältnis zu Redaction N des Romans
Anseïs de Mes*, Dissertation (Greifswald: H. Adler, 1903), 77. This portion of the manu-
script is copied in a modern hand and is barely legible on microfilm.

At the same time, Philippe's translation is a response to more localized phenomena. His fierce attachment to the history and preservation of Metz cannot be overstated, as evidenced by Pierre Demarolle's playful analogy: "le chroniqueur a pour sa ville les yeux d'un amant heureux."[12] This ardent devotion goes far beyond Philippe's historiographical writing. He composed his prose translation during a critical transitional period in the history of Metz. The free imperial city had enjoyed a very favorable economic and political position throughout the Middle Ages, managing to defend itself against incursions by powerful regional enemies, particularly the dukes of Lorraine. Metz had preserved its autonomy under the oligarchic structure of the *paraiges*, six aristocratic families who shared virtually uncontested power, and who had succeeded in coopting the prosperous merchant class. Philippe de Vigneulles himself had fared very well under this system, and had an interest in promoting municipal solidarity. By 1514, however, when Philippe began his prose epic, this solidarity had begun to unravel. Martial Gantelet has documented the decline of civic consciousness in Metz during the late fifteenth and early sixteenth centuries.[13] The city's economy and defenses had been seriously damaged by war with the duchy of Lorraine in the 1470s, and by 1512 Metz was under attack by German mercenaries. The Empire was developing a more German identity, and the merchant class was beginning to resist demands for financial support of the city's defenses.

As the sense of a unified urban identity became more fragile, cultural manifestations of civic pride seem to have become more frequent. Philippe's *Chronique* describes numerous processions celebrating the history and prestige of Metz during this period. As the citizens moved through the urban space with its venerated monuments, it was hoped that they might be reawakened to the image of a strong and cohesive Metz.[14] Philippe commemorates these spectacles in his historiographic works, immortalizing the performances as written text.[15] He also provides detailed accounts of the numerous urban renewal efforts undertaken during his lifetime. Clearly, however, the *Chronique* – for all its copiousness – was not sufficient. As a further testimonial to the city's past greatness, the marvelous feats of epic heroes entered the

---

12 Demarolle, *La Chronique de Philippe de Vigneulles et la mémoire de Metz*, 31.

13 Martial Gantelet, "Entre France et Empire, Metz, une conscience municipale en crise à l'aube des Temps modernes (1500–1526)," *Revue Historique* 301, alt. 617 (2001): 5–45.

14 Gantelet, "Entre France et Empire," 11–12.

15 On late medieval performance and pageantry, see Barbara A. Hanawalt and Kathryn L. Reyerson, eds. *City and Spectacle in Medieval Europe*, Medieval Studies at Minnesota 6 (Minneapolis & London: U of Minnesota Press, 1994); David M. Bergeron, "Stuart Civic Pageants and Textual Performance," *Renaissance Quarterly* 51 (1998): 163–83; Sandra Logan, "Making History: The Rhetorical and Historical Occasion of Elizabeth Tudor's Coronation Entry," *Journal of Medieval and Early Modern Studies* 31 (2001): 251–82.

space of civic discourse, adding another layer of "history" to the endangered municipal consciousness.[16]

When Philippe refers to his translation project in both the *Chronique* and the *Journal*, the very act of prosifying the *chansons de geste* is framed by accounts of local crisis and city-building. In chronicling the events of the summer of 1515, Philippe relates a number of misfortunes that befell the city and surrounding area. He is particularly disturbed by a resurgence of the pillaging raids that had plagued merchants, particularly cloth merchants, for over two years. Although the merchants of Metz had been ordered to avoid the Frankfurt fair for their own protection, travellers from a neighboring town fell victim to thievery:

> Et vellà comment yceulx pouvre mairchant furent prins, détenus, et pardirent grant partie du leur. De quoy c'est moult mal fait à l'empereur de ainssy soubtenir en ces pays yceulx lairons pillairs, qui destruissent et robbe pellerins et merchamps, et ne demende que à mal faire; et n'y ait hommes que seurement ossaicent aller ne venir par ces pays et ampire. Dieu y vueulle provoir! Amen. (*Chronique* IV: 198; cf. *Journal* 283)

> [And that is how these poor merchants were seized and detained, and they lost a good part of what belonged to them. Hence the emperor is wrong thus to tolerate in these parts such pillaging thieves, who harm and rob pilgrims and merchants, and seek only to do evil; and there are no men who would dare to come and go with confidence in this country and empire. May God attend to this! Amen.]

Philippe follows this lament with an entry devoted to his own accomplishments, not as merchant but as author. He records his translation of "ancienne rime en prouse" as well as a "livre contenant cent nowelles," emphasizing that he finished his two books during the very same summer that merchants were being attacked across the region (*Journal* 283).[17] He then returns to matters of broader concern. Here, the *Chronique* and the *Journal* record a number of city renovations. In addition to windmills along the Seille River and walls

---

[16] It is not clear to what extent Philippe was able to reach a wide civic audience in the absence of print publication. We do know that a prominent local family commissioned a copy of the first volume of the *Chronique*, and that his historiographical work was well known in Metz. Given his status as a respected citizen (he was offered a municipal function, which he modestly refused) and his active participation in local cultural events, he clearly had the means to promote his work. See Bruneau's Introduction to the *Chronique*, I: vi–vii.

[17] For the complete passage, see Chapter 1, p. 6. In his historiographical works, Philippe often begins a new paragraph with "En celle dite année." In this particular section, however, he notes more than once that his books and the attacks on merchants occurred in the same year: "aussy en celle année [...] en la meisme année [...] Lesquelles livres furent fait et eschevis en l'an dessus dis"(*Chronique* IV: 198–99, cf. *Journal* 283).

along the Moselle, the city had financed the building of several bridges. This latter project led to a grisly archeological discovery:

> Et, en faisant les fondement de l'ung d'iceulx pont, l'on trouvait merveilleusement grant foison de teste de gens mors gectée et mise en terre l'une sur l'aultre, cen regairder comment; et y avoit aussy plusieurs aultres ossement; mais aulcune d'icelle teste furent trouveé la fasse dessoubz ou de cousté, et bien loing des aultre ossement. Et, pour ce, fault dire et est à croire que au temps passés fut là en ce lieu faicte une bataille et grant tuerie [...] Mais, comment qu'il en fût, il y ait cy loing temps que la chose avint qu'il n'y a ajourd'uy homme vyvant que jamaix, par escripture ny aultrement, en oyt parler, ne que en ce lieu y eust heu baitaille ne melléez.
>
> (*Chronique* IV: 199, cf. *Journal* 283–84)

> [And, while preparing the foundations of one of these bridges, they found a marvelously great quantity of dead people's skulls tossed in and buried carelessly one on top of the other; and there were also some other bones; but some of these heads were found face down or turned aside, and quite far from the other bones. Thus, it must be said and believed that in the past in this very spot there was a battle and great slaughter {...} But in any case, the event occurred so long ago that there is no one alive today who ever heard of it or knew that a battle or skirmish had taken place in that spot, through a written document or otherwise.]

Municipal improvements uncover forensic evidence of past violence, even more disquieting because there is no oral or written record of the turbulent event.

In the chronicle of Philippe's life and times, then, his work on the *mise en prose* is circumscribed textually by traces of aggression and acts of rebuilding. This sequencing of events for the summer of 1515 is not without significance. First, the framing device places the Lorraine epic material squarely within the space of contemporary urban problems, particularly those that plagued the merchant class. Second, by juxtaposing his translation of ancient verse with the discovery of undocumented remains, Philippe evokes a relationship between physical and writerly excavation. Lest the murderous but instructive conflicts of the Lorraine epic fade from public memory, the prosifier unearths and interprets poetic artifacts as a foundation for civic reconstruction.

This link between archeological and literary remnants is further strengthened by another discovery recounted in the *Chronique*. In 1513, the collapse of four houses exposed the remains of ancient city walls:

> car alors fut sairchiez cy perfon que l'on trouva le fon; et encor, en aulcuns lieu, fut cayvé plus baix que yceulx fondement, par quoy fut trouvés, comme j'ay dit devent, la grant magnificence de celle édificacion et premier foncacion. Car dessoubz yceulx fondement furent trouvée de grosse pier de tailles platte et cairée, esquelles y avoit figure et ymaige d'hommes et de

femmez eslevée et entaillée [...] et, avec ce, tout autour d'ycelle ymaige estoient plusieurs ancienne lettre rommaine escriptes, lesquelles nul ne pouoit lire pour leur anciennetés, et n'y avoit causy homme qui sceût entandre que ycelle lettre voulloient dire ne signifier.

(*Chronique* IV: 159, cf. *Journal* 250)

[then they searched so far below that they located the foundations {of the houses}; and further, in some places, they dug below the foundations, where they found, as I said before, the great magnificence of this construction and original foundations. For below these foundations were found large freestones, flat and square, on which sculpted images of men and women were carved {...} and, with this, all around these sculptures were several ancient Roman inscriptions, which no one could read because of their antiquity, and there was practically no one who could understand what these inscriptions meant or signified.]

Philippe's account of the inscriptions on these mysterious carvings parallels his assessment of the forgotten *chansons de geste*. We recall that in the authorial commentary to the prose epic, the verse tales of the city's glorious ancestors are said to have become virtually indecipherable to the people of Metz owing to their "anciennetey." Happily, the translator's craft ensures that the story will be seen and known ("weue et congneuez").[18] In Philippe's chronicle, the excavators and construction workers fulfill a similar role by restoring ancient objects to public scrutiny. Unlike the epic texts, the inscriptions surrounding the old statues are said to defy translation, but these artifacts of the Gallo-Roman period were nonetheless brought to the surface and recycled into the modern cityscape. Philippe assures us that most of the carved stones were subsequently integrated into the facades of the reconstructed houses for all to see ("comme encor ajourd'ui ce moustre," IV: 159).[19] The historical preservation project as Philippe records it thus figures the process of literary adaptation.

Le Livre de la belle Beaultris

The different branches of the cycle function in varying ways with respect to the geopolitical context underlying Philippe's project. While Philippe's major divisions do not correspond precisely to those of the existing cyclical verse manuscripts, it is possible to establish a general correlation between the sections of verse and prose.[20] The following concordance is based on

---

[18] For the complete passages, see Chapter 1, p. 11 and Chapter 2, p. 27.

[19] See Demarolle, *La Chronique de Philippe de Vigneulles et la mémoire de Metz*, 34.

[20] See Herbin, "Approches," 471–472 for the precise correlations of folios (in the prose) and verse numbers in modern editions.

the conventional modern French titles given to the *chansons de geste* and shortened versions of Philippe's book titles as they appear in the prologues and epilogues:

Verse	Philippe's Prose
Hervis de Metz	*Le Livre de la belle Beaultris*
Garin le Lorrain	*Guerin I, Guerin II*
Gerbert de Metz	*Guerin III*
Anseÿs de Metz (*de Gascogne*)	*Yonnet*[21]

Of the three surviving prose versions, Philippe's is the only one to incorporate the branch commonly known as *Hervis de Metz*. It is possible, of course, that the other prosifiers did not have access to the manuscripts preserving this continuation. However, there is some indication that the Burgundian prosifier was aware of the story, as he mentions "old chronicles" that allude to events transpiring in this branch. The *Histoire de Charles Martel* refers specifically to a key innovation of *Hervis de Metz*, the reinvention of the hero's father as a non-noble:

> l'istoire ait en aucunes anciennes croniques, dont cestes dependent, trouvé qu'il ne descendist mie de grant gentillesse sinon du costé de sa mere, ce non obstant touteffois il ne fourligna pas ne oncques il ne fist chose par laquelle il en deust perdre le nom ne estre aucunement reprochié en court de prince ne d'autre seigneur. (*Guerin le Loherain* 73)

> [The story relates in some old chronicles, related to the present tale, that {Hervis} was not descended from great nobility, except on his mother's side; despite this, nevertheless, he never brought shame on his lineage and never did anything that might cause him to lose his good name or in any way invite reproach in the court of a prince or other lord.]

As Valérie Naudet suggests, the narrator seems troubled by accounts of Hervis's mixed lineage, and seeks to downplay any sources that might confirm this ancestry.[22]

---

21 Only the first 1441 lines of *Anseÿs* (as it appears in Arsenal 3143, edited by Green) can be compared to Philippe's *Yonnet*. After this point, the two narratives diverge significantly. See Herbin, "*Yonnet de Metz*," 33.

22 Naudet, *Guerin le Loherain*, introduction, 30. It is true that texts other than the continuation *Hervis de Metz* contain references to mixed lineage. Some manuscripts of the verse *Garin le Lorrain*, a text in which Hervis's pure nobility is not expressly questioned, refer to Hervis as a "villain" in one passage. This may be attributed to the confusion between the Loherain hero and another character in the story, Hervis le Villain. In *Gerbert de Metz*, the Bordelais knights taunt the Lorraine heroes with their ancestor's shady origins (vv. 4864–81), and two of the prologues in the cyclical manuscripts mention (faulty) sources claiming that Hervis was the son of a "vilain." All of these texts, however,

For his part, Philippe, who was clearly determined to render the totality of the story, gives special prominence to the *Hervis* portion of the narrative. This tale is best suited to the glorification of the city's past, as Metz is the focal point of the hero's ascendance to power. In the *Chronique*, where Philippe includes a summary of the Lorraine cycle as part of the city's history, the youthful adventures of Hervis occupy eighty-five per cent of the narrative, while the lengthy and notorious feud between Lorrains and Bordelais is dispatched in a few paragraphs (I: 162–169).

In the verse redactions, Hervis is manifestly the central figure of the branch devoted to Garin's ancestors, as is evident in the jongleur's prologue:

> Bone chanson plast vos a escouter?
> Des Loharans vos voromes chanter:
> [Com]e Hervis li gentis et li bers,
> [Cil] qui fut peres Garin le redotei
> [Et au] cuen Bégue qui tant ot de bontei,
> [To]ute la tresse vos en vorai conter. (*Hervis de Mes* vv. 2–7)[23]

[Do you wish to hear a good song? We want to sing of the Lorrains, how the noble baron Hervis, father of the redoubtable Garin and of Count Begon, who was so full of goodness {...} I wish to tell you the whole story.]

However, in Philippe's reworking, other characters share the spotlight. In fact, the translator is not entirely consistent in the labels he accords to the various books that comprise his adaptation. At the end of the section that corresponds to *Hervis de Metz* in the verse redactions, Philippe describes the preceding narrative inclusively, declaring it to be the story of Garin's parents and grandparents:

> Icy devent est finee la vie et istoire du duc Pier de Louraine et de Aelis sa fille. Paireillement de la belle Beautris fille a Eustaiche le roy de Thir et suer a roy Fleur de Honguerie. Et du noble duc Hervey de Mets son bon mary. (fol. 59r)

[Thus ends the life and story of Duke Pierre of Lorraine and of Aelis his daughter. Likewise that of fair Beatrice, daughter of Eustache, King of Tyre, and sister of King Floire of Hungary. And that of the noble Duke Hervis of Metz, her good husband.]

---

postdate *Hervis de Metz* and may have been influenced by its version of the Lorraine heroes' lineage. See Gittleman, *Le Style épique dans Garin le Loherain*, 211–212 and August Rhode, "Die Beziehungen zwischen den Chansons de geste *Hervis de Mes* und *Garin le Loherain*," *Ausgaben und Abhandlungen* 3 (1881): 123–76, at p. 134.

[23] The sentence is incomplete, leading Herbin to suggest a lacuna in the common ancestor of the extant manuscripts (*Hervis de Mes* 537, note to vv. 4–7).

The noble but spendthrift Pierre, Duke of Metz and Lorraine,[24] makes only brief appearances in the text. This character, however, is the basis for one of Philippe's lengthiest amplifications, and one of the rare instances in which he inserts moralizing commentary. The story opens with an account of the duchy's economic woes, brought about by Pierre's excessive expenditures in tournaments and unrestrained largess toward his vassals. In Philippe's translation, the prose narrator intervenes to assure us that, despite his financial predicament, the ancestor of the Lorraine epic heroes does not resort to the questionable tactics of present-day rulers:

> Or estoit iceluy duc homme de bone conscience et qui craindoit Dieu et qui tenoit son païs bien en paix *sans le taillier ne gabellier*. Par quoy tous merchamps et touttes aultres gens vivoient en paix et se anrichissoient dessoubz luy. *Et n'estoit point iceluy duc comme sont aujourd'huy beaucopt d'aultres princes par la crestientey*, lesquelz pour leur plaisance ou proffiz particulier *gectent une grosse taille et font paier de grant gavelles* a leur subgectz sans çans et sans raison dont le pouvre peuple se sant souvent foullez et apowris. Mais iceluy duc Piere ne le faisoit point aincy. Car jamais n'eust souffris que taille ou levee eussent esté fait par son païs sans grant et juste cause et par bons conseille et dreis et grande // deliberacion sur ce heue et que ce eust esté pour ung grant et juste cas. Et pour ce, considerant que prodigallement avoit despendu, le preus ne voulut icelluy souffrir que son peuple fut foullés ne taillés comme dit est, jay ce que soubz luy y heust de moult grant et riches merchamps.
>
> (fols. 1v–2r, my emphasis)

> [This duke was a man of good conscience who feared God and kept his country in peace *without imposing the taille or gabelle tax*.[25] Thus all merchants and all other people lived in peace and grew prosperous under him. *And this duke was not at all like many Christian princes of today*, who for their own pleasure or particular profit impose a heavy *taille* and force their subjects to pay large *gabelles* senselessly and without reason, causing the poor people often to feel oppressed and impoverished. But Duke Pierre did not act in this way. For he never would have allowed a *taille* or tax to be imposed in his land without a great and just cause, and through good and right counsel after great deliberation, and the reasons for doing so being important and appropriate. Therefore, considering that he had spent prodigally, the worthy man refused to allow his people to be oppressed or taxed, as mentioned, even though many great and rich merchants lived under him.]

---

24 The duke's title, like that of his descendants, does not correspond to historical reality, as there was never a Duke of Metz. See Michel Parisse, "Garin le Loherain dans l'histoire de son temps," *La Geste des Lorrains*, ed. François Suard, Littérales 10 (Paris: Centre de Recherche des Littératures, Université Paris X, Branche française de la Société Rencesvals, 1992), 51–64, esp. 54.

25 A *taille* was a tax paid to a lord, while a *gabelle* was a tax on specified commodities.

Although the duke's merits are described negatively (he is praised for what he does **not** do), the legendary figure serves here as a model of aristocratic behavior, an example that present-day princes would do well to imitate. It is surely no coincidence that Philippe's commentary comes just three years after the Emperor Maximilian's unsuccessful attempt to impose a "grosse taille" on the city of Metz, an incident that Philippe recounts at length in his *Chronique* (IV: 137–40). The champion of civic independence thus manages to chastise both ducal and imperial misconduct in a single gloss. By declaring that modern princes do not measure up to their past counterparts, he implicitly diminishes the status of contemporary dukes of Lorraine; by denouncing excessive taxation, he recalls the city's successful resistance to the Emperor's economic encroachment. Despite his minimal role in the original story, then, Duke Pierre looms large in Philippe's cast of characters.

A more profound modification in Philippe's prose is the gradual displacement of Hervis as the eponymous hero of the first branch. As work on the translation progressed, the first book crystallized around the figure of Beatrice, wife of Hervis and mother of Garin and Begon. Whereas earlier prologues and epilogues defined the branch's material by enumerating three generations of the heroes' forebears, the beginning of the final branch, *Yonnet*, attributes a new and more specific name to the first segment:

> je Philippe de Vignuelle dessus nommés ait eschevis, extraicte et compouseis cest deux livre precedant, *nommeis l'ung la belle Beaultris fille au roy Hutaisse de Thir*, et l'aultre c'est dez mervilleux fait d'airme du Lourain Guerin de Mets, du duc Baigue de Bellin son frere et de tout leur lignie. (fol. 306r, my emphasis)

> [I, the aforementioned Philippe de Vigneulles, completed, translated and composed the two preceding books, *one of which is called Fair Beatrice, Daughter of King Eustache of Tyre*; the other is about the marvelous feats of arms of the Lorrain Garin of Metz, his brother Begon of Belin and their entire lineage].

Ultimately, when mentioning the first branch, Philippe would designate the finished product simply as "le Livre de la belle Beaultris" (*Chronique* IV: 198; cf. *Journal* 283).

This revisionist title draws attention to a character who plays a vital role in the founding myth of the Lorraine lineage. In the verse redactions of *Hervis de Metz*, Beatrice brings royal blood to a genealogy in need, for Hervis is portrayed as the product of a socially hybrid union between Duke Pierre's daughter Aelis and a wealthy cloth merchant.[26] An exotic Eastern princess,

---

[26] See Jones, *The Noble Merchant*, and Kimberlee A. Campbell, "The Reiterated Self: Cyclical Temporality and Ritual Renewal in *Hervis de Metz*," *Transtextualities: Of Cycles and Cyclicity in Medieval French Literature*, eds. Sara Sturm-Maddox and Donald

Beatrice is also great-aunt to Charlemagne, as her brother Floire is declared to be the father of Berte au grand pied.[27] In Philippe's prose, as in the verse, Beatrice's bloodline links the *geste des Loherains* – as lineage and epic cycle – to the most noble of *gestes*, that of "grant roy Charlemaigne de France, lequelle roy Charles fut si vaillant qu'il est mis au nombre des preus" (fol. 6r; the great King Charlemagne of France, King Charles who was so courageous that he counts among the worthies).[28] To a large extent, Philippe's feminized title recognizes and confirms the importance of matrilineal structures in the verse original.[29] Despite the presence of bourgeois blood in their genealogy, Hervis and his descendants are possessed of noble instincts and talents inherited from their noble maternal ancestors.[30]

In addition, the renaming positions Beatrice in the center of the narrative, shifting the focus from the fledgling knight Hervis to his much-disputed bride. In this way, the story becomes aligned with the relatively small number of French medieval epics named after women, such as *Aye d'Avignon, Belle Hélène de Constantinople, Parise la Duchesse* and *Florence de Rome*. These eponymous heroines are complex figures, not to be dismissed as mere pawns in male characters' struggles for land and power. It is true that, as Sarah Kay has observed, the texts in question spin their female protagonists "in a vortex of sexualized violence."[31] Victims of male desire and aggression, they nevertheless assume a great deal of authority by demonstrating moral and discursive prowess, exposing the flaws in the social order that allowed such violence to erupt.[32]

Beatrice already displays common traits with these heroines in the verse redactions of *Hervis de Metz*. Initially promised to an elderly "pagan" king, she is kidnapped, put up for sale, purchased by Hervis, coveted by bandits,

---

Maddox, Medieval & Renaissance Texts & Studies 149 (Binghamton, NY: Center for Medieval and Early Renaissance Studies, State U of New York at Binghamton, 1996), 157–77, esp. 173.

27 *Hervis de Mes* vv. 626–30.

28 This is a reference to the Neuf Preux or Nine Worthies: Joshua, Judas Maccabee, David, Hector, Alexander, Julius Caesar, Charlemagne, Godefroy de Bouillon, and King Arthur.

29 Similarly, sixteenth-century historiography of the French monarchy mobilized female figures to fill gaps in the continuity of royal lineage. Jean Bouchet, in his *Jugement poetic de l'honneur femenin*, closes the gap between Clotaire I and Pepin the Short through the figure of Blitilde. See the edition and commentary by Adrian Armstrong (Paris: Champion, 2006), vv. 2726–37 and Appendix 493.

30 See Jones, *The Noble Merchant*, 21, 68–94.

31 Kay, *Chansons de geste in the Age of Romance*, 158. She refers here to Aye d'Avignon and Florence de Rome, but the same may be said of Belle Hélène.

32 See Kay, *Chansons de geste in the Age of Romance* and, by the same author, "La Représentation de la féminité dans les chansons de geste," *Charlemagne in the North: Proceedings of the Twelfth International Conference of the Société Rencesvals* (London: Grant & Cutler, 1993), 223–240.

and unjustly accused of prostitution. Kidnapped a second time, she becomes the prize in a war between her husband Hervis and the elderly Spanish king championed by her male relatives. Yet, Beatrice is far from being the helpless victim of male aggression in the early episodes of the story. As Kimberlee Campbell has demonstrated, this heroine actively constructs her identity, albeit according to the standards of the epic universe:

> Beatris, like Hervis, creates her "self" through performance, in her case as a worthy wife and mother, exhibiting loving fidelity to Hervis in all circumstances. Her figurative death, when kidnapped from her father's garden and therefore separated from her genealogical identity, and her subsequent performance bring into being a Beatris who is an ideal of womanhood [...][33]

The verse versions, however, tend to efface Beatrice once her identity has been constructed. The ideal wife and mother, no longer able to determine her own fate, becomes a spectator in the male competition for her body. In the branch devoted to *Garin le Lorrain*, Hervis's wife[34] simply disappears from the text after her husband is slain on the battlefield. By contrast, the newly christened *Livre de la belle Beaultris* elevates the maternal figure to a higher status. In Philippe's reworking, she is consistently ranked among the heroes of the lineage in the prologues and epilogues. Her sepulchre in the monastery of St. Arnoult is cited along with those of Hervis and Garin in the parade of tombs that graces the general prologue (fol. 1r).[35] In the second book of his prose translation, Philippe modifies the original verse by linking the deaths of Hervis and his wife. The prose recounts the death of Beatrice as well as her burial in a familiar local monument:

> sa leaulle femme et amie, laquelle menait si grant deuil qu'elle ne vesquist gueire aprés, ains fu noblement encevellis en l'abaiees de Sainct Arnoult devent la pourte la ou encor a presant gissent. (fol. 70r)

> [his loyal wife and beloved, who was in such great mourning that she did not live long afterward, but rather was nobly buried in the abbey of St. Arnoult before the gate, where they still lie at the present time.]

We have seen that such references serve both to authenticate narrative events and to suffuse local sites with historical meaning. Furthermore, by adding a female celebrity to the list of worthies immortalized in his prose, Philippe offers the city a mythical patroness to complement the female saints

---

[33] Campbell, "The Reiterated Self," 173.

[34] Aelis is the name given to Hervis's wife in *Garin le Lorrain*. The continuation, *Hervis de Metz*, gives her a new name and origin.

[35] See Chapter 2, pp. 22–23.

and allegorical figures venerated during urban celebrations. The *Chronique* relates one such elaborate performance, which mobilized all the master craftsmen of Metz in the pre-Lenten festivities of 1511. Parading about the city in a richly decorated chariot, the workers were clad in traditional costumes and assigned various theatrical parts. A local sculptor known for his work on the Champenoise Gate seems to have had the starring role as "ma damme la Cité":

> Or estoit ycellui maistre Jehan abilliez et acoustrés moult richement et triumphanment cellon l'ancienne fasson: c'est assavoir vestus d'une riche tunicque, avec ung gros rouge chapperon faict à bourlet en sa teste. Et tenoit grant gravités: car il représentoit en son personnaige la cité de Mets; et pour ce estoit ainssy acoustrés, moustrant que la cité est anciennes.
>
> (*Chronique*, IV: 94, cf. *Journal* 194–95)

> [Master Jehan was dressed and attired very richly and triumphantly in the old style, that is clad in a rich tunic, with a large red hood made of rough linen on his head. And he had a very serious bearing, for his character represented the city of Metz, and thus he was dressed to show that the city is ancient.]

In a dramatic presentation designed to inaugurate the city's newly remodeled fortifications, the City personified as a maternal figure graciously welcomes the craftsmen into her service, at the behest of "Angiens" (IV: 95). The *Livre de la belle Beaultris* similarly celebrates and preserves the city's cultural heritage, resurrecting a venerated local mother as evidence of Metz's glorious past.

In her study of textual communities in the towns of northern medieval France, Brigitte Bedos-Rezak finds that urban ceremonial and literate accounts thereof "fostered a symbiosis between townspeople's personal experience of urban identity and the city's role both as a site of ceremony and political prestige and as a crucible of communal values."[36] Philippe clearly intended his prose translation to enrich the complementary modes of public ceremonial and historiography, concentrating collective aspirations and memories in representative (female) figures.

Philippe's own contribution to urban ceremonial, the mosaic fabric he produced for St. Mark's feast day in 1507, also featured female images in conjunction with craftsmanship. Recognizing the secular and religious powers of the day, the cloth duly depicted the arms of the local gentry, the pope, the emperor, and the king. However, saintly women occupied the center of the display, which Philippe proudly describes as a masterpiece of needlework. Also given special prominence is the clothmaker's own name:

---

[36] Brigitte Bedos-Rezak, "Civic Liturgies and Urban Records in Northern France, 1100–1400," *City and Spectacle in Medieval Europe*, ed. Barbara A. Hanawalt and Kathryn L. Reyerson, 34–55, at p. 34.

je Phelippe fis une pièce d'oewre à l'agueille la non pareille que jamais on avoit veu: c'est assavoir que ce fut ung draps taillié et cousu ensemble; auquel draps y avoit plus de viiii mil pieces de draps mises et joinctes ensemble, toutes de biais et alaine et sembloit à le veoir qu'il fut peint, tant estoit justement fait. Et y avoit à milieu l'imaige notre dame et sy avoit à destre et à senestre l'imaige ste Katerine et ste Bairbe [...] Et tout à mey lieu du dit draps tout au bout dessoubz furent faits deux bon-hommes habilliés à la moude du temps passé, lesquels tenoient ung écusson [...] et y avoit en escript tout entour du dit escusson: "Phelippe de Vigneulles m'ait fait." (*Journal* 154)

[I, Philippe, made a piece of needlework unlike any that had ever been seen, that is, a cloth cut and sewn together. The cloth was made of more than 9,000 pieces of cloth fitted and joined together, all cut on the bias and in wool, and when one looked at it, it seemed to be painted, so exactly was it made. And in the middle was the picture of Our Lady, and to the right and left the pictures of Saints Catherine and Barbara {...} And in the middle of the cloth at the very bottom were portrayed two little men dressed in old-fashioned garb, who held an escutcheon {...} and all around this escutcheon was written "Philippe de Vigneulles made me."]

This textile portraiture has attracted the attention of modern quilt enthusiasts, as Philippe's ekphrastic journal entry offers a rare first-hand account of early European patchwork.[37] More striking to the literary scholar is the curious resemblance between Philippe's handiwork and the cloth portraits woven by the fair Beatrice in the Lorraine epic. In the early years of her marriage, Beatrice conceals her status as Princess of Tyre, even from her husband Hervis. She is shunned by her vulgar bourgeois father-in-law, who denounces her as a lowly tramp. In the absence of parental support, Beatrice and Hervis fall into poverty, until the young wife and mother devises a scheme to replenish the family coffers. Asking for satin cloth and multicolored thread of gold and silk, Beatrice secretly embroiders the portraits of the Tyrian royal family. She sends Hervis (disguised as a rich merchant) to Tyre to sell the cloth at an exorbitant price, knowing that her estranged family will recognize and pay for her work. Indeed, her brother Floire is thunderstruck upon spotting the work displayed at the fair, as we see in Philippe's prose rendering:

Lequelle quant il le vit tirait sa bride ce arestait et le drapz print a regairder moult fermement. Cy vit et apersust la forme et figure du bon roy son pere, et puis de la royne sa mere. Aprés vit sa forme et figure. Et d'aultre part vit et aperseust la forme et figure de la belle Beaultris sa chier suer, laquelle il tant amoit, par quoy il fut cy estraint a cuer que a bien peu ne cheut de son chevaulx a terre. (fol. 15r)

---

[37] See Janniere, "Filling in Quilt History."

[When {Floire} saw it, he reined in his horse and began to examine the cloth very intently. He saw and noticed the portrait and likeness of the good king his father, and then of the queen his mother. Then he saw his own portrait and likeness. And on the other side he saw and noticed the portrait and likeness of fair Beatrice his dear sister, whom he loved so, and this caused him so much anguish that he very nearly fell off his horse.]

When Floire describes the cloth to his mother, we learn that the artist identi-fied herself in (embroidered?) writing: "'Beaultris ma suer l'ait owrés, car la lettre le dit'" (fol. 16r; This is the work of my sister Beatrice, for the writing says so.)

Following instructions from Beatrice, Hervis doubles the asking price each time King Eustache makes an offer, and sells the cloth for an astonishing 32,000 marks. Beatrice's artistry ultimately enriches her household, reveals her identity as Princess of Tyre, and draws her male relatives to the city of Metz, which Hervis successfully defends against foreign invasion.

Philippe did not invent or even embellish the tale of Beatrice's embroi-dered portraits, for the episode has equal prominence in the verse.[38] Any suggestion that his own masterpiece was inspired by the epic text would be mere conjecture. There is, however, an undeniable intertextual connec-tion between the patchwork described in the *Journal* and the embroidery in the *Livre de la belle Beaultris*. Both are expertly crafted pieces of textile portraiture, displayed in public, with inscriptions identifying their respective makers. At the very least, Philippe seems to have had a particular affinity for the character Beatrice, whose beauty, lineage, and artistry he enlisted in the service of civic remembering. By promoting Beatrice to a titular role, he is able to valorize invention and storytelling alongside the martial pursuits that otherwise dominate the epic narrative.

A Merchant's Tale

The *Livre de la belle Beaultris* intersects in other ways with Philippe's narra-tives of contemporary Metz. Like his historiographical works and comic tales, this branch shows a pointed interest in urban landscapes, characters, and crises. Many of the episodes are situated in Metz, and bourgeois char-acters play an unusually large role in the action, particularly in the earlier portions of the story. The marketplace is the backdrop for the hero's first adventures, as he is plunged into the alien world of the trade fair.

Hervis's father Thieri is an extraordinarily successful merchant, having inherited a sizable fortune that he invested wisely in the cloth trade. When Hervis reaches the age of fifteen and wishes to become a knight, his father

---

[38] The episode has its origins in folk tale. See Jones, *The Noble Merchant*, 35 and note 10.

balks at the expenses involved in battles and tournaments. Thieri proposes instead that the youth try his hand at commerce, insisting that Hervis accompany his paternal uncles to the fairs, where he is to buy and sell prudently. This triggers a series of adventures that highlight the pitfalls of mixed lineage, for young Hervis proves to have little in common with his shrewd and thrifty father. Instead, he has inherited the noble tastes and prodigality of his maternal grandfather, Duke Pierre. Rather than purchasing the textiles ordered by his father, he spends his money on food, drink, lodging, a horse, a falcon, some hunting dogs, and the beautiful Tyrian captive Beatrice. His lack of business savvy generates a number of comic scenes, and while Hervis's uncles find humor in the situation, Thieri becomes enraged, eventually disowning his son. Father and son do not become reconciled until many years later, when Hervis sells Beatrice's embroidered cloth at the fair in Tyre.

In the original verse, these episodes are sites of a lively conflict between competing discourses and value systems. The stock bourgeois figure Thieri displays stereotypical avarice as well as undue anger, and he and his brothers are incapable of discerning the seeds of future greatness in young Hervis's escapades. The hero's choices ultimately reveal superior noble instincts, especially with regard to the purchase of a princess in disguise. He is clearly meant for the life of the warfaring knight: when he and Beatrice are attacked by would-be kidnappers on the return trip to Metz, Hervis distinguishes himself in battle. At the same time, however, the story appears to condemn the noble predilection for extravagance. Hervis, like his grandfather Pierre, brings about the ruin of his family through excessive spending. It is true that the young hero later redeems his earlier commercial disasters by selling Beatrice's cloth in Tyre at a huge profit, but his life as a merchant ends there, as he soon becomes a knight and accedes to the duchies of Metz and Lorraine. The second half of the narrative shifts the focus to Hervis's exploits on the battlefield, as he defends Metz and Lorraine against the kings of Spain, Tyre, and Cologne.

Modern scholars have not been able to agree on the ideological import of the original verse text in the context of thirteenth-century reception. While Joël Grisward argues that *Hervis de Metz* champions its hero's bourgeois origins, Alfred Adler and Philippe Walter maintain that aristocratic blood triumphs in the end, for Hervis's newfound status as warrior and duke effaces both the heritage and the values of the merchant Thieri.[39] These positions are not, in fact, mutually exclusive. As I have argued elsewhere, the bipartite structure of the song allows for both interpretations, allowing an increasingly

[39] See Joël Grisward's review of Alfred Adler, *Rückzug in epischer Parade, Cahiers de civilisation médiévale* 7 (1964): 497–504, esp. 502; Philippe Walter, postface to his translation of *Hervis de Metz*, 197–201; Alfred Adler, "*Hervis de Mes* and the Matrilineal Nobility of Champagne," *Romanic Review* 37 (1946): 150–61; Jones, *The Noble Merchant*, 21.

diverse audience to identify either with the "noble merchant" of the earlier episodes or with the more traditional epic hero of the second half.[40]

How, then, did Philippe de Vigneulles receive and interpret this ambiguous material? As one might expect, given Philippe's own social position, his rewriting tends to valorize the cloth merchant's world view, as articulated in his other works that clearly exemplify mercantile discourse and ideology. In fact, his corpus contains many narratives of merchant life that serve to inform his reception of the Hervis story. Whether serious or comic, these tales reflect a concern for cost efficiency and safe travel, as is evident in the following examples.

The *Cent Nouvelles Nouvelles* contain two comic tales that feature novice merchants stumbling their way through the marketplace. Tale 28 is particularly pertinent here, as it presents a scenario not unlike that found in the *Livre de la belle Beaultris*. A father, having acquired much wealth by the sweat of his brow, decides it is time for his spoiled and silly son to learn the merchant's trade. Advising the boy to be prudent and wise, the father gives him specific instructions about choosing goods:

> "Premier, quant tu viendras à la foire, soit à Paris, soit à Envers, à Lyon ou à Franckfort, ou en aultre lieu, regarde tousjours. Quant tu verras beaucop de gens autour de quelque marchandise, c'est signe que la marchandise est bonne et qu'il y a gain et prouffit et que c'est danrée bien requise."
> (*Cent Nouvelles Nouvelles* 138–39)

> [First, when you arrive at the fair, whether it be in Paris, Antwerp, Lyon, Frankfurt, or some other place, always look carefully. When you see a lot of people crowded around some merchandise, it is a sign that the merchandise is good, and that there is profit to be made and that it is a worthwhile commodity.]

The son, who is wise as a goose (138), sets off merrily for Paris, where he finds crowds of people buying tripe for the noonday meal. Recalling his father's admonition, he purchases tremendous quantities of tripe wherever he can find it, and ships home barrels of the malodorous and worm-infested merchandise. While the neighbors find this hilarious, the father is furious. When his son protests that he was only obeying orders, the weary father concedes that the boy is unfit for the merchant's life, and finds him another trade. The narrator concludes that children must be properly taught early in life, or they will amount to nothing (140). Tale 82, discussed in the previous chapter, ridicules a valet who forgets what he was sent to buy at the fair. The source of the tale is said to be the valet's master, whom the narrator claims to have encountered at the Lendit fair in Paris (325). Thus Philippe represents the marketplace both as a setting for the story and as a locus of storytelling itself.

Indeed, medieval fairs provided an arena for the exchange of narratives as well as commodities, facilitating the circulation of news and other stories. The *Journal* recounts the author's own periodic expeditions to the fairs, particularly the Lendit in Paris, where he learned many of the international events recorded in his historiographical works.[41] Whereas clerkly authors tended to locate the exchange of narrative adventures in the refined spaces of court assemblies, Philippe situates such exchanges in the world of commercial travel and transactions.[42]

Philippe's own travel accounts are imbued with a merchant's pragmatism and restraint. As a young apprentice, he made his first commercial voyage under the supervision of experienced traders. In Frankfurt, everyone was buying, and Philippe made his first purchase, a "futenne" or piece of cotton. However, in Antwerp several days later, where prices were exorbitant, the experienced merchants bought less than half of what they intended, and the young Philippe bought nothing (*Journal* 42–43). Even in his youth, then, the hero of the *Journal* understands the value of money and learns from his merchant mentors. In recalling his later commercial trips, Philippe's *Journal* consistently notes the route taken and the success of the transactions: "je Philippe acteur de ces présentes cronicques m'en aillai à landi à Paris par le chemin accoustumé et retournai, la dieu mercy, et y emploiai en draps environ pour ix.c frants" (*Journal* 310; I, Philippe, author of the present chronicle, went to the Lendit fair in Paris by the usual road and returned, thank God, and there I traded in cloth for about nine hundred francs). Clearly, the *Journal* serves as a counter narrative to the novellas, offering a serious role model for the hapless figures in the amusing cautionary tales.

Thus, it is not surprising that in adapting the story of *Hervis de Metz*, Philippe de Vigneulles filters a predominantly aristocratic discourse through the perspective of a seasoned tradesman. This represents the culmination of a sociocultural process begun in the late twelfth century. Eugene Vance has documented the infiltration of mercantile values and discourses in the chivalric narratives of Chrétien de Troyes. In the context of a new commercial economy, which flourished in the nearby fairs of Champagne, Chrétien created "transcoded" fictions in which aristocratic figures and scenarios subtly betray the influence of the emerging economic paragdigm.[43] Three centuries

[41] See, for example, *Journal* 215.

[42] Eugene Vance argues that the exchange of knights' tales in chivalric romance is already modeled on an emerging monetary economy. See the chapter entitled "Chrétien's *Yvain* and the Ideologies of Change and Exchange" in *Mervelous Signals: Poetics and Sign Theory in the Middle Ages* (Lincoln and London: U of Nebraska Press, 1986), 111–51. See also Demarolle, *La Chronique de Philippe de Vigneulles et la mémoire de Metz*, 23.

[43] Vance, *Mervelous Signals*, 122.

later, Philippe de Vigneulles, an experienced participant in the marketplace, would translate chivalric fictions for a public thoroughly immersed in this now-established paradigm. To be sure, Philippe does not substantiantially modify the epic's general drift, with its valorization of noble prerogatives and warrior virtues. Nonetheless, his narration does occasionally show signs of authorial intervention, especially in those passages devoted to commercial transactions.

Thieri's marvelous prosperity, for example, is seen to derive from a general economic climate conducive to business, a climate that Philippe's prose evokes nostalgically:

> [Thieri] en marchandait comme avoit fait son feu pere, et frequentoit touttes foires et merchiés tant sur mer que sur terre, tellement qu'il assemblait si grant tresors que c'estoit une chose infiniee. Car pour celluy temps estoient les païs si en paix c'on n'y oyoit parler de murtrier ne de larron, mais alloient et frequentoient les pellerins et marchamps a leur volunteis et plaisir. (fol. 2r)

> [Thieri engaged in commerce as his late father had done, and went to all the fairs and markets, by land and sea, so that he amassed such a large fortune that it was an infinite amount. For at that time all lands were at such peace that one never heard of murderers or thieves, but pilgrims and merchants came and went as they pleased.]

This golden age contrasts sharply with the picture of contemporary Metz as it is portrayed in the *Chronique* and the *Journal*. In relating one of many assaults on merchants traveling to and from Metz, the narrator in the *Journal* concludes: "Ainsy dit-on vray, quant on dit, que mairchand resque soubz fortune" (225; thus those are right who say that a merchant lives a risky life).

Philippe's prose, like the original verse, alternately mocks and approves Hervis's behavior at the fairs. He does give special attention to the second fair, which he transfers from the original "Lagny" (in Champagne), to the Paris fair at Lendit, which features so prominently in his other works. In the prose translation, the hero's relapse into profligacy warrants special commentary from the narrator:

> et s'il avoit bien fait des oultraiges en despence a Provins, encor en fit il plus la moitiés a Paris, en mandant journellement gens nombreulx et festoiant les marchamps par cent, par deux cent, et estoit chose de l'autre monde de l'oultraige et despence qu'il faisoit. (fol. 5v)[44]

> [and if he had made outrageous expenditures in Provins, he did so half as

---

[44] This is an anticipatory passage not present in the extant verse manuscripts.

much again in Paris, inviting many people daily and entertaining merchants a hundred or two hundred at a time, and his outrageous spending was out of this world.]

Above all, however, the *Livre de la belle Beaultris* highlights the importance of a fruitful collaboration between the nobility and the bourgeoisie. The original verse epic hints at such a cooperative model, but Philippe's version develops its potential by virtue of small but significant modifications and additions. When Hervis is on the verge of leaving the fair in Tyre, for example, he is threatened with violence by the royal family, who suspect that he can lead them to Beatrice's whereabouts. Local merchants rush to his aid, threatening King Eustache with a boycott, as is seen in the verse:

"E! rois Eustaices, tes cors est parjurez!
Tu pers ta foire, ja mais en nos aez
Ne nos vairas arriere retourner." (*Hervis de Mes* vv. 3853–55)

[Eh! King Eustache, you have betrayed your word! You will lose your fair. Never in our lifetime will you see us return.]

The prose translation amplifies the merchants' speech, elucidating the potential risk to the king's moral and economic viability:

"Sire, vous avés grant tort quant a merchampt faictez desplaisir. Car en ce faisant mentez voustre foy a cause dez foire qui sont franche. Et ce ne le laissez ailler il en poulrait mal venir, et n'y arait merchampz qui plus oysait ailler ne venir, et perdrez la credictes de vostre foire." (fol. 17r)

[Sire, you are very wrong to cause trouble for a merchant. For in doing so, you betray a trust, because fairs are open. And if you do not let him go, evil may come of it, and there will be no merchant who will dare again to come and go, and you will lose the reputation of your fair.]

Collaboration between social groups is thus essential to a city's prosperity. Accordingly, some of Philippe's more substantial amplifications are found in the passages devoted to descriptions of Metz and the valuable contributions of its bourgeois inhabitants. When Hervis and his entourage return to Metz after the expedition to Tyre, for example, the prose lingers over the splendid panorama as it appears to the homesick hero:

Il virent la noble cité de Metz et le douls païs entour, d'yawe doulce, prés, vigne, et gerdin environnee. Puis ce print le noble Hervey a dire "Ha noble cyté de Metz, haulte ellevee de tour et de muraille, coment est tu bien scitueez et assize et fait biaulx veoir tez paillas et maixon! Je croy que entre .xl. cité tu soiez la milleur." (fol. 20v)

[They beheld the noble city of Metz and the pleasant countryside, surrounded by fresh water, meadows, vineyards, and gardens. Then the noble Hervis said: "Ah, noble city of Metz, with your lofty towers and walls, how well you are situated and located, and how lovely it is to see your palaces and houses! I believe that you are the best among any forty cities."][45]

Hervis's return culminates in a joyful reconciliation with his father Thieri, who softens upon discovering his son's newfound wealth and his daughter-in-law's royal lineage. Thieri hastens to atone for his past errors, gathering noble and bourgeois members of the extended family for a mass in Beatrice's honor. Here, Philippe both amplifies and corrects his source, which does not name the bishop and attributes all largess to the nobility:[46]

> A la grant glice ont la dame mené
> Et li esvesques et li amis cherné:
> Grant fut l'offrande qu'i offre li barné!
> *(Hervis de Mes* vv. 5164–66)

[The bishop and family members brought the lady to the cathedral. Great was the donation offered there by the barons!]

Philippe's prose adds historical detail and also recognizes donations by the bourgeois notables in attendance:

> [Beatrice] fut adestree et menee de .iiii. cousté jusque ès la grant eglise en laquelle l'evesque Glondulfe xxxiie evesques de Mets chantait la grant messe. La y olt moult riche offrande de la seigneurie et bourjoiserie qui illec estoit. (fol. 24r)

[Beatrice, flanked on all four sides, was led and taken up to the cathedral where Bishop Glondulfe, thirty-second bishop of Metz, sang high mass. There were many rich donations on the part of the lords and bourgeois who were there.]

Later in the text, when Metz is under siege by the King of Spain, civic solidarity is essential to survival. The original verse declares that Metz was

---

45 The verse redactions are more succinct:
> De Mes choisirent le grand palais listé,
> Les augues douces, les vignes et les prés:
> "Mes, dist Hervis, tu fais tant a loer!
> Ne cui meillour en .XIIII. cité!" (*Hervis de Mes* vv. 4697–4700)

Herbin notes that in Philippe's version, even King Floire, Hervis's adversary, utters a speech in praise of Metz ("Approches" 49).

46 Böckel notes the amplification but not the modification: *Phillipp de Vigneulles Bearbeitung des Hervis de Mes*, 37.

surrounded on three sides, and that the people defended themselves fearlessly (vv. 9767–70).[47] Philippe's prose stresses the plight of the citizens as well as their capacity for resistance:

> vous dirons de ceulx de Mets et du puissant roy d'Espaigne, lequelle thient la cité en grant subjection, car essigiee estoit en trois partie, et souvent y donne de merveilleux et fier assault. Mais aucy il trowe bien a qui parler car comme gens de bon couraige il ce deffande en resistant contre sa grant et merveilleuze puissance. Et estoit le poupullaire bon et vuis ansamble.
>
> (fol. 56r)

> [I will tell you about the people of Metz and about the powerful King of Spain, who held the city in subjection, for it was besieged on three sides, and often attacked marvelously and fiercely. But also he met his match, for as they were people of great courage, they defended themselves and resisted his great and marvelous strength. And the people were good and vigilant together.]

This would have been a familiar and even inspiring scenario for Philippe's contemporaries, who often united in their resistance to foreign attack. Once again, the translation gestures toward the author's historiographical works, which celebrate the courage and spirit of his fellow citizens in times of war. The *Chronique* and the *Journal*, for example, recount an attempted invasion by Duke Nicholas of Lorraine in 1473. The duke is portrayed as a diabolical predator:

> O couraige mallin, escorpion satanicque, cuer insaciable, plains d'envie et de mallice, serait tu jamaix soullés? Quant, pour ung peu de gloire vaine et mondaigne, veult et ais bien le couraige de ung cy noble peuple destruire et mestre à fin! (*Chronique* III:1)

> [O evil spirit, satanic scorpion, insatiable heart full of envy and malice! If, for the sake of a little vain and worldly glory, you wish and intend to destroy and bring to an end such a noble people, will you ever be satisfied?]

Though the duke had the advantage of surprise and superior force, his men were no match for the people of Metz. A clever baker outwitted the advancing army and was seconded by the general populace, who fought bravely until the arrival of professional soldiers:

> Et ce temps pendant le peuple se esmeut aux armes et sortissoient de leur maison sans tenir ordre ne mesure et comme gens de couraige, nus et

---

[47] In Herbin's edition, see the variants to v. 9767.

deschaulx comme ils estoient, avec pal et massue et avec bèche et howes ou aultres hutancilles, tel que chacun les powoit trower, se mirent au devant en deffandant leur corps et leurs biens et tinrent bon et tres virillement se deffendirent jusques tant que aulcuns hommes d'arme fussent armés et venus. (*Journal* 4–5; cf. *Chronique* III, 3)

[And meanwhile, the people were moved to take up arms, and they left their houses without order or moderation, and as courageous people, naked and without shoes as they were, with stakes and clubs, with spades and hoes or other utensils, whatever each could find, they charged forward defending themselves and their possessions, and they stood fast and defended themselves bravely until some men-at-arms were armed and had arrived.]

Once again, then, the epic material proves suitable to the author's overall interest in recognizing and preserving his beloved city and its diverse inhabitants. While Philippe's translation is scrupulously faithful to its verse sources, the prose is far from being a neutral reproduction of fixed and immutable content. Rather, the *Livre de la belle Beaultris* forms part of a multigeneric project designed to keep the city's past ever present in times of turmoil and uneasy transition.

The Great Feud

In both verse and prose redactions, the rest of the cycle forms a unit fairly distinct from the tale of Beatrice and Hervis. In adapting the succeeding branches, Philippe is ever vigilant in his attention to civic pride; yet these narratives also bring into play another hallmark of his writing, namely the "culture of worry" that permeates his historiographical works.[48] The stories of Garin, Gerbert, and Yonnet provide him a springboard simultaneously to glorify the embattled heroes of Metz and to deplore the needless suffering occasioned by feudal warfare.

The city of Metz itself plays a much smaller role in the remaining branches of the Lorraine epic. In fact, it is probable that the original verse *Garin le Lorrain*, the core of the cycle, was not composed by a poet from Metz or even the duchy of Lorraine. Based on a careful examination of the song's narrative geography, Michel Parisse situates its origins in the Champagne region. The original poet(s) chose "Lorraine" as the homeland of epic heroes,

---

48 Pierre Demarolle writes of a culture of worry in the *Chronique*, but in that work the author's anxiety is not where one might expect it. His *inquiétude* is directed less toward the risks inherent in seasonal disturbances, epidemics and wars, and more toward a crisis of belief and confidence. Demarolle cites particularly Philippe's uneasiness about changes in the world order, including the defeat of Christians at the hands of the Turks and the Reform movement in the Church. See his "Tourments et inquiétudes," an article primarily focused on the last book of Philippe's chronicle.

Parisse believes, primarily because of an age-old tradition that portrayed the knights of this region as particularly bellicose.[49]

Whether the foundational text was conceived in Champagne or farther eastward, audiences in both Lorraine and Metz quickly adopted Garin as a local hero. Codicological evidence suggests that the cycle enjoyed great favor in the region, as an entire group of verse manuscripts, known as the "Lorraine group," were copied in the regional dialect in the thirteenth century.[50] Archival evidence shows that the city of Metz and the duchy of Lorraine each laid claim to Garin le Lorrain as a native son. Garin's birthday was already being celebrated annually in Metz cathedral when the dukes of Lorraine began to proclaim the great warrior as their ancestor in the mid-fourteenth century. Raoul de Lorraine founded the collegiate church of Saint-Georges in Nancy in 1341, where he established a memorial service to commemorate the illustrious member of his lineage "chascun an a tous jours maix, a teil jour com on le fait en l'englise de Mes" (every year from this day forward, on the same day it is done in the church of Metz).[51]

Philippe de Vigneulles clearly sought to revive the competition, as his translation predictably endeavors to associate Garin with the city of Metz. This is evident not only in his frequent allusions to the hero's burial place in the Metz cathedral,[52] but also, once again, in the politics of naming. The verse redactions most often refer to Garin with the epithet "Li Loherens Garins," and consistently use this epithet in the prologues and epilogues that enumerate the cycle's principal characters.[53] Philippe's prose does not attempt to erase the hero's traditional appellation, as he duly entitles the second, third and fourth books of his translation the books of "le Lourains Guerin." At the same time, he frequently amplifies the epithet to include Garin's birthplace, particularly at the beginning or end of a book, referring to "le Lourains Guerin *de Mets*" (fol. 189r, my emphasis). In manuscript *v*, the addition "de Mets" is very often inserted above the line, suggesting that the author revised his draft to give heightened emphasis to the city. Moreover, Lorraine assumes a secondary and contiguous status in Philippe's topographical descriptions. At the beginning of the *Yonnet* section, he recapitulates the subject matter of the earlier books, namely "la noble lignie du jantil duc Guerin *de Mets*, d'icelle dicte noble cité et du païs de *Louraine qui est joindant*" (fol. 305r, my emphasis; the lineage of the noble Duke Garin of

[49] Michel Parisse, "Garin le Loherain dans l'histoire de son temps," 62.

[50] See François Bonnardot, "Essai de classement des manuscrits des *Loherains* suivi d'un nouveau fragment de *Girbert de Metz*," *Romania* 3 (1874): 195–262.

[51] Mathias Auclair, "Le Preux et le saint: Garin le Lorrain et Saint Gengoult, ancêtre des ducs de Lorraine," *Romania* 117 (1999): 245–57. The "donation" is quoted on p. 247.

[52] See Chapter 2, p. 22.

[53] See Gittleman, *Le Style épique dans Garin le Loherain*, 214. The verse texts also make use of a secondary epithet, "li dus de Mes," but it is used with less frequency.

Metz, of that noble city and of *the adjoining region of Lorraine*). He even attributes the epithet "Lourain Guerin" to the collective voices of Metz, introducing the Garin branch as "la vie et histoire du noble duc Guerin [...] c'on dit *a Mets* le Lourain Guerin" (fol. 59r, my emphasis; the life and story of the noble Duke Garin ... who is known in Metz as Garin le Lorrain). These periodic interventions in the prose effect a constant return to a site that might otherwise be eclipsed by the dynamics of the inherited story. Thus the narrator's not-so-subtle reminders foreground the birthplace of his protagonists and target audience, though numerous events unfold against the backdrop of Paris, Lyon, Flanders, Cologne and Gascony.

The branches devoted to Garin, his son Gerbert and grandson Yonnet are further distinguished from the *Livre de la belle Beaultris* by their compositional strategies and generic features. As we have seen, the story of Hervis and Beatrice incorporates numerous motifs associated with the romance of adventure, whereas succeeding branches correspond more closely to the conventions of earlier epic. This is particularly striking in the dynamics of plot resolution. The *Livre de la belle Beaultris* reaches a peaceful closure, while the other books relate a perpetually renewable narrative of violence. This divergence is mirrored in the illustrations that accompany Philippe's prose in manuscript *h*. The peace agreement between Hervis and the Kings of Spain and Tyre is duly represented in the sole miniature accompanying the *Livre de la belle Beaultris*. Although the illustration has been lost, it is preserved in the partial edition published by Maurice de Pange, with the caption "Comment les deux Roys avec Beautris la belle vinrent au devant du duc Hervey" (How the two kings along with Fair Beatrice came before Duke Hervis).[54] The image depicts the couple's embrace, observed by the newly-vanquished princely figures, and framed by the towers of Metz. Conversely, the three remaining miniatures mark key junctures in the development of the the reiterated conflict between two feudal houses: the battle of Ancerville and the death of Hervis in *Guerin I*; the arrival of the Lorrains and Bordelais at Genivaux, where Garin will meet his death (*Guerin III*); and a hunting scene, which precipitates a quarrel between Lowis and Yonnet that will lead to Gerbert's assassination (*Yonnet*). Another miniature, already lost at the time of de Pange's publication, was originally placed at the beginning of *Guerin II*, and likely depicted the death of Begon, which opens this book.

The germs of conflict are present from the early pages of *Guerin I*. Hervis, whose lands are under attack by "pagan" forces, fails to obtain the help of King Pepin thanks to the machinations of the Bordelais knights Hardré and Magis, "desquelle n'y avoit plus fellon en .l. païs. Que Dieu les puissent confondre car oncque en leur vie il n'amairent leur voixin!" (fol. 68r; there were no more treacherous than they in fifty lands; may God strike

---

54 De Pange, *La Chanson de Garin le Loherain mise en prose*, 26 bis.

them down, for never in their lives did they love their neighbors!) Hervis is forced to enlist the aid of King Anseÿs of Cologne, and succeeds in fending off the attackers. However, the Lorraine hero is slain on the battlefield, and Anseÿs treacherously seizes Metz, depriving Hervis's descendants of their birthright.

The feud between the lineages of Lorraine and Bordeaux begins in earnest after Hervis's death, when his sons Garin le Lorrain and Begon de Belin incur the wrath of their closest companions, of the "Bordelais" lineage. A dispute arises after the knights of both houses have agreed to defend King Thieri de Maurienne against Saracen invasion. While the cowardly Bordelais desert their fellow knights on the battlefield, the Lorraine heroes distinguish themselves in battle, thereby earning the favor of both King Thieri and King Pepin. Thieri, who has been mortally wounded by a Saracen arrow, offers Garin his land and his daughter Blanchefleur, and Pepin agrees to the match. This sends the Bordelais Fromont de Lens into a jealous rage, and harsh words soon give way to blows. The verse versions clearly mark this event as the inception of a bloody and protracted war:

> Ilec comence le grant borroflement
> donc furent mort chevalier ne sai cant!
> chasteax brisiez et viles a noient,
> deserité en furent li enfant. (*Garin le Loherenc* vv. 2146–49)

[There begins the great quarrel from which I know not how many knights died, castles and towns were destroyed, children were disinherited.]

In his prose, Philippe de Vigneulles adds to the anticipatory passage a comparison to the greatest of all epic wars:

> Helas! Adoncque acomansait la grant malle [heure] et le hutin pour le quelle mourut tant de noble gent qu'il n'est a dire ne [penser]. Car plus de .iiii. mil personne et tant que plussieur grant personnaige et [gens de] bien moururent pour cest follie ycy. Ne oncque pour l'amour d'Ellainne que fut trainé par Paris, filz a roy Priant, par qui fut destruict Troie, ne mourust autant de gens qu'il fist pour ce huttin cy [...]. Car mainte femme en desmeurairent sans maris et mainte pucelle [sans] amis, mainte anffans en furent desherités et orfellin, maintez [chastiaulx], ville et maixon en furent depuis ruees par terre airxe et brulee, et ce fut grant pitiet et domaige comme cy trowés lisant ce [lire ou] acouter le voullés. (fol. 82v)

[Alas! Thus began the great evil and quarrel for which so many noblemen died that one can neither say nor imagine it. For more than four thousand people and many great personages and distinguished men died for this folly. Nor did as many people die for the love of Helen, who was taken away by Paris, son of King Priam, who brought about the destruction of Troy, as died in this conflict. For because of it, many women lost their husbands and many maidens their lovers, many children were disinherited and orphaned, many castles, towns and houses were later crushed to the ground and burned, and it was a great pity and shame, as you will read here if you wish to read or hear it.]

Thus the Trojan War itself pales before the bitter feud between Lorrains and Bordelais. This rather banal allusion not only allows Philippe to display his knowledge of classical tradition. It also gives him the opportunity to argue implicitly for the literary value of a cycle less renowned than the epics of antiquity or the celebrated Carolingian songs of France. This value is measured in part by the number of casualties and the scope of material destruction, factors that seem to contribute to the "great excellence" of the Lorraine material.

The Cycle of Death

Though the narrative as a whole dramatizes the cumulative effects of the great feud, Philippe's prose gives special prominence to the deaths of individual heroes. These episodes clearly appealed to his imagination, since they furnish the subject matter for five of the six extant illustrations in manuscript h.[55] The deaths of great Lorraine warriors occur at or near the beginning of each book, and in the case of Garin and Begon, this placement represents a departure from the verse redactions. Now, I do not mean to suggest that Philippe radically revised his sources in calling attention to such scenes. Death and dying are among the most frequent and vivid events in the Old French epic, and the hero's final moments nearly always occupy a privileged place in the textual economy, constituting both a lyrical interlude and a source of narrative development.[56] The death of a hero as rebirth of narrative is entirely consistent with patterns of conflict in the genre as early as the *Chanson de Roland*, and played an especially important role in the extension of the Lorraine cycle. Moreover, Jean-Charles Herbin shows convincingly that while Philippe's division between books does not match the branch divisions in any extant

---

55 P. 270, full-page miniature depicting the death of Hervis; p. 734, full-page miniature depicting the prelude to Garin's death; p. 735, historiated initial depicting the murder of Garin; p. 1150, full-page miniature depicting the prelude to Gerbert's death; p. 1151, historiated initial depicting the murder of Gerbert. See the reproductions in De Pange, *La Chanson de Garin le Loherain mise en prose*. The manuscript shows evidence of a missing full-page miniature preceding the death of Begon: see Herbin, "Notice du manuscrit *h*," 235.

56 On death in the *chanson de geste*, see Pierre Le Gentil, "Réflexions sur la mort dans les chansons de geste," *Mélanges offerts à Rita Lejeune* (Gembloux: J. Duculot, 1969), II, 801–09; Pierre Jonin, *Pages épiques du moyen âge français* (Paris: Société d'Édition d'Enseignement Supérieur, 1970), II, 361–65; Peter Haidu, *The Subject of Violence: The Song of Roland and the Birth of the State* (Bloomington and Indianapolis: Indiana UP, 1993), 17–35, 120–34.

cyclical manuscript, he may have followed a lost version in which Garin's and Begon's deaths inaugurated new songs.[57] Even if we assume limited intervention on Philippe's part, however, his prose subtly tailors the death narratives to fit a certain view of the world. Without altering the course of events found in his source material, the translator models the deaths of legendary heroes after the real-life fatalities recorded in his histories of Metz.

In considering Philippe's treatment of death in the last book of the *Chronique*, Pierre Demarolle finds that the author's thematic perspective is not death itself in the context of human experience (as it was for Villon), but rather the rupture of equilibrium occasioned by unforeseen events.[58] Demarolle situates Philippe's outlook in the collective culture of worry or anxiety that informed late medieval society in crisis.[59] The focus on sudden misfortune is certainly palpable in the *Chronique* and *Journal*, where "fortunes et adversités" seem to define the existence of the author and his fellow citizens. This lexicon also permeates the prose *Guerin* and *Yonnet*, depicting a world dominated not only by feudal warfare but also by chronic insecurity. A comparative study of the passages devoted to the heroes' deaths will demonstrate that in Philippe's adaptation, marvelous feats of arms are subordinated to the power of misfortune and the treachery of evildoers. More than the verse or the other two prose adaptations, his version tends to dramatize the unexpectedness of the fatal blow dealt to each major figure of the Lorraine lineage. More precisely, the heroes themselves seem unaware of imminent death, or inclined to assume great risk despite objections raised by their wives and companions. Each death is preceded by a triumph or truce, a respite that begs to be shattered in the iterations of feudal hostility.

Thus Hervis's death in *Guerin I* is characterized as an unfortunate twist of fate that follows on the heels of a glorious victory. Having successfully routed the invading Saracen forces, Hervis pursues the fleeing survivors and is slain by an enemy arrow. The verse redactions emphasize the hero's mighty pursuit:

> Paien s'en fuient, si ont les tres guerpi;
> del gaaing furent li plusor enrichi.
> Hervis les enchace qui molt ert de grant pris.
> .ii. liues granz dure li fereïz.
> En cele chace, la fu Hervis ocis
> d'un quarrel fort [...] (*Garin le Loherenc* vv. 990–95)

[The pagans flee, the have left their tents; many had become rich from plunder. The worthy Hervis pursues them, and the combat endures over two full leagues. In this pursuit Hervis was slain by a strong arrow.]

---

[57] Herbin believes that the prosifier was following a version reflected in the lacunary manuscript *I* (Dijon 528). See "Approches" 480.
[58] Demarolle, "La Mort dans l'univers mental."
[59] Demarolle, "Tourments et inquiétudes," 27.

The anonymous *Prose de l'Arsenal* is characteristically terse, providing only the bare facts: "Més ung Teurc fery Hervis, le nafra de si grant plaie que tantost morut" (4; but a Turk struck Hervis and inflicted such a great wound that he died at once). The Burgundian prose is also brief, but does add a regretful note blaming the hero for pursuing his enemy:

> Et quant il perceu les Sarrazins mettre en desarroy, lors encommença il la chasse *non mie comme bien advisé*, car il fut occis d'un carrel d'arbalestre en la presence de ses meilleurs amiz, quy de ce meschief furent tant dolans et esbahis qu'ilz en perdirent sens et entendement.
>
> (*Guerin le Loherain* 79, my emphasis)

[And when he saw the Saracens in disarray, he began his pursuit, *which was ill-advised*, for he was killed by a crossbow bolt in the presence of his closest friends, who were so grieved and astounded by this misfortune that they lost their senses.]

Philippe de Vigneulles's version further underscores the role of misfortune ("meschief"). His prose amplifies the hero's final moments by dwelling on the honorable motives that led to his unfortunate demise:

> Et furent yceulx tout desconfis et le rest ce mist en fuite et abandonnairent tref et pavillon auquelle fut cy grant richesse tant que quiconque vouloit gaignier jamais ne veoit son powre jour. Le noble duc Hervy de Mets, non cowoitant a l'avoir forcque a l'onneur, // courust aprés les fuitif luy et ces gens et les enchaissait deux grant lue et demy. Parquoy le grant meschief vint a celle poursuite et y olt une perde inrecowrauble. Car en courant que le noble duc faisoit aprez et destranchait Hongre, Wandre et Sarrains il fut ferus d'ung quairiaulx ou trait d'airboullette de bais de quoy on usoit pour ce tamps et duquelle copt il mourust, dont ce fut moult grant domaige a toutte crestienté de la mort d'ung cy noble et vaillant homme.
>
> (fols. 69v–70r)

[And they {the Saracens} were defeated, and the rest put to flight, and they abandoned their tents, where there were such great riches that whoever wanted to enrich himself would never see poverty. The noble Duke Hervis of Metz, who didn't covet the goods, only honor, went after the fleeing army with his men and pursued them for a full two and a half leagues, which pursuit led to great misfortune and irreparable loss. For in pursuing and cutting down the Hungarians, Vandals and Saracens, the noble duke was struck by a quarrel or crossbow bolt such as they used at that time, and he died from this blow. The death of such a noble and valiant man was a great loss for all Christendom.]

The bishop Henri de Châlons, brother of Hervis, is also distressed upon hearing of the great warrior's demise, which Philippe's version alone terms "l'infortune du noble duc Hervy" (fol. 70r).

Hervis's sons and grandson are not slain on the battlefield like their illustrious forefather. Rather, they are all victims of murder, a crime that receives
particular attention in Philippe's historiographical works. In fact, the *Journal*
and the *Chronique* (especially Book V) display far more interest in homicide and accidental death than large-scale military confrontations, which the
author knew only indirectly. Notorious crimes and executions in Metz are
frequently related in detail, alongside other tabloid-worthy events. In 1510,
for example, a butcher's servant bludgeoned his master and the master's pregnant wife to death as they slept, slit the corpses' throats, murdered the servant
girl, and then calmly sat down to a meal of roasted meat. Philippe devotes
several pages to the cold-blooded crime, declaring it to be the strangest, most
detestable and most cruel deed he has ever heard of (*Journal* 188–91; *Chronique* IV: 86–89). On January 16, 1520, the people of Metz were shocked
to learn that a local baker had fallen prey to some murderous villains upon
returning from mass:

> ung homme estimé de homme de biens, tué et inhumainement murtri
> [...] y olt on ne scet encore quel malvais garnement, traystres lairons, qui
> entrèrent en la maison, on ne scet comment, et murtrirent tellement le dit
> Husson, que l'on luy veoit tout les cerviaulx de la teste et avec ce il avoit
> ung des yeulx hors de la teste plus groz, que ung euf.
>
>   (*Journal* 372; cf. *Chronique* IV: 301–02)

> [a man considered a good man, killed and inhumanely murdered {...} no
> one yet knows what hoodlums or treacherous thieves entered the house,
> no one knows how, and they killed Husson in such a way that his brains
> had spilled out of his head, and in addition one of his eyes lay outside his
> head, larger than an egg.]

The thieving murderers terrorized the city for a long time, causing the Messins
to cower in their homes in an atmosphere of general insecurity:

> tellement, que l'on ne parloit d'aultre chose et se bairroient et se enser
> roient les ungs et les aultres en leur maison, que c'estoit merveille de veoir
> la peur, que le puple avoit, et n'estoit nul assuré tant ès rues comme ès
> maisons. Dieu par sa graice y veuille pourveoir. Amen.
>
>   (*Journal* 373; cf. *Chronique* IV: 304)

> [so that people talked of nothing else, and shut themselves up and crowded
> together in their houses, and it was amazing to see the fear that the people
> had, and no one was safe either in the streets or in the houses. May God
> through his grace provide for them! Amen.]

As Demarolle has noted, Philippe's accounts of murder are once again
relatively unconcerned with death in its metaphysical dimension. He focuses
instead on attendant circumstances such as the perpetrator's motives, the

victim's blissful ignorance of danger, the manner in which the act is committed, the mutilated body and the horrified reactions of those who discover the corpse.[60] For this narrative framework, the Lorraine epic provided Philippe with a veritable gold mine, as Begon, Garin and Gerbert are all struck down in exceptional – indeed sensational – circumstances.

The death of Begon is perhaps one of the most memorable casualties in the Old French epic.[61] Throughout the Middle Ages, this emotionally and symbolically charged episode captured the imagination of illuminators and chroniclers, and there is even some evidence that the segment once existed as a separate poem.[62] In all versions, Begon's death occurs in the wake of a rare interval of peace between Lorrains and Bordelais, during which the embattled hero returns to his wife and sons in Belin. He enjoys seven and a half years of peaceful domestic life (which the verse summarizes in two lines), but inevitably begins to grow restless. He has not seen his brother Garin in seven years, and moreover, he has heard about an extraordinary wild boar that roams the forest of Vicoigne near Valenciennes. Despite his wife's reservations, Begon resolves to hunt the wild boar and offer the beast's head to Garin.

The hunting expedition proves to be the supreme test of the hero's skill and endurance. The boar is marvelously large and powerful, his tusks and footprints so massive that he is said to be a demon (*Garin le Loherenc* vv. 9739–44). Begon succeeds in slaying his adversary, despite the animal's spectacular flight from the forest across the equivalent of 60 kilometers ("granz .xv. leues," v. 9759) into the territory of the Bordelais warrior Fromont. As Begon rests beside his prey, he is discovered by a woodsman, who brings reinforcements from the Bordelais clan. Believing the knight to be a mere poacher, Fromont's vassals seek to kill the intruder.[63] Although he defends himself valiantly, killing several of his attackers, Begon is mortally wounded by the woodsman's nephew.[64] When his body is brought to Fromont, the latter immediately recognizes his adversary. Far from rejoicing, however, Fromont

---

60 Demarolle, "La Mort dans l'univers mental," 26–27.

61 See Catherine M. Jones, "The Death of Bégon Revisited," in *"Por la soie amisté"*: *Essays in Honor of Norris J. Lacy*, ed. Keith Busby and Catherine M. Jones (Amsterdam & Atlanta: Rodopi, 2000), 235–46. Begon's death was also of great interest to certain Romantic writers and scholars of the nineteenth century.

62 See Édward Le Glay, *Fragments d'épopées romanes* (Paris: Techener, 1838), 96.; and Jean-Charles Herbin, "Géographie des chansons de geste: itinéraires de *Garin le Loherain*," *La Géographie dans les textes narratifs médiévaux*, ed. Danielle Buschinger and Wolfgang Spiewok, *Etudes médiévales de Greifswald* 62, Series 3, vol. 38, 59–79.

63 One of the vassals, Thiébaut du Plesseïs, is a long-standing enemy of Bégon. In BnF, fr. 4988, he seems to have guessed Bégon's identity from the beginning, but the manuscript tradition in general does not offer a coherent picture of Thiébaut's responsibility in Bégon's death. See Gittleman, *Le Style épique dans Garin le Loherain*, 257–60.

64 In the Burgundian prose, Begon is killed by the forester's son (*Guerin le Loherain* 296).

deplores the cowardly murder of France's most worthy knight, not to mention the probable repercussions of Begon's death, and the incident indeed rekindles the hostilities.

All three prose versions mention the seven-year truce that precedes the wild boar hunt. True to its abbreviated form, the *Prose de l'Arsenal* merely states that the time passed with no conflict (25). The Burgundian prose amplifies the passage, filling the seven years with courtly pastimes:

> Et vesquirent tresbien l'espace de sept ans en ce point ensemble et se entremettoient les nobles hommes de aler chasser, voler et vivoient du demaine de leurs seignouries en toute plaisance et deduit de gibier.
>
> (Guerin le Loherain 288).

> [And they lived together very well for a period of seven years, and the noblemen occupied themselves in hunting and hawking, and they lived off their seigneurial domains quite agreeably and pleasurably, with plenty of wild game.]

For his part, Philippe de Vigneulles mentions the precise length of the truce four times, but finds the time to be utterly devoid of interest:

> Et ne fut faictes choses lesdit .vii. ans et demi durant *qui soit digne de memoire* jusques a ung jour comme cy aprés ou second livre vous serait dit et contés ce lire ou acouter vous le voullés. (fol. 145r, my emphasis)

> [And nothing was done for the duration of those seven and a half years *that is worth remembering*, until one day, as will be told and related to you presently in the second book, if you wish to read or hear it.]

For Philippe, the time of peace has narrative worthiness only insofar as it will be shattered on the fateful day leading to Begon's death.

Philippe's prose is particularly attentive to the drama of Begon's murder as it unfolds in a series of anticipatory passages. In all versions, verse and prose, Begon's wife Beatrice tries in vain to dissuade her husband from venturing into enemy territory, for her heart tells her that Begon will never return alive.[65] Both Philippe and his Burgundian counterpart dwell on Beatrice's supplication, emphasizing her prescience to foreshadow the hero's imminent death. However, the Burgundian prose soon attenuates the suspense when the narrator remarks: "Adont luy respondy le noble duc, quy avoit a mourir ainsi que par adventure il luy estoit predestiné" (*Guerin le Loherain* 289; thereupon the noble duke, who had to die as he was predestined to do, responded to her). When Begon takes leave of his family, the *Prose de l'Arsenal* and the

---

[65] *Garin le Loherenc* vv. 9609–11; *Prose de l'Arsenal* 26; *Guerin le Loherain* 289; Philippe's prose, fol. 14v.

Burgundian narrative are dispassionate, noting Beatrice's great sadness and stating that Begon would never again see his two sons (*Prose de l'Arsenal* 26; *Guerin le Loherain* 289). These matter-of-fact renderings diminish the pathos of the original verse, in which the jongleur interjects his own lament: "Dex! quel domage, c'onques puis ne les vit!" (*Garin le Loherenc* v. 9637; God, what a shame! For he never saw them again!) Philippe, however, who clearly wishes to retain the poignancy of the scene, effects a subtle modulation from verse to prose:

> Et la belle tout en plourant lez lairme a l'ueil pareillement le baisait et acoullait. Helas! elle avoit cause de pleurer et c'elle eust sceu la piteuse aventure elle ce fut pasmee de doulleur. Car jamaix plus ne le vit en vie comme cy aprez il serait dit. (fol. 146v)

> [And the lovely lady, weeping, with tears in her eyes, also kissed and embraced him. Alas! she had every reason to cry, and if she had known about the piteous outcome she would have fainted from sadness. For never again did she see him alive, as will be told afterward.]

In Philippe's version, the narrator's exclamation recalls the affective quality of the jongleur's intervention. At the same time, the prose translation thickens the premonitory statement by condoning the heroine's grief and adding a layer of conjecture. Later in the episode, when Begon's companions leave him alone in the forest during the pursuit of the wild boar, Philippe once again retains and amplifies the jongleur's warning of impending doom. The verse narrator laments: "seul ont Begon en la forest gerpi, / Dex! quel dolor et quel domage a ci!" (vv. 9770–71; they left Begon alone in the forest; God! what a misfortune and what a shame this is!) Philippe's prose both exclaims and explains: "Et laissairent le duc en la fourest. Hé Dieu! quelle dommaige ce fut de l'avoir abandonneis, et le grant mal qui en advint! Car oncque puis ne le virent" (fol. 147r; And they left the duke in the forest. God! what a shame it was that they abandoned him, and what great evil came of it, for they never saw him again). Thus, in rendering the inexorable moves leading to the hero's death, Philippe is not content merely to transcribe them. Rather, his style is at once marked by nostalgia for the jongleur's voice and by the prosifier's desire to adduce explanations embedded in subordinate clauses and circumstantial complements.[66] Intent upon preserving the heightened suspense of the moment, he locates an intermediate space between the jongleur's performative mode and the clarifying tendencies of prose adaptation.

All versions of the story emphasize in varying ways Begon's final moments, which include a lament for his wife, sons, and kinsmen. Philippe, however, gives more attention than the others to the abuse suffered by the

---

66 See Rasmussen, *La Prose narrative française du XVe siècle*, 42–43.

hero's corpse at the hands of the Bordelais. The verse relates the post-mortem crime succinctly:

> Li .iii. gloton li sont sore fichié:
> chascuns le fiert de son tranchant espié,
> desi qu'as doiles li fist el cors fichier.
>
> (*Garin le Loherenc* vv. 10,005–07)

[The three wicked ones attacked him; each strikes him with his sharp lance, planting it into the body all the way up to the shaft.]

The *Arsenal* and the Burgundian prose state only that the perpetrators pierced Begon's body after his death.[67] Philippe embellishes, adding more gory details and overtly condemning the villains' brutality. His chapter title sets the tone: "Coment Thiebault le malvaix murtreus et ces complisse ont inhumainement fraipeis le noble duc et plusieurs copt lui ont donneis de puis qu'il estoit mort" (fol. 148v; how Thibaut the evil murderer and his accomplices struck the noble duke inhumanely and dealt him several blows after he was dead). The chapter itself multiplies the accusations of savagery before lingering on the violation of the corpse:

> Et alors que Thiebault lequelle Dieu maldie et les trois glout qu'il ait en sa compaignie virent le noble duc mort aincy que aveis oÿ, cy ce aprouchairent du corps et comme murtreus de bois et gens inhumains plain de cruaulteis cen pitiet ne compaicion ont le noble duc ferus de leur espiedz parmi le corps de grant copt jusques au manche, tellement que fer et fust lui font baignier dedans son sancque [...] (fol. 149r)

[And when Thibaut (may God curse him!) and the three evil ones in his company saw the noble duke dead, as you have heard, they approached the body, and like stealthy murderers of the woods, inhuman people full of cruelty, without pity or compassion, they dealt great blows to the noble duke with their lances, right up to the shaft, so much that they bathed both head and shaft in his blood.]

The repeated designation of "noble duc" eloquently contrasts the victim's elevated status with his ignominious death and mutilation. Subsequent passages further cloak the hero in sacrifical imagery. In Philippe's account as in all others, Begon is laid on an altar-like table in place of the wild boar, wrapped in deerskin, and surrounded by bright candles (fol. 150r). Begon's death is thus fraught with mythical overtones, but Philippe does not capitalize on them, turning quickly to the shock and horror felt by each successive character who learns of the incident (fols. 150r–150v).

---

[67] *Guerin le Loherain* 297; *Prose de l'Arsenal* 27.

Guerin III opens with the murder of Garin, a premeditated crime engineered by the Bordelais Guillaume de Monclin. Like his brother before him, Garin is slain during a truce, engaging in a peaceful activity that makes him vulnerable to attack. Having vowed to atone for his sins by taking up the cross and making the voyage to Jerusalem, Garin gathers together his enemies to ask their forgiveness and secure the safety of his son Gerbert. In response, the Bordelais ambush the mighty duke and kill him in the chapel of Genivaux.

We have seen that the Burgundian prose version elaborates on Garin's repentance and crusading ambitions.[68] The *Prose de l'Arsenal* reduces the episode to a concise summary (44–45). For his part, Philippe is far more attentive to establishing structural links between the deaths of Begon and Garin, revealing a latent pattern of domestic tranquillity followed by sudden violence. He frames the two episodes in very similar ways, employing the transitional space between branches to depict a warrior at rest, basking in the temporary absence of conflict. Echoing the juncture between *Guerin I* and *Guerin II*, the opening sentences of *Guerin III* (heading and text proper) relate and reiterate the duke's unusual sojourn at home with his family:

> Coment de puis ces guerre aincy menee le noble duc fut l'espaisse de trois ans en sa bonne cité de Mets a repos sans mener guerre ne huttin a vosin qu'il eust // [...] le noble duc demourait a Mets luy sa femme et son filz Gilbert, lequelle moult il amoit, en sa privees masgnie. Et luy estant en repos a celle noble cité comme dit est, fist [...] et repairer toutte lez plaisse par le païs et mist touttez chose en ordennance [...]. Car il fut l'espaisse de trois ans avec sa femme et son filz cen avoir ne mener guerre.
>
> (fols. 189r–189v)

> [How, after waging these wars, the noble duke spent three years in his good city of Metz in peace, without waging war or battle on any of his neighbors {...} the noble duke stayed in Metz with his wife and his son Gerbert, whom he loved very much, in his private household. And since he was at peace in this noble city, as mentioned, he had all the structures in his domain rebuilt and repaired, and put everything in order. For he spent three years with his wife and son without waging war.]

Although the verse does not say so explicitly, Philippe's prose states three times that Garin went to his meeting with the Bordelais accompanied by few of his own men:

> Et ledit Guerin, sans panser a malz de son cousté, y aillait bien simplement, car il y allait a petitte compaignie et tout desairmés et desgairnis. Mes cez annemis plain de cautelle et traïson y vinrent a grant nombre de gens qui estoient airmés a la cowerte [...] (fol. 190r)[69]

---

68 See p. 45 of the present chapter.
69 Cf. fol. 189r, chapter title: "le noble duc y allait bien simplement et a petitte

[And Garin, without thinking about any evildoing on his part, went there very simply, for he went with very few companions, completely unarmed and unequipped. But his enemies, full of cunning and treachery, came there with a great many men who were armed covertly.]

Caught in an ambush, Garin defends himself like a lion (fol. 190r). When the fatal blow strikes, Philippe's prose narrator intervenes more emphatically than any other version to condemn the perpetrators:

Et cheut illec en grant pitiet devent l'aultel. Par quoy ce fut grant domaige et incrowraible perde de la mort d'ung telz personnaige que aincy meschante- ment firent morir. Car il estoit prince vertueulx et beaulx ne oncque en sa vie ne fist faussise ne traÿson. Et quant les inumains murtreus oyrent fait du noble duc tout leur plaisir il laissairent le corps illec gisant entre lez aultre mort tout estandus. Toutte en haiste il c'en fowirent, car tropt doubtoient lez bourjois de la cité qu'il n'aillisse aprés pour les tuer. (fol. 191r)

[And he fell there piteously before the altar. This was a great shame and irrevocable loss, the death of such a figure whom they killed so wickedly. For he was a virtuous and handsome prince, and never in his life did he engage in dishonesty or treachery. And when the inhuman murderers had done as they pleased with the noble duke, they left the body lying there outstretched among the other dead. In great haste they fled, for they greatly feared that the bourgeois of the city might follow and kill them.]

As did his brother's, Garin's body undergoes mutilation, this time at the hands of a well-meaning municipal official. The verse introduces a mayor or provost who bursts into the chapel:

Vit son seigneur devant l'autel gesir:
cuida morz fust, que il ne fust pas vis!
– Encor i est l'ame, ce m'est avis –
Li meres tint son seignor por martir:
hauce .i. vooge que antre ses braz tint,
le braz senestre li a copé par mi.
En blanc argent le metra, ce a dit.
Li dus se pasme quant l'angoisse senti,
oevre les iauz, a son major a dit:
"Amis, biau frere, por coi m'as tu ocis?"
                                    (*Garin le Loherenc* vv. 16,094–103)

[He saw his lord lying in front of the altar. He thought that he was dead, that he was no longer alive! His soul is still there, I believe. The mayor considered his lord a martyr. He raises a halberd that he held in his arms,

compaignie" and fol. 190r, "Et le noble duc Guerrin y estoit venus comme j'ai di tout simplement et a petitte compaignie."

and cut Garin's left arm in half. He will put it in shining silver, he said. The duke faints when he felt the pain, opens his eyes. He said to his mayor, "Friend, dear brother, why have you killed me?"]

The duke pardons his assailant and expires (v. 16,107). It is no coincidence that Garin had just mentioned Longinus in his last prayer, asking God to forgive his sins just as He forgave the "mortal blow" that pierced Christ's body (vv. 16,063–67). Typology thus associates Garin's death with the Crucifixion in the verse redactions. In the manner of other celebrated epic heroes such as Roland and Vivien, Garin merits apotheosis and joins the ranks of the holy martyrs.

All of the prose translations include the incident of the amputated arm, but exploit it in very different ways. The *Prose de l'Arsenal* retains all the facts, but converts Garin's plaintive question into a flat indirect statement, diminishing the pathos of the scene: "Lors soy despasma Garin et lui dit que mal faisoit de le tuer" (45; Then Garin came to and told him he was wrong to kill him).

The Burgundian prose amplifies the beginning considerably to establish the pious motives of the relic-seeker, who is transformed into a knight.

> Il le regretta sur tous autres princes, disant en soy meismes que la mort avoit ravy le plus sage, le plus large, le plus courtois et le plus catholicque et le plus vaillant chevallier du monde, et a ce qu'il povoit comprendre disoit en soy que le bon prince estoit vray martir, et que Dieu l'avoit moult aimé, quy avoit souffert qu'il receust couronne de martir en si digne lieu comme devant l'autel d'une tant sainte chappelle. Lors le chevallier se advisa que Nostre Seigneur pourra en temps advenir faire pour luy plenté de moult beaulx miracles, et pour ce il delibera se possible luy estoit que de celluy saint corps en emporteroit aucun membre. (KBR 8, fol. 8v)

> [He lamented the loss of {Garin} above all other princes, telling himself that death had taken the wisest, most generous, most courtly, most Catholic and most valiant knight in the world, and he told himself that as far as he could understand, the good prince was a true martyr, and that God had loved him very much, having allowed him to receive the crown of martyrdom in such a worthy place, before the altar of such a holy chapel. Then the knight realized that Our Lord might in time bring about many beautiful miracles for him, and thus he wondered whether it was possible to take away a part of this holy body.]

When Garin feels the blow, he eloquently questions the knight, who declares tearfully that he was convinced Garin's soul had left his body. Garin's response is both courtly and Christlike: "Certes le noble duc luy pardonna debonnairement et en ce faisant il rendy son ame a Dieu par glorieux martire" (KBR 8, fol. 9r; truly the noble duke pardoned him graciously and in doing so gave up his soul to God in glorious martyrdom).

Philippe, on the other hand, underplays the religious imagery, omitting the reference to Longinus as well as Garin's exchange with his accidental tormentor. Instead, he dwells on the unfortunate timing of the amputation:

Cy antrait ledit prevost en la chaipelle et en grant pleur et lamentacion baisoit // son sire et la bouche, le nef et le visaige, car il le cuidoit mort et tués. Mais non estoit encor. Sy print ledit maire son espee et cuidant que le noble duc fut mort comme dit est, cy lui coppait ung bras en intancion de l'ampourter et de le faire envaisseler en or ou en argent pour l'amour qu'il avoit a son seigneur. Car il le tenoit pour martir. Mais ledit duc qui encor avoit vie owrit lez yeulx [...] (fols. 191r–191v)

[The mayor entered into the chapel, and crying and lamenting kissed his lord's mouth, nose, and face, for he believed him to be dead and gone. But he wasn't yet. The mayor then took his sword, and thinking that the noble duke was dead, as mentioned, he cut off one of his arms with the intention of taking it and having it enclosed in a gold or silver vessel for love of his lord. For he considered him a martyr. But the duke, who was still alive, opened his eyes]

In Philippe's retelling, the provost still considers Garin a martyr, but the relic is cherished as a reminder of the feudal bond rather than a vector of miracles. Recalling emphatically that Garin is "not dead yet" (like Monty Python's plague victim), the narrator makes the sacred secondary to the sensational. Unlike the verse original or the court-commissioned prose, Philippe does not sublimate the inherent violence of the scene, nor does he exploit its potential for transcendence.

The final branch of the cycle opens with yet another homicide. Following the beginning of *Anseÿs de Metz (Gascogne)*, Philippe's *Yonnet* recounts the death of Garin's son Gerbert at the hands of his own nephew Louis. Louis is the son of Gerbert's cousin Hernaut and the Bordelais Ludie, a bitter and shrewish woman who seeks revenge on the Lorraine clan for their role in her brother's death. After quarreling with his cousin during a falcon hunt, the young Louis is easily convinced to obey his mother's order to kill Gerbert, who is playing chess with his kinsmen during a joyful family gathering at Pentecost. The boy sneaks up behind his uncle, strikes him on the head with a sword (or a chessboard in *Anseÿs*), and splits his skull, killing the mighty Gerbert instantly. The ingredients of the episode will by now seem quite familiar. In time of peace, Gerbert ventures into a potentially dangerous environment, much to the distress of his wife. Believing that all is well, he engages in noble pastimes in the safety of his brother's castle. He is murdered treacherously, and his death triggers a new war between the two lineages. The parallels between Gerbert's murder and that of his father Garin are reinforced by the illustrations in MS *h*: the historiated initials depicting these events both show the victim being struck from behind as he looks over his left shoulder.[70]

Once again, the Burgundian prose champions repentance, inserting a long passage in which Gerbert confesses his sins to a lady who happens to be passing through the room when the crime occurs. He has a heavy conscience, and given his condition, cannot recall all of his transgressions, but makes a valiant effort, evoking pity and compassion in his listener (KBR 9, fol. 15r).[71]

Philippe includes no such confession. He lingers over his motifs of preference: the hero's cheerful departure from the safety of his home, his wife's sense of foreboding and the pleasant distractions that precede Gerbert's murder (fols. 307r–309r). In fact, the prelude to the crime bears a remarkable resemblance to Philippe's own brush with death as he relates it in the *Journal*. When Gerbert arrives to celebrate Pentecost with his cousin, the beginning of the feast is marked by music and dancing, but the narrator warns that the revelry will be short lived:

> Et aincy ce demenoient escuiers et damoiselles en dance, chanson et biarolle en passant le tampts joieusement pour acomancement de celle feste. Mais helas! la joie tournerait en doulleur, car ainsois que le vespre soit venus lez ferait Ludie triste et dollans comme il vous serait dit ycy. (fol. 307v)

> [And thus squires and damsels engaged in dance and song, passing the time joyously at the beginning of this feast. But alas! joy would turn to sorrow, for before evening arrived Ludie would make them sad and miserable, as will be told to you here.]

The translator has invented neither the amusements nor the narrator's lament on the reversal of fortune, for they are also present in the verse original (*Anseÿs de Mes* vv. 125–31). It is striking, however, that in the *Journal*, the home invasion that will lead to the abduction of Philippe and his father is framed in precisely the same way. The crime is preceded by a family gathering, where Philippe happily plays the rebec:

> adonc tous se mirent à danser de tant bon couraige que merveille et ne voulloient que Phelippe laissait le juer, tant y estoient boutes et eschauffés, meyme son père qui estoit tant joyeux que merveille et furent ainsy jusques près de minuit en joie et en déduit. Helas! com pouc que durait celle joie, car s'ils eussent seu le grant malz c'on leur pourchassoit, ils heussent

---

[70] Pp. 735 and 1151. Similarly, the full-page miniature of Hervis's death on the battlefield shows the hero being struck from behind as he looks over his left shoulder (p. 270).

[71] The Burgundian translator clearly used a different verse manuscript, which may have contained Gerbert's confession. Nonetheless, the passage is consistent with the religious fervor that informs this version of the cycle.

laissié le chanter et le danser et se fussent mis à plorer ou à regairder comment ils se poroient saulver. (*Journal* 44)

[then all began to dance with marvelous good humor and didn't want Philippe to stop playing, they were so lively and excited, especially his father who was marvelously joyful, and they remained in joy and pleasure until almost midnight. Alas! how briefly this joy would last, for if they had known the great evil that was about to befall them, they would have put aside singing and dancing, and would have begun to cry or to figure out how to save themselves.]

Here, the narrator implies the lesson to be learned from such narratives: happinesss is fleeting, it prefigures adversity, and one must be on one's guard even when one feels most secure.

Also conspicuous in *Yonnet* is the narrator's righteous indignation toward Ludie, an outsider who bears much responsibility for Gerbert's killing. In the prologue, she shares the blame for the ultimate destruction of the great lineage:

Et coment parmi ledit Lowis et par le conseille de damme Ludie sa mere ce reesmeut de nowiaulx la guerre, laquelle ne print jamaix fin tant qu'il en y eust nés ung en vie et que tout en fut destruit. Car enfin en moururent tous exceptés le roy Gerin lequelle c'en aillait tenir a boix en exille et ne sceut jamaix homme qu'il devint [...] (fol. 306r)

[And how by means of Louis and by the counsel of Lady Ludie his mother, the war was rekindled and never ended until not a single one remained alive, and all was destroyed. For in the end, all died except King Gerin who went into exile in the woods and no one ever knew what became of him.]

To be sure, Ludie is portrayed in all versions as an evil woman. When narrators and characters mention her, they often invoke the wrath of God ("que Dieus puist maleïr!"), but Philippe goes further. He qualifies more frequently the lady's proper name, alternating between the neutral "damme Ludie" and pejorative epithets ("la folle Ludie" "Ludie la faulce femme" "la traisteresse dame Ludie") or simply referring to her as "la fourbe femme" or "la malvaise femme." In his revisions to MS *v*, he often adds these qualifiers to his first draft, as though he found his initial condemnations to be insufficient (fols. 307v, 309r, 309v).

Thus, while the first book of Philippe's prose pays homage to the good mother Beatrice, *Yonnet* is the story of motherhood gone astray. Bad mothers similarly haunt the *Chronique* and the *Journal*, although these figures are generally guilty of infanticide.[72] Jody Enders has examined the role of

---

[72] See, for example, *Journal* 146, cf. *Chronique* IV: 25–26; *Journal* 291–92, cf. *Chronique* IV: 215–16.

murderous mothers in Philippe's chronicle and in the legendry of early sixteenth-century Metz. She argues that Philippe and his contemporaries "retrofitted" a fictional infanticide from a 1513 production of the *Mistere de la Sainte Hostie* onto the local Messin crime scene.[73] This blurring of boundaries suggests that Philippe made connections between the real crimes he committed to text and the textual crimes he witnessed on stage. Enders situates such conflations "in the context of local anxieties about history repeating itself" in the case of certain types of criminals, including foreigners.[74] A similar process is at work, I believe, in the author's translation of the violent crimes that define the Lorraine epic. In the context of Philippe's corpus, the murder of an epic hero does not merely signify martyrdom and an unbroken cycle of feudal violence. These crimes also participate in an intertextual network of ignoble deeds assembled by a chronicler seeking to thrill and forewarn his public in risky times.

The preceding discussion does not claim to be a comprehensive analysis of narrative technique in Philippe's five-volume adaptation. The episodes studied are, however, representative samples of the Messin author's approach to *translatio* on the level of storytelling. Comparison with the other prose versions of the Lorraine cycle is illuminating. The *Prose de l'Arsenal* reduces the verse texts to a threadbare summary of events. Conversely, the Burgundian prose tends to inflate courtly and pious traits that are merely hinted at in the original. Philippe de Vigneulles intervenes far less than either of his predecessors, and yet his derhyming reflects a highly personal interpretation of the inherited material. By foregrounding the figures and events that conform to his world view, he subordinates these excellent stories to a new narrative logic.

---

[73] Enders, "Theater Makes History: Ritual Murder by Proxy in the *Mistere de la Sainte Hostie*," *Speculum* 79 (2004): 991–1016. This antisemitic mystery play compounded infanticide with host desecration. Enders shows convincingly that Philippe's chronicle linked the real and theatrical events, contributing to a cultural climate that justified the persecution of Jews.

[74] Enders, "Theater Makes History," 994.

4

The Craft of *dérimage*

The late medieval derhymer was long portrayed as a well-meaning but inept hack. Representative of the first wave of studies devoted to the *mises en prose* is Pierre Le Gentil's assertion that the prosifiers simply did not understand the requirements of their task: "Les mises en prose ont été faites dans l'équivoque par des hommes qui, à une nostalgie sincère du passé, ne joignaient pas assez de sens historique et philologique pour opérer une véritable résurrection littéraire."[1] In fact, it is the modern medievalist who is often afflicted with misplaced nostalgia. Philippe de Vigneulles's contemporaries did not valorize transparent readings of original verse texts, nor did they expect translators to efface their voices. These weighty adaptations, admittedly alien to modern sensibilities, are better understood in light of recent theories of translation. Lawrence Venuti, for example, attempts to dismantle modern expectations of invisibility, declaring that accuracy in translation is not absolute, but historically determined. The viability of a given translation does not depend on the communication of an idealized essence, but is rather "established by its relationship to the cultural and social conditions under which it is produced and read."[2] With the publication of every new edition and critical study, it has become clear that even amateur translators such as Philippe de Vigneulles did apply their own sense of history and language to an endeavor that was encouraged and appreciated by cultivated audiences.

Furthermore, the compositional and discursive strategies involved in late medieval *dérimage* are more varied than earlier scholarship would have us believe. Although certain practices were common to all types of prosification, each practitioner developed a distinctive (if not always systematic) set of interpretive processes for replacing Old French verse with Middle French prose. I have already explored patterns of adaptation with regard to specific areas of content in which Philippe was highly invested as both citizen and writer. The present chapter examines his approach to prosification from a

---

[1] Pierre Le Gentil, "Jean Wauquelin et la légende de Girard de Roussillon," *Studi in onore di Italo Siciliano*, Biblioteca dell'Archivum Romanicum 86 (Florence: Leo S. Olschki, 1966), I, 623–35, at p. 635.

[2] Lawrence Venuti, *The Translator's Invisibility: A History of Translation* (London & New York: Routledge, 1995), 18.

broader, formal perspective. In Philippe's work, the most revealing interventions are located in the following areas: compilation and organization of the cyclical material, amplification, abridgement, derhyming, lexical updating and modes of discourse. In the absence of Philippe's actual verse sources, comparison between verse and prose must remain approximate. However, we are fortunate that extant versions of Philippe's prose contain revisions in the author's own hand, thus offering a glimpse into the translator's evolving conception of his work. Repackaged by an earnest antiquarian, the Lorraine prose epic may be read as a compelling record of reflection on structure, style and intelligibility.

Compilation, Segmentation, and Junctures

Philippe's adventure in translation unfolds as a parallel story, told in the prologues and epilogues that frame each branch of the prose adaptation. In addition to providing insight on authorial intention and audience expectations, the paratextual commentary depicts the labors of a diligent historian. Philippe reminds us incessantly of the length of the old songs he has inherited, and periodically repeats the conventional apologies for his lack of skill and understanding. The prologue to the last book, *Yonnet*, is more specific in its portrait of the author at work. Once he had completed his translation of the *Livre de la belle Beaultris* and the three books of the *Lourain Guerin*, Philippe wondered whether there might not be another sequel. He describes his quest for new manuscripts, anxious to discover what became of Gerbert, Yonnet, and the other surviving members of the Lorraine clan. Did the great feud ever begin anew?

> je Philippe dessus nommeis ait sairchiez, tournés, remireis et anquerir plusieurs ancienne istoire, voullume, livre et cronicque, desirant et appetant pour savoir mon quelle fut la fin [...] Et pour ce aprés ce que j'eus asseis serchiez j'ez troweis en aulcune ancienne istoire et cellon aulcuns aultre acteur ce qu'il en avint, et coment parmi ledit Lowis et par le conseille de damme Ludie sa mere ce reesmeut de nowiaulx la guerre, laquelle ne print jamaix fin tant qu'il en y eust nés ung en vie et que tout en fut destruit [...] Et jay ce que le livre ycy devent nommeis le Lourain Guerin n'en mest rien, touttefois aultre istoire despandant de cest, come j'ez dit devent, le mect. Et aultre istoirien en ont escript toutte en la fourme et manier ou au moins en subtance, comme la teneur s'ansuit. (fol. 306r)

> [I, the aforementioned Philippe, searched, turned pages, examined and scrutinized several ancient stories, volumes, books and chronicles, desiring and wishing fervently to find out the end {...} And thus after I had looked hard enough I found in an old story and according to another author what happened to them, and how by means of Louis and by the counsel of his mother Lady Ludie, the war was rekindled and never ended until not a

single one remained alive, and all was detroyed {...} And although the
aforementioned book called the *Lourain Guerin* includes nothing about
this, nonetheless another story connected to that one, as I said before, does
include it. And other historians wrote about it according to the form and
manner, or at least substance, of what follows.]

In order to reconstruct the "vraye histoire" in its entirety, Philippe was thus
obliged to join material from several disparate documents: "l'ez retrait au
moins malz que j'ez peu de trois ou quaitre ancienne istoire et l'és remis,
concordez et join[c?]g" (fol. 306r; I extracted it as best I could from three
or four ancient stories which I put together, combined and joined). It is not
entirely clear whether he refers here to the final branch or to the translation as a whole. In either case, for Philippe, prosifying the Lorraine epic
involved many of the same tasks as chronicle writing: "assambler, joindre, et
concorder" (*Chronique* IV: 1; assembling, joining and reconciling). He uses a
similar vocabulary to describe the fabrication of his portraits in cloth: "plus
de viiii mil pièces de draps mises et joinctes ensemble" (*Journal* 154; more
than 9,000 pieces of cloth put together and joined).

   The verbs *remettre, concorder, joindre* and *assambler* designate not
only the material collection of diverse elements, but also their purposeful
assembly. As Douglas Kelly has amply demonstrated, the language of *join-
ture* was used throughout the Middle Ages in both literary and nonliterary
contexts "to refer to any combination of elements, however unwieldy, untidy,
or heterogeneous."[3] In the case of verse romance, authors such as Chrétien
de Troyes employed sophisticated rhetorical techniques to conjoin disparate tales into a coherent and pleasing configuration. The principle of *bele
conjointure* evoked in the prologue of *Erec et Enide* valorizes a seamless
and harmonious combination that obscures articulations. This concept also
underlies Philippe's textile masterpiece, where the 9,000 pieces of cloth were
so expertly joined that, according to its maker, the finished product looked
like a painting (*Journal* 154). Conversely, the prose romance and epic *mise
en prose* typically demonstrate more overt links between parts, revealing the
breaks between interlaced or successive branches of narrative. These junctures are sites of metalanguage that foreground the narrator's voice and the
prosifier's art. The artful juxtaposition of episodic material constitutes a *bele
desjointure*.[4] Although Philippe does not use this term, it aptly describes his
chronicle and his prose epic, both of which call attention to discontinuities

---

   3 Kelly, *The Art of Medieval French Romance*, 15.
   4 Kelly, *The Art of Medieval French Romance*, 17–22. The *mises en prose* display
varying degrees of disjuncture. The *Histoire de Charles Martel*, like Philippe's prose,
separates cyclical branches into clearly defined books. The author of the *Guillaume
en prose* strives for more cohesiveness: although he divides the text into chapters and
paragraphs, he masks the hiatus between disparate epic songs. See Suard, *Guillaume
d'Orange*, 147.

in source material. In the *mise en prose*, these discontinuities are offset by the prologues and epilogues. Organized according to the genealogy of heroes and conflicts, the thresholds of each book recall and announce the principal narrative threads that bind the work.

Like most late medieval prose writers, Philippe is also attentive to internal structure. As he states in his general prologue, he reworked the verse into prose "par chapitre."[5] These narrative divisions do not correspond to the laisses of his verse sources, the contours of which are motivated by lyric as well as narrative exigencies. Rather, Philippe's chapters organize the unwieldy content into digestible segments, generally about one folio in length.[6] Unlike those of the Arsenal and Burgundian prose versions, however, Philippe's chapter boundaries do not correspond strictly to episodes, in the sense of completed events circumscribed by spatial and temporal limits.[7] Rather, his divisions are more often triggered by shifts of perspective and deferred closure.

The death of Begon is a case in point, revealing significant differences in structure and segmentation among the various versions. The verse epic relates the episode in eleven laisses, beginning with Begon's decision to hunt the wild boar and ending with the departure of his body from Fromont's court in Lens (*Garin le Loherenc* vv. 9550–10,262). Formal markers define the contours of the segment. With only one exception, the extant verse manuscripts display a clear juncture at the beginning of the episode, generally in the form of a prominent or historiated initial.[8] As a closure device, a transitional formula separates Begon's death from its consequences in the opening of laisse 110: "Huimais dirons" (*Garin le Loherenc* v. 10,263; henceforth we will tell). The intervening laisses vary considerably in length and composition, with a high frequency of lyric overlap in the relatively short laisses devoted to the death itself.

Philippe's fellow prosifiers consolidate this material into a single cohesive narrative unit. The *Prose de l'Arsenal* relates the content in one brief chapter, framed by "Or dit li contez" and "Or dirons de Rigaut" (26–28; now the tale says / now we will tell about Rigaut). The Burgundian *Histoire de Charles Martel* devotes one lengthy chapter to the event, beginning with an authenticity formula: "L'istoire anchienne racompte que" (*Guerin le Loherain* 288;

---

5 The reference to chapter divisions is found in the revised prologue of MS *h*, p. 6.

6 MS *v* crowds as much text as possible into its pages, which measure 21x25 cm. The pages become less aerated as the work progresses. The number of words per page is quite variable, depending on rubrics and corrections, with an approximate average of 550.

7 Valérie Naudet notes that in the *Histoire de Charles Martel*, "les chapitres paraissent comme des unités narratives, centrés, autant que faire se peut, sur un événement comme la mort de Begon, l'adoubement de Girbert, le mariage des frères lorrains ou de Pépin" (*Guerin le Loherain*, Introduction, 14).

8 *Garin le Loherenc*, laisse 99, beginning at v. 9550. For a detailed account of this juncture in the manuscript tradition, see Jean-Charles Herbin, "Approches," 482.

the ancient story tells that) and ending with a transitional device: "Si s'en taist a tant le conte pour le present" (301; here the tale breaks off for the time being). Philippe's version, on the other hand, adapts the delaying tactics of verse to the machinery of prose. Like the verse poet, he divides the material into eleven segments, but his chapters are not coterminous with the laisse divisions. Rather, Philippe's prose incorporates cliffhangers, prolonging the hero's death by pausing at key junctures in the fateful hunting scene. For example, when Begon becomes isolated in the forest and sounds his horn, Philippe inserts a chapter break to defer the arrival of the murderous Bordelais:

> Puis ait cournés par trois fois son corne d'ivoire pour ces chiens ras-sambler. Mais ce fut une piteuse cornee pour lui, car par ycelle moureut le noble duc comme cy aprés vous serait dit. (fol. 147v)

> [Then he sounded his ivory horn three times to round up his dogs. But this blowing of the horn was unfortunate for him, because it led to the noble duke's death, as will be told to you afterward.]

The beginning of the next chapter shifts focalization to the forester who will denounce Begon, inserting the standard transition formulas of prose narrative:

> Or vous lairés a pairler du noble duc et de tous ces serviteur et vous dirés du fourestier et gairde du bois, lequelle incontinent qu'il eust oÿ ce cornet d'ivoire aincy doulcement sonner, pas a pas ce aprouchait du lieu et de loing espiait le duc car nullement n'oisoit aprouchiés de luy. (fol. 147v)

> [Now I will stop talking to you about the noble duke and all his attend-ants, and I will tell you about the forester and guardian of the woods, who, as soon as he had heard that ivory horn sound so softly, approached the place step by step and observed the duke from afar, for he didn't dare approach him.]

This juncture is at variance with the segmentation of the verse, which depicts the blowing of the horn and the forester's gaze in one laisse, only to reit-erate and amplify the forester's role in the next, in a classic example of epic *enchaînement* (*Garin le Loherenc* vv. 9824–48). As François Suard points out, laisse structure in the *chansons de geste* animates dramatic content through intricately woven patterns of incantation that modulate between lyric and narrative exigencies.[9] Segmentation in the *mise en prose* is a func-tion of narrative alone, but Philippe does seek to heighten dramatic effect by suspending the action in the midst of a crisis. Like the jongleurs, he

---

[9] Suard, *Guillaume d'Orange*, 163–64.

also attends to the mechanics of linking. He consistently inserts anticipatory phrases at chapter's end, followed by *rappels* or reminders at the opening of the next chapter. However, these bridges between chapters are quite different from the interstrophic repetitions one finds in the *chanson de geste*. Epic *enchaînement* involves the repetition of an event or utterance in a new assonance, with subtle changes in aspect or vocabulary; it tends to suspend time and create a lyric pause. Derhymed epic *enchaînement*, on the other hand, calls attention to the procedure of linking, as the narrator advertises his efforts to augment the readability of the text.[10]

Philippe also follows established convention by adding explanatory intertitles or headings at the opening of each chapter.[11] However, his headings are considerably longer than those found in other *mises en prose*, which typically provide a fairly concise overview of the chapter's content. The following example confronts a chapter title from Philippe's prose with its equivalent in the *Histoire de Charles Martel*:

Philippe de Vigneulles, *Guerin I*	*Histoire de Charles Martel*
Coment le noble roy Thierey, voiant son dernier jour venir, mandait tout lez plus grant de son païs, auquelle il fist promestre de tenir sa seulle fille a royne, damme et maitresse, et de ce en firent foy et omaige. Et coment par le conseille de Joffroy fut envoiés querir le duc Guerin auquelle le roy donnait sa fille en mariaige avec tout son païs. Et le noble duc la print par condicion telle que cil plaisoit a roy Pepin. Et aprez ce fait ce fist oster le quairiaulx de la teste et aincy mourut le roy Thierey. (fol. 80r)	Comment le roy Thierry de Morienne donna sa fille en mariage au gentil duc Guerin le Loherain a tout son royaulme par le consentement des barons de ses paiis. (*Guerin le Loherain* 104)

---

[10] On *enchaînement*, see Jean Rychner, *La Chanson de geste: Essai sur l'art épique des jongleurs* (Geneva: Droz, 1955), 74–80. On transition formulas in the *mises en prose*, see Doutrepont, *Les Mises en prose*, 473 and Suard, *Guillaume d'Orange*, 152–56.

[11] I refer to Philippe's chapter titles alternately as *tituli*, "intertitles" or "headings," as they are not rubricated. Keith Busby uses the term *"titulus"* to designate "a simple indication of the content of the item to follow"; a "rubric," on the other hand, is "an extra-diegetic comment, often related to a miniature of historiated initial." See *Codex and Context: Reading Old French Verse Narrative in Manuscript*, 2 vols. (Amsterdam & New York: Rodopi, 2002), 195, note 83. In MS *v*, the intertitles disappear temporarily after the first ten chapters of the *Livre de la belle Beaultris* (fol. 5v), and resume again toward the end of that book (fol. 57r). However, there are markers at the junctures between chapters, to signal the need for headings in a future revision. The missing *tituli* appear in the table at the beginning of the work, copied by Auguste Prost. For the text of the titles found in MS *h* see Maurice de Pange, *La Chanson de Garin le Loherain mise en prose*.

Philippe de Vigneulles, *Guerin I*

[How the noble King Thierry, seeing his final day arrive, sent for all the important barons of his land. He made them promise to regard his only daughter as their queen, lady and sovereign, and they swore fealty and homage to her. And how, on the counsel of Joffroy, Duke Garin was sent for, and the king gave him his daughter in marriage along with his entire kingdom. And the noble duke accepted her on the condition that it might please King Pepin. And after this was done, King Thierry had the arrow removed from his head, and thus he died.]

Histoire de Charles Martel

[How King Thierry of Maurienne gave his daughter in marriage to the noble Duke Garin le Lorrain, along with his kingdom, with the consent of the barons of his lands.]

The *tituli* reflect the translators' conception of essential narrative information. For the Burgundian author (or rubricator), this information is limited to the principal actors, the bestowal of daughter and kingdom, and the consent of vassals. Philippe's heading, which is three times longer, adds considerably more circumstantial detail: the reasons for the King Thierry's decision, the nature of the exchange between Thierry and his barons, the manner in which Garin was summoned, and Garin's conditional acceptance and Thierry's death. Rather than mere titles, Philippe's headings are digests that add another interpretive layer to the rewriting.

Pierre Demarolle finds little stylistic differentiation between titles and chapters in Philippe's translation, and he concludes that Philippe did not have a sufficiently rigorous conception of titles as discourse to detach them in his mind from the translated text. Demarolle bases his judgment on a stylistic analysis of the titles in MS *h*, as edited by Maurice de Pange.[12] Indeed, the headings do become longer as the work progresses, and the titles increasingly duplicate the narrative information carried by the text proper. However, an examination of MS *h* itself demonstrates that Philippe actually shortened many of the titles as they had appeared in *v*, often crossing out several lines of text and reducing the level of narrative detail.[13]

In addition, MS *v* contains a revealing emendation that attests to the translator's attention both to *mise en page* and to the language of titles from the

[12] Pierre Demarolle, "De la narratologie à la syntaxe: les titres des chapitres de la mise en prose de *Garin le Lorrain* par Philippe de Vigneulles," *Rhétorique et mise en prose au XVe siècle*, ed. Sergio Cigada and Anne Slerca (Milan: Vita e Pensiero, 1991), 245–55, at p. 255.

[13] See, for example, pp. 341, 925, 1053, 1074.

beginning of his project. In *Guerin III*, he commits a *saut du même au même*, and in so doing neglects to insert a chapter break and heading. He corrects the error by placing marks at the appropriate insertion points, and also adding instructions for the revised copy:

> Prenés ce coment ycy et mectés le ou livre aprés ou il y ait telz ansaigne ✠ et acomensés ledit coment aprez ces mot ycy qui s'ansuive [...] Reprenés ou livre a telz ansaigne car je avoie obliez le coment et tout cey devent escript. (fol. 222r)

> [Take this "how" here and put it in the following book, where this sign ✠ is, and begin that "how" after the following words {...} Resume in the book at this sign, for I forgot the "how" and everything written before this.]

It is not clear whether he omitted a passage from an earlier draft of the translation, or a passage to be translated from the verse. The correction does show, however, that the proper placement of junctures was essential to his craft. His instructions also show that he had a name for the heading or intertitle: the *coment* or "how" that generally serves as the first word. While some of his *tituli* begin with the preposition *de* followed by a nominal syntagm, the vast majority display the pattern *coment* + subject + verb, a structure that is often repeated several times in the longer titles.[14]

There is thus clear evidence that Philippe did make the mental leap from paratext to text. His intertitles were subject to significant editing in both extant versions of the translation. For him, the principal function of the chapter heading appears to reside in its capacity to express actions and process. That this function coincides with the event-centered prose narrative does not imply that the translator perceived no difference between them. Rather, to the extent that the *coment* incorporates an increasing proportion of the chapter's contents, it competes with the following line-by-line derhyming.

In effect, Philippe's lengthier headings, minus the *coment* formula, may be compared to the Arsenal prose redaction of the Lorraine cycle, which, being highly abridged, contains no intertitles itself. There is no evidence that Philippe knew the Arsenal prose, but his titles are not unlike its encapsulated version with respect to length and choice of content. The following title from *Guerin III*, which introduces Gerbert's expedition to Cologne, correlates rather closely to the Arsenal text:

---

[14] As Demarolle notes, there are also bicephalous headings, which combine clauses beginning with "de" and "Coment." See his "De la narratologie" 248–49.

Philippe de Vigneulles, *Guerin III* (title)

Coment le vaillant duc Gilbert, Gerin et Malvoisin conclurent tous trois ensamble de c'en ailler devent Collongne et pour ce faire en parlairent a la royne, laquelle leur donnait mil home en change et en fist Gilbert maistre e capitaine. Et coment il arivairent a Collongne et trowairent le roy trés courroussés de ce que ce jour il avoit perdus deux de ces filz. Mais aulcunement fut resjoÿs pour la venue du duc Gilbert et de Gerin. (fol. 221r)

[How the valiant Duke Gerbert, Gerin and Mauvoisin decided, all three together, to go off to Cologne, and in order to do this, spoke of it to the queen, who gave them a thousand men and made Gerbert master and captain of the troops. And how they arrived in Cologne and found the king very angry, for he had lost two of his sons that day. But he was somewhat cheered by the arrival of Duke Gerbert and Gerin.]

Prose de l'Arsenal (text)

et lors enprist Gerbert d'aler secourir le roy Anseïs et la roine luy bailla mil chevaliers sans l'ascent du roy poiés pour ung an. Il trova le roy a Couloigne, qui avoit combatu lez Sarrasins, més trop y avoit il perdu car il avoit perdu ses deux filz et .X. ses neveux et mil chevaliers; bien estoit courrocé et plus le fut quant il sceut la responce le roy et bien fut joieux quant il sceut la venue Gerbert. (55–56)

[and then Gerbert set out to go and help King Anseïs, and the queen gave him a thousand knights without the consent of the king, paid for one year. He found the king in Cologne, where he had fought the Saracens, but he had lost too much, for he had lost his two sons and ten of his nephews and a thousand knights; he was very angry, and even more so when he learned of the king's response, and he was very happy when he learned of Gerbert's arrival.]

While the comparison shows slight differences in the choice of detail, Philippe's chapter title renders the sequence of events and the king's affective state just as completely as the Arsenal text proper, which describes itself as a "roman" (88, 148).

Extracted from the whole, whether read in the table at the beginning of the manuscript or distributed throughout, Philippe's titles stand alone as an elaborate synopsis, and a far more thorough one than the those provided by other *mises en prose* of the period. They furnish not only a narrative map, but also a plausible alternative to the complete translation. At the turn of the twentieth century, Philippe's *tituli* continued to fulfill this function when Maurice de Pange published them along with the miniatures from MS *h* to revive the work for his own contemporaries.[15] This publication, while partial

---

[15] De Pange acknowledges his debt to the Count of Hunolstein, who gave him access to the manuscript and allowed him to publish excerpts (*La Chanson de Garin le Loherain mise en prose* I).

in nature, is entirely consistent with the spirit of the prosifier's endeavor. While Philippe spent considerable time and effort on the comprehensive *dérimage*, he was certainly not averse to the digest as a means of disseminating the tale. We may recall that his *Chronique* summarizes the same material in a highly condensed form (I: 162–69). In a very real sense, then, Philippe de Vigneulles may be credited with three distinct rewritings of the Lorraine cycle, supplementing the verse with a long version (the derhymed text), a medium version (combined intertitles), and a short version (chronicle summary).

The junctures between branches and episodes are the most salient *loci* of amplification in Philippe's adaptation. The following section examines additions to the original verse in the translation proper.

Amplification

A number of late medieval *mises en prose* augment the original songs with new characters, episodes, marvels, and/or moral commentary.[16] Philippe's additions are far more modest. As we have seen, he does occasionally intervene to condemn the Bordelais (and the Saracens, who make only brief appearances) or to caution contemporary rulers. Generally, however, Philippe's amplifications serve to clarify or emphasize the letter of the text, and involve the addition of a few words or phrases. As Jane H. M. Taylor has shown, such interventions are no less illuminating than the large-scale transformations effected by accomplished translators such as Chaucer and Gower: "it is possible that lack of sophistication and carefully pedestrian renderings may afford better evidence of reception than the responses of creators in their own right."[17] Philippe's microadditions attest to the hermeneutic value of minor stylistic variations. I will first consider the types of clarification employed in the prose, and secondly the figure of *accumulatio* as a form of emphasis.

Derhyming implies fundamental modifications of the formulaic language found in the *chansons de geste*.[18] The following examples demonstrate Philippe's rendering of a structural pattern routinely used to depict a character's reaction to something heard or seen. The translated passages show a range of intervention, from minimal to moderate amplification:

---

[16] See Doutrepont, *Les Mises en prose*, 495–532.

[17] Jane H. M. Taylor, "Translation as Reception: Boccaccio's *De Mulieribus Claris* and *Des cleres et nobles femmes.*" *Por le soie amisté: Essays in Honor of Norris J. Lacy*, ed. Keith Busby and Catherine M. Jones (Amsterdam & Atlanta: Rodopi, 2000), 491–507, at p. 493.

[18] On epic formulas and motifs, see Rychner, *La Chanson de geste*, 126–53 and Jean-Pierre Martin, *Les Motifs dans la chanson de geste: Définition et utilisation* (Lille: Centre d'études médiévales et dialectales, Université de Lille III, 1992).

Prose

Lors que le noble duc l'antant, il fut tout effraiez. (fol. 153v)

[When the noble duke hears this, he was quite horrified.]

Le noble duc Hervy voiant cest desconfiture fut presque enraigié. (fol. 64v)

[The noble Duke Hervis, seeing this defeat, was nearly out of his mind.]

Quant Fromont oyt la relacion du messaigier, Dieu scet c'il fut estonnés et perdus. Et fut dollans jusques a la mort. (fol. 197v)

[When Fromont hears the messenger's account, God knows if he was astounded and distraught. And he was mortally sad.]

Verse

Li dus l'antent, a poi n'anrage vis. (*Garin le Loherenc* v. 10,779)

[The duke hears this, he almost takes leave of his senses.]

Hervis le voit, le sen quide desver! (*Garin le Loherenc* v. 430)

[Hervis sees this, he thinks he will lose his mind!]

Fromons l'entent, le sen cuida changier. Molt fu dolanz Fromons li posteïs. (*Garin le Loherenc* vv. 539–40)

[Fromont hears this, he thought he would lose his mind. The powerful Fromont was very sorrowful.]

The Old French verse is paratactic, juxtaposing the formula "*x* + object pronoun + verb of perception (*antandre, veoir*)" with the character's equally formulaic reaction ("*x* + expression of wild rage"). Philippe's prose converts the first sentence into a subordinate clause that emphasizes the causal relationship between perceiving and reacting. The second and third examples go further, specifying the antecedent of the object pronoun so that the cause of the knight's rage or sorrow might not be lost on the reader.

Philippe's prose adds a small number of historical asides to explain proper names or objects that might be unfamiliar or confusing to the modern reader. After mentioning a Joffroy of Lusignan, for example, the narrator hastens to add that this was not the famous son of Mélusine, Joffroy of the large tooth (fol. 169r). In his portrait of the future wives of Garin and Begon, he notes a change in women's hair styles: "puis laissant ailler leur crins par dessus leur espaillez cellon le tampts de leurs" (fol. 120r; then letting their hair fall back over their shoulders, as was the custom in that time). Certain military terms or practices merit explanation, including the weapon used to kill Hervis. The verse describes that object as "un quarrel fort" (*Garin le Loherenc* v. 995; a strong arrow), a term glossed in the prose as "ung quairiaulx ou trait d'airboullette de bais de quoy on usoit pour ce tamps" (fol. 70r; a quarrel or crossbow bolt such as they used at that time). Toponyms that might be misunderstood by a Metz reader are occasionally clarified or differentiated. The prosifier specifies, for example, that the Clermont destroyed by the Lorrains is not "Clermon en Airgonne, ains est en tirant devers Biavais" (fol. 188v; not Clermont in Argonne [near Metz], but rather on the way to Beauvais).[19]

In fact, Philippe's clarifications are very often associated with time and space, both of which are profoundly modified in the shift from performance to written verse to prose.[20] His spatio-temporal amplifications fall within three major categories: the sequence of story events, the spatial configuration of the fictional world, and the space-time of enunciation.

The construction of story time is among the most radical differences between the *chansons de geste* and their later adaptations. In his study of temporal notations in thirteenth-century French verse epics, Bernard Guidot finds that such texts follow a rather fuzzy chronology. Periodic allusions to feast days and duration of events are largely formulaic, and epic time is impalpable, irreducible to the measures of real time.[21] The *mises en prose*, on the other hand, are more concerned with temporal precision. Translators frequently add dates and other points of reference to clarify sequence and duration within the tale, and to situate story time within a historical framework.[22]

In light of Jacques Le Goff's well-known essay on changing perceptions of time in the Middle Ages, it would be tempting to suggest that Philippe de Vigneulles, an experienced and prosperous merchant, fully represents in his prose the "merchant's time" that had gradually permeated Western European culture since the late twelfth century.[23] However, the rigorous measuring of time so necessary to the merchant's professional life does not regulate Philippe's translation of the Lorraine cycle. His prose does not add such precise temporal notations that we might reconstruct fictional time with any degree of accuracy. Philippe seems to have reserved this sort of effort for his *Chronique* and his *Journal*. He does not insert actual dates into the *mise en prose*, with the notable exception of the year in which Hervis is said to have married Beatrice.[24] Yet he does regularly highlight the chronology of events by adding temporal conjunctions and adverbial phrases, particularly in the opening sentences of his chapters:

---

19 See Herbin, "Approches," 494–495 for this last addition and several others. Philippe also specifies that Lyon is "dessus le Rosne" (fols. 74v, 75r; on the Rhône).

20 See Catherine M. Jones, "Espace, temps, réécriture: La mise en prose des *Loherains* par Philippe de Vigneulles," *Les Chansons de geste*, ed. Carlos Alvar and Juan Paredes (Granada: U de Granada, 2005), 325–35.

21 Bernard Guidot, "Mesure du temps et flou chronologique dans quelques chansons de geste du XIIIe siècle," *Le Temps et la durée dans la littérature au Moyen Age et à la Renaissance* (Paris: Nizet, 1986), 55–70.

22 Doutrepont, *Les Mises en prose*, 485–88.

23 Jacques Le Goff, "Au Moyen Age: temps de l'Eglise et temps du marchand," *Pour un autre Moyen Age* (Paris: Gallimard, 1977), 46–65.

24 This is in a chapter heading. See de Pange, *La Chanson de Garin le Loherain mise en prose*, 14; Herbin, "Approches," 496.

Prose	Verse
Aprés ce que celle paix fut aincy faictes comme *cy devent* avés oÿ, laquelle gaire ne durait comme *cy aprez* oÿrés, le roy ait apellés le noble duc Guerin de Mets et comme tout resjoïs il luy ait dit [...] (fol. 111r, my emphasis)	Li rois parole, qui fu de toz oïz, Garin apele, belement si li dit [...] (*Garin le Loherenc* vv. 5595–96)
[*After* this peace had been made, as you heard *before*, which did not last long, as you will hear *afterward*, the king called the noble Duke Garin of Metz, and seeming delighted, he said to him]	[The king speaks, and everyone hears him. He calls Garin, and says to him graciously]
Quant celle baitaille ou saillie fut aincy finee comme avés oÿ, et *que* Fromon avec lez siens en grant doulleur fut retournés dedens la ville, *lors* le duc Baigue bien joieulx de la victoire ait *pour ce meisme jour* convoyez le roy a disner dedens ledit gerdin en son tref et pavillon. (fol. 104r, my emphasis)	Begues semont l'enperëor Pepin q'o lui menjuce laienz en son jardin; (*Garin le Loherenc* vv. 4785–6)
[*When* this battle or sortie was thus finished, as you heard, and *when* Fromont with his men had returned to the city in great distress, *then* Duke Begon, quite delighted with his victory, invited the king *on that very day* to eat in the garden in his tent or pavilion.]	[Begon invites Emperor Pepin to eat with him in his garden.]

This tendency to avoid sharp breaks between narrated events is characteristic of prose *enchaînement* in all prose genres of the period.[25] Like many of his fellow derhymers, Philippe equips the threshold of each chapter with a sequential overload, attenuating the temporal vagueness of the verse.

Prose translation also modifies the impression of omnitemporality conveyed by the *chansons de geste*. Once again, François Suard's study of the prose *Guillaume* offers a valuable contrastive analysis, distinguishing temporal perspectives in the traditional epic from standard practices in the *mise en prose*. Suard writes of the verse epic's vocation to recapitulate all of the moments contributing to its story. The *chanson de geste* reaches out of

---

[25] See Doutrepont, *Les Mises en prose*, 473; Rasmussen, *La Prose narrative française du XVe siècle*, 71–75; Suard, *Guillaume d'Orange*, 152–56.

the text, conjugating past, present, and future in the same mode. Prosifiers, on the other hand, tend to dismantle this eternal present in favor of a linear, dramatic development.[26] Philippe is no exception, but his interventions seek a middle ground: he retains the juxtaposition of multiple time frames, but takes care to untangle the relationship between anticipation, flashback, and primary narrative.

This process is quite evident in a passage from *Guerin I* that enumerates the descendants of Hervis de Metz. It is early in the story, and Hervis has just returned to Metz after assuring the coronation of young King Pepin. His family welcomes him joyously, and though the children are still quite young, the tale flashes forward to three distinct moments in the future:[27]

Prose

Et la .viie. et dernier fille du duc Hervy fut mariee en France et d'icelle saillit deux filz. Le premier fut apellés Hue du Mans et fut conte du Maine. Et l'aultre fut nommés Guernier seigneur de Droiez. Mais je lairez a parler d'eulx et revenrés a ma matier et vous dirés *des tampts que* cez anffans au duc Hervy estoient encor // bien jeune et que *nulle de cez fille n'estoient encor point mariee*. Ce reassamblairent *derechief* les Wandre et Hongre [...]
(fols. 67v–68r, my emphasis)

[And the seventh and last daughter of Duke Hervis was married in France, and she bore two sons. The first was called Hue du Mans and he was Count of Maine. And the other was named Garnier, lord of Dreux. But I shall stop speaking of them and

Verse

de la setiemme, Hue del Mans oissi, Garniers li preuz, icil qui Dreues tint. Or le lerom ester del duc Hervi. Dirons des Woandres, que Dex puist maleïr!
(*Garin le Loherenc* vv. 819–22)

[From the seventh sprang Hue du Mans, and the valiant Garnier, who held Dreux. Now we will leave aside Duke Hervis, and we will tell of the Vandals, may God curse them!]

[26] Suard, *Guillaume d'Orange*, 167.

[27] Most of the verse redactions insert the episode right after Hervis's marriage and before the birth of his children, thus creating another proleptic level. However, the manuscripts containing the *Hervis* branch reconcile the hero's marriage as it is told in that tale with the earlier version related in *Garin le Lorrain*. Manuscripts N and T insert a distinctive version of the genealogy in a lengthy addition, which indicates that the daughters were born within a "terme" of fifteen years, but this addition does not include any transition between the prolepsis and the Vandals' invasion. See Herbin's edition of *Hervis de Mes*, Annexe XXIV, vv. 657–701.

Prose (cont.)

return to my subject and tell you
about *the time when* these children of
Duke Hervis were still very young,
and *none of his daughters were yet
married*. The Vandals and Hungarians
assembled *once again*]

In the original verse, the jongleur relates the hero's return, and then lauches into a digression on events in the distant future. He lists Hervis's seven daughters, their marriages to worthy knights, their illustrious sons, and the lands eventually acquired by these descendants. The jongleur moves almost imperceptibly between the main story line and future events, placing on the same level the family reunion, the daughters' marriages (first-degree prolepsis), the birth of grandsons (second-degree prolepsis), the chivalric careers of those grandsons (third-degree prolepsis) and the Vandal invasion. His transition formula underlines the introduction of new actors rather than a shift in time frame.[28] By contrast, Philippe's transition seeks to avoid all possible confusion between immediate events and anticipatory statements. He adds circumstantial locutions to draw a line of demarcation between two very distinct time periods, the imminent barbarian attack (during the early childhood of Hervis's offspring) and the later eras of marriage and childhood. After the genealogical digression, Philippe's prose goes on to specify that Hervis spent many days and weeks with his family before receiving the news of the invasion (fol. 68r). To some extent, then, Philippe's version demystifies epic temporality by refusing to elide the junctures between discrete moments in story time.

In the passage from performed epic to written prose, the representation of space also demanded elucidation. Like his modifications of time, Philippe's reworking of space is subtle but significant. His prose generally adopts the primary mode of spatial perception found in the *chansons de geste*, that is to say one based on a subjective linearity that privileges itinerary over expanse.[29] He reproduces the venerable topos of the *voyage éclair*, in which long journeys are condensed into short, rapid accounts punctuated by toponyms. However, the prose does expand the fictional space in certain contexts, notably the initiation of speech by a character in formal or ceremonious scenes.

<hr/>

[28] It must be noted, however, that the poet does use different tenses for these events: preterite for the marriages, and passé composé for the Vandals' mobilization of troops in the ensuing narrative.

[29] On space perception in the *chansons de geste*, see Alain Labbé, "Itinéraire et territoire dans les chansons de geste," *Terres médiévales*, ed. Bernard Ribémont (Paris: Klincksieck, 1993), 159–201 and "Sous le signe de saint Jacques: chemins et routes dans la représentation épique de l'espace," *L'Épopée romane*, Civilisation médiévale 13 (Poitiers: U de Poitiers, Centre d'études supérieures de civilisation médiévale, 2002), 99–116.

This intervention occurs most often in council episodes, where the narrator prepares a baron's utterances by declaring his presence in the room:

Prose	Verse
L'abbé de Cluny *luy estant illec presant* ce dressait alors en piedz et dit [...] (fol. 61r, my emphasis)	Adonc parla li abbes de Clugni: (*Garin le Loherenc* v. 99)
[The Abbot of Cluny, *who was present there*, then rose to his feet and said]	[Then the Abbot of Cluny spoke]

Although they mention the place of assembly, the verse models introduce the councillors rather abruptly, giving their name and prefacing their speech with a curt ("Adonc parla "), sometimes accompanied by a vertical movement ("s'en est levez" [he rose], *Garin le Loherenc* v. 71). Philippe's derhyming slows the series of verbal interventions in order to define the space of the speakers. To be sure, the addition of the parenthetical "lui estant illec presant" is formulaic, and typical of the "diffuse style" of the period.[30] The formula is nonetheless revealing of a certain mentality. Without launching into a detailed description, the derhymer takes care to situate his characters "illec" before reporting their actions or words, thereby expanding the circumference of individual discourse.

Other passages magnify even further the zone surrounding speaking subjects. Before engaging in a duel with Begon, for example, the traitor Bernard de Naisil addresses King Pepin:

Prose	Verse
Bernaird du Naisil *estant illec presant*, et *voiant que* le preux duc Baigue n'estoit de rien esbahis, ains estoit tout deliberés d'entrer en champs, *sy ce aprouchait* derechief ledit Bernaird du roy et humblement luy ait priés. (fol. 114r, my emphasis)	"Droiz empereres, por Dieu," Bernarz a dit. (*Garin le Loherenc* v. 6021)
[Bernard de Naisil, *being present there*, and *seeing that* the worthy	["Righteous emperor, in God's name," said Bernard.]

---

30 The corresponding passage in the *Histoire de Charles Martel* similarly introduces "L'abbé de Clugny, *quy estoit la present*" but then proceeds to emphasize the tone and motivation of the speaker: "fut de telz propos tant tourblé qu'il ne se fust pour riens tenu de parler et dist si hault que bien fut entendu" (*Guerin le Loherain* 61; he was so troubled by these words that he would not have kept from speaking for anything, and he said so loudly that he was heard well).

Prose (cont.)
duke Begon was not a bit frightened,
but was rather quite determined
to proceed to the battlefield, that
Bernard again *approached* the king
and humbly beseeched him.]

In the verse redaction, Bernard's entreaty is uttered rather hastily after a series of exchanges between Pepin and the Lorraine knights. Having declared Bernard's arrival on the scene twenty-five lines before, the jongleur does not bother to remind us of the character's location. The prose version, however, reestablishes Bernard's presence, explains his motivation, and precedes his request by a movement toward the king. Moreover, the addition of circumstantial locutions is accompanied by a fleeting change of focalization, allowing us to see Begon's resolve through his adversary's eyes. Godzich and Kittay confirm that the *dérimages* often subordinate verbs of action to verbs of perception, allowing internal cognition to organize textual space.[31]

Philippe also adds spatial markers to indicate the relative position of individuals and groups. In the following passage, Hervis de Metz arrives in Soissons, which is under siege by Saracen forces:

Prose

Le menus peuple pareillement ce
recomendoit a Dieu qu'il les woussist salver et deffandre, qu'il ne
fussent honnis ne vergongniés, mais
peussent estre leur ennemis vaincus
en essaussant saincte crestienté.
D'aultre part estoit le noble duc
Hervy qui chevauchoit luy et ces
gens. Et en son airmee avoit fait .x.
eschielle auquelle on peult veoir mil
pennon vanteller a vans et mil banier
desploiees. *D'aultre coustés* firent
les Sarasins leur gens armer [...] (fol.
64r, my emphasis)

[The common people also prayed God
to save and protect them, so that they
might not be dishonored or shamed,
but that their enemies be defeated
and Holy Christianity exalted. *On
the other side* was the noble Duke
Hervis, who was riding forth with his

Verse

[La veïssiez] menue gent qui ont Deu
reclamé,
qu'essaucement ait la Crestïenté,
que il ne soient honi ne vergondé.

XIV

Hervis chevalche, li gentix et li ber,
a .x. eschieles qu'il ot fet deviser.
La veïssiez maint penon venteler
et mil banieres desploier et mostrer.
Li Sarrazin firent lor gent armer,
(*Garin le Loherenc* vv. 406–13)

[There you would have seen the
common people imploring God to
exalt Christianity, that they might not
be dishonored or shamed. Hervis the
noble and valiant rode forth, with the
ten battalions he had formed. There
you would have seen many pennons

---

[31] Godzich and Kittay, *Emergence of Prose*, 34–35.

Prose (cont.)
men. And he had formed ten battalions, in which one could see a thousand pennons waving in the wind,
and a thousand unfurled banners.
On the other side the Saracens
commanded that their men be armed]

Verse (cont.)
waving, and a thousand banners
unfurled and displayed. The Saracens
commanded that their men be
armed.]

The prose is a near-literal rendering of the verse, with one important distinction. The verse depicts successively and without transition the people's prayers,
Hervis and his men mounted on horseback, and the arming of Saracens. The
derhymed version composes a more analytical picture, dividing the space
into three visual fields by inserting prepositional phrases. Once again, the
nuance may be attributed, at least in part, to fundamental differences between
signifying practices: Godzich and Kittay maintain that the characters in verse
occupy distinct places by virtue of the jongleur's gestures, which fix them in
space. Prose, which works in the textual and visual space of written culture,
is often obliged to delimit fields of action through purely linguistic means.[32]
The problem is somewhat more complex, since the actual performance of
surviving verse epic is questionable.[33] It is perhaps more accurate to suggest
that abrupt spatial shifts became part of the epic tradition, and may have been
alleviated by their place at the beginning of the laisse or line. In the absence
of such markers as assonance and the decasyllabic line, the prosifier felt the
need to compensate with clarifying devices.

These innovations in the temporal and spatial dimensions of the fictional
world are framed by a new space-time of enunciation specific to prose epic.
The following is a translation of the verse "Li rois estoit respassez et gariz"
(*Garin le Loherenc* v. 1987; the king was healthy again and cured):

> *Durant ce tampts que* ces guere ce faisoie en Mourienne *comme cy devent
> avés oÿ*, fut le roy Peipin a Lion *dessus le Rosne au quelle lieu* fut tresfort
> mallaide. Mais la Dieu mercy *aprez plussieurs journee* il fut tous saincts
> et regueris. (fol. 81r, my emphasis)

> [*During the time that* this war was being waged in Maurienne *as you heard
> above*, King Pepin was in Lyon *on the Rhône, and in that place* he was
> very ill. But by the grace of God, *after several days* he was completely
> well and cured.]

In addition to the clarifications of story time and space, Philippe frequently
employs circumstantial locutions to structure his tale, peppering the narration with temporal deictics: "comme cy devent avés oÿ"; "comme cy aprez

---

32 Godzich and Kittay, *Emergence of Prose*, 34.
33 See Andrew Taylor, "Was There a Song of Roland?"

oÿrés" (as you heard before; as you will hear afterward).[34] He thus borrows from epic tradition the vocabulary of oral transmission, very often expressing the reader's role in auditory terms and representing the narrator as a reciter. Other interventions, however, stress the written nature of his work. For example, in order to help his readers wade through the numerous characters that populate his epic, the narrator-translator supplies navigational markers along the way:

> Alors en la mellee est arivés Aliaume le seigneur de Pontis, chevalier wail-lant aus airmes et en retenés bien le nons car de luy et de Amauris cy devent nommez cerait maintes fois parlés ycy aprés. (fol. 65 bis r)

> [Then into the melee arrived Aliaume, Lord of Ponthieu, a knight valiant in battle, and remember his name well, for both he and Amauri, named above, will be spoken of many times after this.]

> Entre lesquelles y olt plussieurs waillant homme aus airme et gens de grant reputacion comme en lisant vous trowanrés. Et mectés vostre entante a en retenir les nons et de combien chascun leur aparthenoit. Car plus-sieur fois vous cowanrait retourner a ce chaip[it]re ce bien voullez l'istoire entandre. (fol. 67r)

> [Among these names there were several knights valiant in battle and men of great reputation, as you will find while reading. And make an effort to remember their names and how they were related. For otherwise you might need to return to this chapter several times if you want to understand the story well.]

These admonitions differentiate minor figures from the major players whose names and alliances will be essential to the proper understanding of later episodes. Philippe does make allowances for those readers who may have a poor memory for names, as he envisions potential "returns" through the material space of the book. His signalling devices thus point up the substitu-tion of a visual-spatial method of recall for the oral/aural memory of recita-tion.

In this respect, Philippe's *dérimage* seems at first glance to be rather conventional. By multiplying temporal and spatial deictics in the narrator's commentary, he is following standard practices of French prose writing that

---

[34] See, for example, Charles Brucker, "Mises en prose et genres littéraires à la fin du moyen âge: la quête du vraisemblable," *Travaux de littérature* 13 (2000): 29–47, at p. 33; Rasmussen, *La Prose narrative française du XVe siècle*, 72; Sophie Marnette, "Du décasyllabe à la prose: narrateur et point de vue dans la mise en roman du cycle épique de Guillaume," *L'Épopée romane au moyen âge et aux temps modernes*, ed. Salvatore Luongo (Naples: Fridericiana Editrice Universitaria, 2001), II, 753–81, especially 762–65.

date back to the thirteenth century.[35] Despite similarities in narrative discourse, however, individual works display subtle differences. Sophie Marnette has studied in detail the relationship between narrator and reader/listener in a body of works including eight *chansons de geste* and nine prose works dating from the thirteenth to the fifteenth century. Of the prose works in Marnette's corpus, the *Guillaume d'Orange* is the only text derived from Old French epic.[36] Among other linguistic traits, she examines spatio-temporal references to the activity of enunciation and the use of first and second person in narrators' commentary. Marnette finds a relatively high percentage of second-person utterances in the prose *Guillaume*, a trait that aligns the text with earlier *chansons de geste* and distinguishes it from prose romances such as the *Mort Artu* or the *Roman du Comte d'Artois*. This suggests that a prose text derived from epic may tend to conserve ties with the discursive patterns of the *chansons de geste*, in which the narrator-jongleur strives to maintain contact with the audience.

Adopting the methodological criteria used by Marnette, I have undertaken a similar analysis of an excerpt from MS *v* of Philippe's prose.[37] The excerpt covers approximately twenty-five folios at the beginning of *Guerin I* and includes the translator's prologue, the exploits of Hervis de Metz, and the first stages of the conflict between the houses of Lorraine and Bordeaux (fols. 59r–84v). I compared this passage with the corresponding sections of the *Prose de l'Arsenal* (3–9) and the *Histoire de Charles Martel* (*Guerin le Loherain* 52–114) as well as the verse original (*Garin le Loherenc* vv. 1–2352). The results suggest that Philippe is singularly preoccupied with the space-time of narration. The excerpt in question displays a higher frequency of spatial and temporal deictics than the corresponding passages in the other two prose versions of the Lorraine cycle. Moreover, the proportion of these deictics in Philippe's prose is superior to that of all the texts examined by Marnette.[38] In the majority of cases (63%), the use of deictics involves either

35 See Suzanne Fleischman, "Discourse as Space / Discourse as Time. Reflections on the Metalanguage of Spoken and Written Discourse," *Journal of Pragmatics* 16 (1991): 291–306; Michèle Perret, "De l'espace romanesque à la matérialité du livre. L'espace énonciatif dans les premiers romans en prose," *Poétique* 50 (1982): 173–82; Sophie Marnette, "Du décasyllabe à la prose."

36 Marnette, "Du décasyllabe à la prose" and, in more detail, *Narrateur et points de vue dans la littérature française médiévale: Une approche linguistique* (Bern & New York: Peter Lang, 1998).

37 Marnette explains her methodology in "Du décasyllabe à la prose" 754, note 3. For verse texts, her percentages are based the number of occurrences of a given reference per total number of verses in the work. For prose, she has attempted to homogenize the results by using the syllable as a basic unit, and the decasyllable as a system of reference. She transforms the number of total lines of the text into a number of syllables, and then divides by 10.

38 Prose *Guillaume* 1.05%; Philippe's prose 1.67%; *Prose de l'Arsenal* 0.8%; *Histoire*

a verb or a pronoun in the second person plural, but Philippe also employs the first-person singular and the first-person plural far more often than the other prose works.[39] It appears that Philippe strives to maintain contact between narrator and reader more insistently than other prose redactors. His revisions to MS *v* are consistent with this pattern throughout the work, for references to the space-time of narration (as well as direct address to the reader) are occasionally added above the line for emphasis.[40] Even in the absence of oral performance, or perhaps to compensate for that absence, Philippe embraces the phatic function of discourse so essential to the jongleur's narrative voice.

The text of MS *v*, including its numerous revisions, also attests to a limited propensity for *accumulatio*, a propensity that Philippe shares with all late medieval prose writers.[41] He does not often indulge in the lengthy enumerations that one finds in the prose *Guillaume* or the *Histoire de Charles Martel*.[42] However, like other prosifiers, he regularly uses synonymic doublets for emphasis. This practice is in some ways faithful to the spirit of verse epic, which also draws on the stylistic convention of "binomials," defined by Yakov Malkiel as a "sequence of two words pertaining to the same form-class, placed on an identical level of syntactic hierarchy, and ordinarily connected by some kind of lexical link."[43] Philippe does not consistently translate the binomials in the verse, although he does so on occasion.[44] More often, he supplies his

---

de Charles Martel 0.79%. The corresponding passage in verse (*Garin le Loherenc*, éd. Gittleman) has a frequency of 0.76%.

[39] With the slight exception of the *Prose de l'Arsenal*, which employs the "Or dirons" formula fairly often. Statistics are as follows: Frequency of second-person plural: prose *Guillaume* 1.6%; Philippe's prose 2.16 %; *Prose de l'Arsenal* 0%; *Histoire de Charles Martel* 0.96%; verse *Garin le Loherenc* 2.8%. First person singular: prose *Guillaume* 0.03%; Philippe's prose 1.01%; *Prose de l'Arsenal* 0%; *Histoire de Charles Martel* 0.24%; verse *Garin* 0.97%. First person plural: prose *Guillaume* 0%; Philippe's prose 0.71%; *Prose de l'Arsenal*, 0.80%; *Histoire de Charles Martel* 0.005%; verse *Garin le Loherenc* 1.4 %.

[40] In the following examples, supralinear additions are in italics: "moureut le noble duc comme *cy aprés* vous serait dit" (fol. 147v; the noble duke died, as will be told to you *afterward*); "En ces entrefaictes et que l'ost fut aincy despairtis *comme oÿ aveis*" (fol. 197r; in the meantime, and when the army had left *as you have heard*).

[41] See Rasmussen, *La Prose narrative française du XVe siècle*, 26, 36, 46.

[42] See Suard, *Guillaume d'Orange*, 226–34.

[43] Yakov Malkiel, "Studies in Irreversible Binomials," *Lingua* 8 (1959): 113–60, qtd. in Taylor, "Translation as Reception," 494. On synonymic doubling in the *chanson de geste*, see Arnulf Stefenelli, *Der Synonymenreichtum der altfranzösischen Dichtersprache* (Vienna: H. Böhlaus, Kommissionsverlag der Österreichischen Akademie der Wissenschaften, 1967).

[44] For example, the verse "respassez et gariz" (*Garin le Loherenc* v. 1987; well again and cured) becomes "saincts et regueris" (fol. 81r; well and cured). Here, Philippe transfers the prefix *re*- to the second element. The verse "Trove les chiens ocis et afolez / forment en fu correciez et irez!" (*Garin le Loherenc* v. 9794–95; he found the dogs dead and killed and was angered and infuriated by it) is rendered as "trowant ces chiens mort

own synonyms or near-synonyms, forming doublets that often result from later revision. In the following examples, all typical of Philippe's prose, the italicized words have been added above the line or in the margin:

1. ledit Hervey luy dit et contait (fol. 4r; Hervis told and recounted to him)
2. a vous me recomande *et vous prie* (fol. 18v; I beg and beseech you)
3. ung messaigier lequelle dit et contait les nowelle (fol. 61v; a messenger who said and told the news)
4. a eraisnier et a deviser (fol. 87v; to address and to speak)
5. vous serait dit *et contés* (fol. 145r; it will be told and recounted to you)
6. Gilbert lequelle disoit et afermoit (fol. 225r; Gerbert, who said and affirmed)
7. le dit son seigneur lui mandoit et prioit (fol. 307r; his lord commanded and beseeched him)
8. merveilleusement coursé et marey (fol. 18v; marvelously angry and irate)
9. tués et mis a mort (fol. 62v; killed and put to death)
10. deshonnourés et honnis (fol. 79v; dishonored and shamed)
11. d'ire et de couroux (fol. 80r; from wrath and anger)
12. pitiet et domaige (fol. 82v; pity and shame)
13. nawrés et plaiez (fol. 146r; hurt and wounded)
14. vergongne *et honte* (fol. 148v; shame and humiliation)
15. conctrict et repantant (fol. 189v; contrite and repentant)
16. desairmés *et desgairnis* (fol. 190r; unarmed and unequipped)
17. dueil et desplaisance (fol. 200r; sorrow and displeasure)
18. cautelle et mallice (fol. 222r; deceit and ruse)
19. infidelles et mescreans (fol. 3r; infidels and nonbelievers)
20. donner secours *et les ayder* (fol. 64r; give aid and help them)
21. *confondre et* mauldire (fol. 261r; confound and curse)
22. acoustree et paree (fol. 109v; dressed up and adorned)
23. soulleis *et ramplis* (fol. 147r; sated and full)
24. saisis *et tenant* (fol. 190v; in possession of and invested)
25. toutes la proie *et le butin* (fol. 193r; all the plunder and booty)
26. baisant et acoullant (fol. 223r; kissing and embracing)
27. l'ousait faire *ne entreprandre* (fol. 306v; dared not do or undertake)

Middle French prosifiers often use synonyms to clarify an unfamiliar or archaic term, and Philippe's binomials occasionally fulfill that function.[45] His additions are partly stylistic in nature, building a network of binary structures into cadence of the prose. Based on the passages he was able to consult and transcribe from MS *h*, Jean-Charles Herbin has determined that

---

et occis fut merveilleusement coursés et desplaisant" (fol. 147v; finding his dogs dead and killed he was marvelously angered and unhappy).

[45] See Tylus, *Histoire de la Reine Berthe et du Roy Pepin*, Introduction, 59.

some of Philippe's later revisions reverse the order of doublets, perhaps in the interest of sonority. In some cases, the revision brings the *dérimage* closer to the original verse by switching words with tonic vowels in /i/ to the second position, thereby recreating the dominant assonance of the verse. In others, a concern for rhythm seems to dictate the reversal.[46]

Additions to MS *v* indicate similar stylistic choices.[47] In example 16 above, the addition of "desgairnis" repeats the negative prefix *des-* for emphasis, but supplies a past participle in /i/ for tonic variation. Many of the appended synonyms seem purposefully differentiated from the first term by number of syllables, thus providing rhythmic modulation ("vergongne *et honte*"; "la proie *et le butin*"; "faire *ne entreprandre*"). Others are parisyllabic, creating a balanced binary rhythm with the tonic vowel again providing variation ("soulleis *et ramplis*"; "saisis *et tenant*").

As Jane H. M. Taylor has observed, however, the intended effect of synonymic repetition in late medieval prose was not only decorative. "Binomial pairs are emphatic, persuasive: they serve, in fact, the better to develop and argue a case."[48] In her analysis of a fifteenth-century translation of Boccaccio's *De Mulieribus claris*, Taylor finds that synonymy is "ideologically selective": the anonymous translator consistently chooses lexemes with pejorative connotations to condemn women.[49] No such pointed conclusions can be drawn from Philippe's use of doubling or tripling. Nonetheless, two patterns do emerge. A first set of binomials is linked to discourse itself, and involves verbs of speaking or telling (as in the first seven items in the preceding list). In both dialogue and narration, Philippe often doubles such verbs, as do other prosifiers of the period.[50] In the prose *Histoire de la Reine Berthe et du Roy Pepin*, one such pair is found among the rare marginal additions to the late fifteenth-century manuscript, when the narrator declares that Charlemagne's exploits were "merveille grant ouÿr *parler et dire*" (a great marvel to hear related and told; italics reflect addition).[51] Prosifiers thus emphasize the high stakes involved in transmission and reception, whether the utterances in question are associated with characters or with authorial voices.

---

[46] Herbin, "*Yonnet de Metz*," 38–39.

[47] It must be noted that supralinear additions to *v* are not consistently incorporated in *h*. For example, the binomial "desairmés *et desgairnis*" (fol. 190r) is absent from the corresponding passage in *h* (p. 736). Occasionally, the second term is added above the line in both manuscripts: "toutes la proie *et le butin*" (*v*, fol. 193r and *h*, p. 746). This suggests that the omitted revisions may be due to scribal inattention. In any case, both versions are replete with newly created binomials, with additions following similar patterns.

[48] Taylor, "Translation as Reception," 501.

[49] Taylor, "Translation as Reception," 503–07.

[50] For example, the *Histoire de Charles Martel*: "Si racompte et certiffie l'istoire" (*Guerin le Loherain* 146; the story tells and asserts); "Adont le conte Ysoré respondy et dist" (*Guerin le Loherain* 154; then Count Ysoré responded and said).

[51] *Histoire de la Reine Berthe*, 139 and note 54.

Another salient group of binomials in Philippe's prose covers a number of semantic fields related to physical or moral distress, specifically death, injury, mourning, shame, anger and betrayal (as in examples 8–18). The frequency of the device increases in emotionally charged contexts where he seeks to heighten pathos or peril. The following passage, which represents Aelis's grief over the murder of her husband Garin, contains a high concentration of synonymic pairs, which I have marked in bold print; the one synonym added after the fact in MS *v* is italicized.

Prose

entre ces aultre **plaintes et lamentacion** disoit aincy: "Helas, Gilbert, mon chier anffans, pas vous ne scaveis encor que a celle journees avés perdus. Las, las, **doullante et esgairees**, que ferons nous, **las doullans chetif**! Ha Fourtune" dit elle, "que tu nous est **contraire et perverce**! Mort vint a cest heure et nous vint querir." Or n'y ait homme qui sceut raconter les *doulleur et* **complaintes** qui adoncques furent faictes des deux damme **serourge et suer** pour leur **seigneur et mary**. Tant en ont fait et cy grant dueille ont demené que dans trois jour aprés **moururent et deviairent de cestuy monde** et furent ensevelie toutte deux ensamble en l'abaihiees de Sainct Arnoult devent les mur de la cité de Mets en ung meisme **sercus et monument** et au plus pres de leur aultre parans et amis. (fol. 192r)

[amidst the other **complaints and laments** she spoke thus: "Alas, Gerbert, my dear child, you do not yet know what you have lost on this day. Alas, alas, **grieving and distraught**, what will we do, **poor sad feeble** ones! Ah, Fortune!" she said, "how **contrary and perverse** you are to us! Death came now and looked for us." Now there is no one who could tell the *mourning* **and complaints** that were uttered then by the two noble **sisters-in-law and**

Verse

Atant ez vos la bien fete Aäliz,
cele renforce et **le duel et le cri**!
Bien le saichoiz, Aäliz, Bëatriz,
les .ii. serors, puis que fu morz Garin
que ne vesquirent que .ii. mois et
   demi!
A Saint Hernol les ont en terre mis:
en .ii. sarquels de marbre vert et bis
furent li cors des .ii. duchesses mis.
(*Garin le Loherenc* vv. 16,133–40)

[Then behold the lovely Aelis, who redoubles **the mourning and the wailing**! Know well that Aelis and Beatrice, the two sisters, did not live two and a half months after Garin's death! They were buried at St. Arnoult: in two coffins of green and gray marble the two duchesses were laid to rest.]

Prose (cont.)
sisters for their lord and husband.
So many did they utter and so much
did they grieve that within three days
they **died and left this world**, and
the two of them were buried together
in the abbey of St. Arnoult near the
city walls of Metz in the same **coffin
and monument**, as near as possible
to their other relatives and friends.]

The verse redaction does contain one pair of monosyllabic synonyms ("le duel et le cri"), which Philippe translates into the more elaborate "plaintes et lamentations." In the following sentences, synonyms and near-synonyms proliferate, with the doubling of virtually all verbs, nouns and adjectives related to sorrow and death. While this is an extreme example, it is in keeping with Philippe's general tendency to dramatize misfortune. In depictions of strife, peril and grief, one even finds the occasional synonymic triplet: "guerre, dissancion ne noise" (fol. 190r; war, strife and dispute); "comme homme anraigiez, forcenés et hors du sanc" (fol. 191r; like a man enraged, crazed and out of his mind); "marris, triste et dollant"(fol. 2r; afflicted, sad and sorrowful); "les grans dueilz, pleurs et lamentacion"(fol. 124r; the great mourning, tears and lamentation). Synonymic doubling and tripling in Philippe's prose, then, is not ideologically selective so much as preoccupied with human frailty, adversity, and a taste for the sensational.

While binomials can be found on nearly every page of this text, it is important to note that Philippe's use of *accumulatio* is restrained by comparison with the rhetorically elaborate *Histoire de Charles Martel*. In recounting Aelis's mourning and death, the Burgundian prose embellishes the episode with a rolling enumeration characteristic of clerkly prose. I reproduce below the beginning of the passage:

> en estoient dolantes come bien le moustrerent, car elles demenerent tel et si aspre dueil que au bout de trois jours elles morurent de desplaisir trés angoisseusement, mais ce ne fut mie sans grans regrets, sans trés piteuses lamentations, sans griefs gemissements, et sans grande habondance de lermes [...] (KBR 8, fol. 10v)

> [they were sorrowful and made this quite evident, for they carried on such bitter mourning that by the end of three days they died of grief with much anguish, but not without deep regrets, or without very piteous lamentations, or without painful moaning, or without a great abundance of tears]

The full scene occupies an entire page, as the women lament not only the death of Garin, but also all the catastrophes that have befallen them since the beginning of the great wars. Thus the Burgundian translator has undertaken far more than a simple *dérimage*, rendering a fairly sober account with considerable rhetorical flourishes. By contrast, Philippe's prose takes once again the middle ground, amplifying the original with modified binary rhythms that both recall and embellish the cadence of verse epic.

Abridgement, True and False

Although Philippe did not hesitate to add emphasis or to fill in gaps he perceived in his verse sources, amplification was not among his explicit priorities. On the contrary, one of his most emphatically stated goals is abridgement, an intervention that he justifies in the general prologue:

> Pourquoy je advertys a tous les liseurs et auditeurs d'icelle histoire que moi l'escripvain l'ais abregiés et que en l'ancienne histoire y ait de grant proces de parolles lesquelles j'ay lessié pour eviter prolixitez. (fol. 1v)

> [For this reason, I inform all readers and listeners of this story that I the writer have abridged it, and that in the ancient story there are long, drawn-out passages that I have omitted to avoid prolixity.]

He reiterates his concern for brevity in the secondary prologues and epilogues, and also in the text proper. Jean-Charles Herbin finds 220 occurrences of abbreviation formulas in the work, with the highest concentration in the *Livre de la belle Beaultris.*[52] The revised general prologue in MS *h* paradoxically amplifies the theme of abridgement. Like Marie de France, Philippe believes that the "modern" mind demonstrates greater subtlety ("les esperit deviengne tout les jours plus agut et soubtilles").[53] Confident that his audience will appreciate the condensation, he chooses from the source (the *istoire*) only that which is useful. To document his method, he conscientiously directs the reader's attention to the formula he will use to signal the *abbreviatio* procedure: "partout la ou vous trovaireis ainsy escript 'pour abregiés' quant ainsy trovereis lisant" (wherever you find the words "to abbreviate" when you are reading).[54]

The abridged passages are crucial to the understanding of Philippe's craft, since his choices indicate the elements he considers worth remembering (fol. 145r) as well as those he deems useless. First of all, Philippe frequently excises certain kinds of redundant material from the original. Although he most often retains anticipatory statements, he tends to dispense with *rappels* that do not occur at the beginning of a chapter. For example, when the reluc-

---

[52] Herbin, "Approches," 500.
[53] MS *h*, p. 6.
[54] MS *h*, p. 6. This passage is excised from *v* (fol. 1v).

tant merchant Hervis returns from the fair in Provins, his outraged uncle reports his antics to Thieri in a detailed reprise, which Philippe shortens considerably:

Prose

et pour abregier, ledit son frere luy contait tous le fait et luy dit coment ledit Hervis avoit fait si mervil-leuse despance en convoiant les marchamps, comme aveis ouÿs. (fol. 5r)

Verse

"Li vostre filz, quant venins a
    Provins,
[Avecques] nos ne vot ostel tenir,
Un en retint del tot a son plaisir,
De marcheans lor manda .IIII.XX.,
Et l'ondemain en remanda .VIII.XX.,
Puis .XII.XX, enaprés .XVI.XX.;
Sire, .M. mars que d'argent que d'or
    fin
Despandit bien li vostre filz Hervis!"
(*Hervis de Mes* vv. 504–11)

[and, to abbreviate, his brother told him the whole story, and told him how Hervis had incurred such marve-lous expenses by sending for the merchants, as you have heard.]

[Your son, when we came to Provins, did not wish to lodge with us. He retained lodging that suited him, and sent for eighty merchants; the next day he sent for one hundred and sixty merchants, then two hundred and forty, after that three hundred and twenty. My lord, your son Hervis spent a thousand marks in silver and gold!]

The verse recapitulates numbers of guests and amounts spent, details not worth repeating in the translator's opinion. Presumably, since he links the modern taste for abridgement with increased subtlety of mind, Philippe assumes that his audience will retain this information, reminding them that they have already "heard" the full story.

Secondly, in the very frequent transfer from direct to indirect discourse, Philippe tends to reduce and summarize the original's dialogue. When Hervis negotiates the purchase of a horse, a falcon, and hunting dogs, the verse includes traditional epithets and fillers that are excised in the prose:

Prose

pour abregier demandait au jowancel s'il vouldroit point vandre le chev-aulx, le falcon avec les chiens. (fol. 4r)

Verse

Il l'i apele, belement li a dit:
"Escuier frere, por Deu qui ne menti
Me venderoies cel destrier arrabi
Et [ces] brochés et cel levrier de pris
[Et cel faucon, n'i wel metre en
    obli]?"
(*Hervis de Mes* vv. 374–76)

Prose (cont.)

[To abbreviate, he asked the young man if he wouldn't like to sell the horse, the falcon and the dogs.]

Verse (cont.)

[He called him, and said to him graciously: "Brother squire, in the name of God who has never lied, would you sell me the Arabian steed, and the pointers, and the worthy greyhound, and the falcon, which I mustn't forget?"]

The translator eliminates from Hervis's request all but the bare nominal facts of the transaction: "le chevaulx, le falcon avec les chiens." Epithets such as "arrabi" and "de pris" are unnecessary, since the animals have already been qualified in a previous passage. The translation also suppresses emphatic formulas such as "pour diu qui ne menti." Such elisions alter considerably the direct, formulaic, incantatory mode of the original. In fact, epic forms of repetition are largely replaced by the translator's frequent abridgement formulas.[55]

The third and most conspicuous form of abridgement, the summary proper, condenses large portions of the narrative by suppressing the particulars of a given episode. In the *Livre de de la belle Beaultris*, for example, Philippe radically condenses a tournament between the counts of Bar and Flanders, an event that occupies over four hundred lines in *Hervis de Metz*:

> Cy acommence le grant tournoy duquelle je ne veult gaire parler [...] De vous dire et conter toutte lez chose qui furent faictez ne dictez audit tournois ce n'est pas mon intancion car j'aroie troptz affaire [...][56] Car il me souffit seullement de dire comme aprez toutte chose faicte ledit Hervey fist tant qu'il print ledit conte de Flandre. (fols. 11r–11v).

> [Thus began the great tournament, about which I do not wish to tell very much {...} It is not my intention to tell and relate all the things that were said and done at that tournament, for I would have too much to do {...} For it is sufficient for my purposes to tell only how after all was done, Hervis finally succeeded in capturing the Count of Flanders.]

Sufficient for the translator's purposes, then, is the hero's victory. The summary is indeed quite frequent in accounts of battle, as in the following version of a passage that occupies four laisses and thirty lines in the original verse: "pour abregiez le noble Hervey a l'aide des Braibanson faisoit tant

---

55 In MS *h*, Philippe occasionally excises the "pour abregier" signal (e.g. p. 18), but generally retains or even amplifies the intention to abbreviate.

56 In MS *h*, the clause "car j'aroie troptz affaire" is crossed out and replaced with "je seroie trop prolixe et enoieulx" (p. 58). In revising, then, Philippe justifies his abridgement in terms of audience reception rather than economy of labor on the part of the translator.

de vaillance" (fol. 33r; to abbreviate, the noble Hervis, with the help of the Brabançons, accomplished such worthy deeds). Once again, a brief statement of the hero's valor furnishes the content that the translator considers worthy of commemoration. Further detail would only bore the public: "Et pour abregiez y olt cy grant murtre et cy grant tuerie que ce tout vouloie dire et conter leur fais et vaillances tropt seroie prolixes et ennuieulx" (fol. 101v; and to abbreviate, there were so many deaths and so much killing that if I wished to tell and relate their deeds and acts of valor it would be too wordy and boring). In this respect, Philippe's adaptation differs considerably from the *mises en prose* commissioned by the dukes of Burgundy, which tend to amplify both tournaments and battle narratives.[57] Unhampered by the tastes and ambitions of a noble patron, Philippe does not dwell on the rituals of aristocracy, but privileges end results over process.

Curiously, Philippe's use of the *brevitas* formula does not always imply a shortening of the original text. Departures from standard *abbreviatio* come in two distinct forms. In the first instance, the translator announces his intention to abbreviate, but fails to produce a text significantly shorter than the original. The following example from the *Livre de la belle Beaultris* is typical of the discrepancy between stated objectives and actual practice. The scene involves a group of wicked squires who have conspired to kidnap the fair Beatrice; once they have succeeded in spiriting her off to the woods, they cannot decide who among them will be the first to deflower her:

Prose

et ce prinrent a dire beaulcopt de folz langaige que je laisse ad cause de briefté, en faisson telle qu'il la voulloient avoir a leur plaisir, la voullant defflourer. Et disoit l'ung d'entre eulx qu'il l'avoit premier apersus ou vergier et qu'il devoit avoir son pucellaige. L'aultre dit que non et qu'il l'avoit prinze le premier. Et le thier dist qu'il en aroient melley et qu'il estoit plus hault homme dez aultre, par quoy l'onneur en devoit estre a lui. (fol. 7r)

Verse

Li uns parla, com jai oïr porez:
"Mi compagnons, envers moi entendez
De ceste dame k'avomes conquesté:
Jeu en ferai premiers mes volantez.
Et pius en faites chascuns de vos son [és]!"
Et dist li atres: "Qu'est ceu que [dit] avez?
Je l'apersui ens ou vergier ramé:
Premierement en doi faire mon gré!
Son pucelaige avrai senz demorer!"
Et dist li tiers: "Certes vos i mentez!
Plus haus hons sui et de grant parenté,
Si en doi faire premiers mes volantez!"
(*Hervis de Mes* vv. 1151–62)

---

[57] See Danielle Quéruel, "Des mises en prose aux romans de chevalerie dans les collections bourguignonnes," 179. See also Suard, who notes a similar amplification of chivalric feats of arms in the prose *Guillaume* (*Guillaume d'Orange* 308).

Prose (cont.)

[and they began to say a lot of crazy things, which I will omit in the interest of brevity, to the effect that they wanted to take their pleasure with her, wishing to deflower her. And one of them said that he had seen her first in the garden, and that he should have her maidenhood. And the second said no, that he had captured her first. And the third said that there would be a fight, and that he was of higher rank than the others, so that the honor should be his.]

Verse (cont.)

[The first one spoke, as you will now be able to hear: "My friends, listen to me: I will be the first to have my way with this lady we have won. Then each of you can screw her." And the second one said, "What did you say? I saw her first in the tree-filled garden; I should be the one to have my way with her first! I will deflower her at once!" And the third one said, "Surely you are lying! I am of higher rank and come from a great family, and thus I should be the first to have my way with her!"]

While the original text represents this exchange by means of direct speech, the translator, unwilling to reproduce all of this "folz langage," summarizes it by means of indirect discourse. A glance at the two versions shows, however, that the translation contains approximately as many words as the original. Philippe has reduced the model's rhetorical accents to a degree by suppressing introductory and concluding formulas such as "envers moy entendés!" and "Qu'est ce que dit avés?" He also eliminates the synonymic repetition in v. 1161. In transferring the exchange to indirect discourse in prose, he nonetheless employs the rather heavy-handed use of subordinate clauses that Suard finds so common in the prose *Guillaume*.[58] Ironically, his lengthy variation on the *brevitas* formula also undermines the abridgement process. For Philippe, then, distilling the original text does not preclude the substitution of a "grant proces de parolles" on the translator's part. In fact, the modern narrator's voice often functions to stifle the voice of both jongleur and character, drawing attention away from the content and focusing on his own editorial decisions. This sort of autonomous metadiscourse, which both reveals and dissembles its own purposes, is not unusual in the documents of the period.[59] In Philippe's prose, such discrepancies occur quite frequently in passages involving characters' speech (*langaige, parolle, propos*). Those utterances ostensibly sacrificed in the cause of brevity tend to materialize in a more overtly mediated form.

A second type of false abridgement involves the use of a *brevitas* formula in conjunction with material that is simply not present in the original. This practice is fairly common in Philippe's translation, and is generally used as a form of hyperbole. After faithfully rendering a father-son reunion, for example, the translator declares that so many words were exchanged that he cannot reproduce them all (fol. 16r). Occasionally, however, the procedure

---

58 Suard, *Guillaume d'Orange*, 201–03.

59 Luce Guillerm finds that gaps between signifying practice and its accompanying metadiscourse are "inevitable" ("L'Intertextualité démontée" 63).

reflects Philippe's own reconstruction of events not recounted in the original. When Hervis's maternal grandfather departs for the Holy Land, Philippe provides the following account: "Et le duc s'en vint oultre meir. Lequel pour abregier fit tant par ces journees qu'il vint en la terre au Sarazins en laquelle il fut moult longuement [...]" (fol. 3r; and the duke went off overseas; to abbreviate, he made such progress in his travels that he arrived in Saracen lands, where he stayed a long time). In fact, this passage represents an addition rather than an abridgement. The original text relates only Duke Pierre's departure, leaving the actual voyage to the reader's or listener's imagination. The translator apparently feels the need to fill that gap, if only very briefly. Philippe thus abridges not the actual text of the original but the story as he has recreated it. In structuralist terms, he has condensed the *histoire* rather than the *récit*. The "istoire" he cites as his source thus incorporates both of these notions: like the translators of the prose *Guillaume*, he conceives of his source in terms of reconstructed content as well as textual support.[60] As a translator of both the telling and the told, he selects from the "istoire" the information pertinent to his design, all the while mindful of the contemporary reader's taste for conciseness.

De-versifying and Updating

Other modifications of the source material do not involve significant lengthening or abridgement of the text, but reflect an attempt to unfetter and modernize the verse as literally as possible. Unlike some derhymers, Philippe does not reproduce entire lines of verse word for word.[61] The rare decasyllabic phrases in his prose are vestiges of epic rhythm, but they do not duplicate the actual epic verse. Witness the prose decasyllable "Illec y olt ung merveilleux huttin" (fol. 64v; in that place there was a marvelous battle), which retains only the final word of the verse "Grans fu la noise et fier fu li hutins (*Garin le Loherenc* v. 449; great was the din and fierce the battle).[62] One finds an occasional verse left nearly intact. To the original "frans chevaliers, corageus et hardiz" (*Garin le Loherenc* v. 10,791; noble knight, courageous and bold) the translator adds only a monosyllabic interjection: "Ha! franc chevalier couraigeux et hairdis!" (fol. 153v).

Philippe also tends to conserve the epic formula "la veïssiez" (there you would have seen), an imperfect subjunctive clause that serves as a compact form of direct address to the listener. This commonplace of battle narratives

---

60 Suard, *Guillaume d'Orange*, 11.

61 Godzich and Kittay, *Emergence of Prose*, 28. See, for example, the prose *Fierabras* edited by Jean Miquet (Introduction 35).

62 Herbin gives several examples of decasyllabic and alexandrine lines in *Yonnet*, none of which represents a verbatim rendering of verse lines or phrases. See his "*Yonnet de Metz*" 34–35.

in the *chansons de geste* heightens the sense of immediacy, drawing the listener into the diegetic world as a hypothetical witness. Philippe's translation maintains this complicity, reproducing the verbal form and modifying the syntax:

Prose	Verse
Adoncques weissez vous grosse pairier, angiens et mangoniaulx pour toutte abaitre et affronder [...] Et la y weissiés feu et la flammes saillir par les fenestre (fol. 193v)	La veïssiez ces perrieres venir, Ces mangonniax et jeter et flatir [...] La veïssiez ces granz flames issir. (*Gerbert de Mez*, vv. 116–17, 124)
[Then you would have seen huge rock-throwing machines and mangonels for knocking down and destroying {...} And there you would have seen fire and flames shooting out of the windows.]	[There you would have seen rock-throwing machines arriving, mangonels throwing and hurling rocks {...} There you would have seen great flames shooting out.]

Philippe is also fairly conservative in his treatment of conventional battle motifs. The motif of single combat with a lance is among the most formulaic units of content in the Old French epic.[63] The jongleurs depict major duels according to an established sequence, as the knight spurs his horse, strikes a fatal blow, and fells his adversary. The paradigm appears from the earliest pages of *Garin le Lorrain*, when Hervis de Metz confronts the Saracen invaders:

> Le destrier broche des esperons d'or fin;
> encontre lui revient li dux Hervis.
> Godin failli, mes li dux le feri
> si com Deu plot, et le Saint Esperit:
> trenche l'auberc et le cuer et le piz.
> Li fers fu chauz, ne pot l'acier sofrir.
> Parmi l'eschine li fet le fer saillir,
> mort le trebuche del destrier ou il sist.
> Puis tret l'espee, s'en a la teste pris.
>
> (*Garin le Loherenc* vv. 516–24)

[He spurs his horse with golden spurs; Duke Hervis comes toward him. Godin faltered, but the duke struck him, and as it pleased God and the Holy Spirit, he slices through the hauberk to the heart and the chest. The blade was hot, the metal could not withstand it. He thrusts the blade through the spine, strikes him dead from the horse he was mounted on. Then he draws his sword, and took off his head.]

---

63 Rychner, *La chanson de geste*, 139–48.

Philippe's prose preserves the classic progression as it appears in the verse, giving a far more literal translation than either the *Prose de l'Arsenal* or the *Histoire de Charles Martel*. The *Prose de l'Arsenal* eliminates this particular duel altogether, noting only that Hervis attacked the Saracens and waged a fierce battle ("Si ferit sur les Sarrazins et moult y ot cruelle bataille" (1). The *Histoire de Charles Martel* tends to rework single combat with a broad sweep, eliding the conventional step-by-step account in favor of a more comprehensive depiction:

Philippe de Vigneulles, *Guerin I*

Cy broichait le chevaulx des esperon d'ore et d'ung grant couraige ce rescomendait a Dieu et encontre dudit Godins c'en vait ferir et Godins contre de luy. Mais le Sarrasins faillit et aincy comme il plut a Dieu l'ait essignés cy biens le noble duc Hervy qu'il luy paissait et fer et fust tretous parmy l'eschine ung grant piedz et demi. Et le trebuchait mort enmey le champs. Puis ce fait ait tirés son espeis et du Sarrasins ait prins le chief. (fol. 65r)

[He spurred his horse with gold spurs, and with great courage commended himself to God, and went to strike Gaudin, and Gaudin did the same. But the Saracen faltered, and as it pleased God, the noble Duke Hervis hit him so well that he thrust both blade and handle a good foot and a half into his spine. And he knocked him dead on the field. After this, he drew his sword and took the Saracen's head.]

Histoire de Charles Martel

il rencontra l'admiral sarrazin, contre lequel il se aborda. Lors encommencerent au trenchant des espees ung merveilleuz estour quy dura longuement. Mais a la fin le noble duc fist tant qu'il luy trencha la teste. (*Guerin le Loherain* 66)

[He encountered the Saracen admiral and approached him. Then with their sharp swords they began to fight a marvelous battle that lasted a long time. But in the end, the noble duke succeeded in cutting off his head.]

The Burgundian translator reworks the passage considerably, substituting a panoramic view of swordsmanship for the up-close, formulaic iteration that Philippe's version preserves. Philippe adds the articulations of prose ("Puis ce fait") without substantially modifying the conventional syntagm.

However, even when rendering a passage according to the letter of the text, Philippe's prose tends to reorder or inflect the verse model. In the following example, the young Hervis assures Beatrice that he will never abandon her, for, having purchased her at great expense, he wishes to protect his investment. Italicized words in the verse indicate pertinent variants that may reflect the text found in Philippe's verse sources:

Prose

"Car vous estez tout mon chactez et
chier vous ait acheteis. Et pour ce
se j'ay du bien vous en arez et se
j'ay du malz vous souffrerez. Se je
mange vous mangerez et se je jeune
vous jeunerez." (fol. 8v)

Verse

"Vos cors est miens, quant je l'ai
achaté;
Si m'aïst Deus, vos estes mes chatez!
*Ou que je voise, avec moi en
vendrez,*[64]
Se je jeüne, avec moi jeunerez,
[*Se je manjue ausi vous mengerez*]
Et mal et bien avec moi prenderez
[*soufferez*]!"
(*Hervis de Mes* vv. 1653–57)

[For you are entirely my possession
and I have paid dearly for you. And
therefore if good comes to me you
will have some, and if evil befalls me
you will suffer. If I eat, you will eat,
and if I fast you will fast.]

[Your body is mine, for I have
purchased it; by God, you are my
possession! Wherever I go, you will
go with me. If I fast, you will fast, if
I eat you will eat, and you will take
the good and the bad with me.]

The extant verse models are distinguished by the presence or absence of the
third and fifth lines, but agree on the ordering of content. Philippe alters
this order, and changes the third to the second person at the beginning of
Hervis's decidedly uncourtly pronouncement, personalizing (if not softening)
the hero's rather crass proprietary speech.

   Elsewhere the translator unpacks the verse by strategically rearranging the
exact words found in the source. When the treacherous bishop Lancelin is
murdered and dismembered by the Lorraine heroes, for example, the verse
postpositions the verbs according to a typical Old French syntactic pattern. In
converting the model to the subject-verb-object word order of Middle French
prose,[65] Philippe's prose places the emphasis on the more gruesome details:

Prose

Et les gens dudit evesque qui aprés
venoient recuillairent les piece et les
mirent en des sacque (fol. 194v)

Verse

Si conpaignon le troverent issi.
Les pieces font par le chanp recoillir,
Dedenz .i. sac asanbler et gesir.
(*Gerbert de Mez* vv. 204–06)

[And the bishop's men, who came
afterward, gathered the pieces and
placed them in sacks).

[His companions found him thus.
They have the pieces gathered in the
field, assembled and placed into a

---

   64 A variant found in mss. NT. For all variants in this passage, indicated in brackets,
see Herbin's edition of *Hervis de Mes*, p. 74.
   65 On the complex changes in word order from Old to Middle French, see Marchello-
Nizia, *La Langue française aux XIVe et XVe siècles*, 413–17.

Verse (cont.)

sack. (*lit.*: The pieces they have in the field gathered, into a sack assembled and placed.]

By relocating the body parts and sacks to the end of their respective clauses, the prose syntax gives these nouns special prominence.

Other "close" translations retain the verb used in the original verse, but modify verbal aspect:

Prose	Verse
lesquelle retournoye d'une guere (fol. 6r)	D'une grant guerre estoient retornez. (*Hervis de Mes* v. 916)
[who were returning from a war]	[They had returned from a great war.]
ung chaudeau auquel plussieurs herbes furent destrempees (fol. 124r)	herbes destrenpe, en .i. chaudel les mist. (*Garin le Loherenc* v. 7068)
[a broth in which several herbs had been steeped]	[He steeps herbs, puts them in a broth.]

In the first example, the prose converts a completed action to the imperfect, showing the characters' return unfolding in time. In the second, Philippe takes the opposite tack, transposing an active verb to the passive voice and perfective aspect.

Even when he preserves nominal or verbal units of expression, then, Philippe strives to rearrange and reorient the verse model.[66] This makes it difficult to judge the extent to which Philippe's lexical modifications represent stylistic choices or updated equivalents of Old French words and expressions he considered archaic. The problem is further compounded by our lack of precise information as to when a given word fell out of usage in a given region.[67] A thorough review of Philippe's lexicon is beyond the scope of the present study.[68] Generally speaking, however, the derhymed text is tran-

---

[66] In his essay on *Yonnet*, Herbin comes to a similar conclusion, which I believe is valid for the translation as a whole: "Tout se passe comme si Philippe de Vigneulles avait soigneusement évité de conserver les vers de son modèle" (*Yonnet de Metz* 35).

[67] See Tylus, *Histoire de la Reine Berthe*, Introduction, 57–58. On lexical changes in Middle French, see Marchello-Nizia, *La Langue française aux XIVe et XVe siècles*, 445–56.

[68] Several linguists have studied morphological, syntactic and lexical features of Philippe's other works. See Paul Hirschbühler, "L'Omission du sujet dans les subordonnées V1: *Les Cent Nouvelles Nouvelles* de Vigneulles et les *Cent nouvelles nouvelles* anonymes," *Travaux de linguistique: Revue internationale de linguistique française* 25 (1992): 25–46; France Martineau, *La Montée du clitique en moyen français. Une étude de la syntaxe des constructions infinitives*, Diss. U of Ottawa 1992 and "Le Placement

sitional in nature, hovering between lexical patterns that had begun to fade from use and the significant innovations associated with Middle French.[69] Unlike many professional writers of the period, Philippe does not embellish the prose with Latinisms.[70] Many of his lexical substitutions do reflect documented changes in the French language between the twelfth and the sixteenth centuries. For example, he regularly updates the locution "par mautalent" ("angrily, spitefully") with formulations such as "bien aigrement elle l'en reprint" (fol. 221v) or "comme en reprouchant" (fol. 224r).[71] Some apparent modernizations, however, are offset by the retention of Old French words or meanings in other passages. For example, he translates "mires" ("doctor" in Old French) with the newer Middle French term "medecins" in one section (fol. 105r), but uses "mire" elsewhere (fol. 65r).[72] He replaces most instances of the verb "choisir," which meant primarily "to notice" or "to perceive" in Old French, a meaning that persisted into the sixteenth century, preferring "apercevoir" ("aperçut," fol. 7r) and "regarder" ("resgairdait," fol. 122v). In one passage, however, he reverses the trend by translating "voir" with "choisir" ("choisy," fol. 77v).[73] This not only confirms that the endangered words and meanings were still viable (and even competitive) in the lexicon of early sixteenth-century Metz,[74] it also suggests once again that Philippe deliberately sought to intervene in the semantic and rhythmic structures of his sources. In the cases cited above, the translator's choices effectively disrupt

---

des pronoms objets dans les constructions infinitives chez Philippe de Vigneulles," *Revue québécoise de linguistique théorique et appliquée* 7 (1988): 157–73; Barbara Vance, "Null Subjects in Middle French Discourse," *Aspects of Romance Linguistics*, ed. Claudia Parodi, Carlos Quicoli, Mario Saltarelli, María Luisa Zubizarreta (Washington D.C.: Georgetown UP, 1996), 457–74; Maryse Hasselmann, "Ademise et non adevise: Note sur un terme technique du droit messin présent dans la *Chronique* de Philippe de Vigneulles," *Études de langue et de littérature françaises offertes à André Lanly*, ed. Bernard Guidot (Nancy: U de Nancy, 1980), 155–64.

[69] See Marchello-Nizia, *La Langue française aux XIVe et XVe siècles*, 445.

[70] See Marchello-Nizia, *La Langue française aux XIVe et XVe siècles*, 448–52. As examples of extreme Latinization, Suard cites the prose versions of *Anseïs de Carthage* and *Mabrian* (*Guillaume d'Orange* 210).

[71] Similarly, Marchello-Nizia notes that Froissart consistently replaces "talent" with "voulenté" (*La Langue française aux XIVe et XVe siècles* 455).

[72] The Larousse *Dictionnaire du moyen français* affirms that "mire" was considered archaic in the sixteenth century (Algirdas Julien Greimas and Teresa Mary Keane, Paris: Larousse, 1992), 417.

[73] See *Garin le Loherenc* v. 1634.

[74] Indeed, Huguet and the electronic site "Bases du moyen français" provide many examples of "choisir" meaning "to see, perceive, notice" in the sixteenth century, including the works of Clément Marot and Jean Lemaire de Belges. See Edmond Huguet, *Dictionnaire de la langue française du seizième siècle* (Paris: Champion, 1925–73), III, 272–73, and the *Dictionnaire du Moyen Français* (DMF), *Base de Lexiques de Moyen Français* (DMF1), ATILF/Équipe "Moyen français et français préclassique" 2003–2005, <www.atilf.fr/blmf>.

the rhythms of decasyllabic verse, lengthening or shortening the number of syllables with semantically equivalent terms.

Modes of Discourse

Prosifiers of the Middle French period rendered the speeches and dialogues of the Old French epic in very different ways. Each of the three *mises en prose* of the Lorraine cycle takes a distinct approach to the problem. The translator of the anonymous *Prose de l'Arsenal* allows only five examples of direct speech, eliminating most utterances found in the verse and converting others into a condensed form of indirect discourse.[75] The Burgundian version privileges oratory, and is given to inflating a few lines of direct discourse into an elaborate speech. Philippe's approach is neither extreme nor systematic. As noted above, he summarizes many direct utterances, particularly accounts of previously reported events, such as those contained in messengers' pronouncements and the contents of letters. His summaries are more detailed than those found in the *Prose de l'Arsenal*, however, and they often absorb the direct address into a moralizing commentary. Such is the method he applies to one of the rare amorous speeches found in the Lorraine cycle, which the three versions render in characteristic fashion. When the (married) Queen of Cologne attempts to seduce Gerbert, the verse presents her verbal advances in four lines:

> Dist la roïne: "Gerbers, molt estes ber!
> Par maintes foiz voz ai oï loer.
> Donnez me .i. don que voz voel demander,
> Vo druerie, s'il voz plaist, me donez!"
>
> (*Gerbert de Mez* vv. 3834–37)

[The Queen said: "Gerbert, you are quite valiant! Many times have I heard you praised. Grant me a boon that I wish to ask of you: please give me your love!"]

The *Prose de l'Arsenal* merely reports the queen asked for his love ("le pria d'amours" 56). The *Histoire de Charles Martel* expands the request into a lengthy declaration of love, complete with courtly rhetoric, to which Gerbert responds with suitable gallantry (KBR 8, fols. 124r–124v). Philippe, for his part, paraphrases the queen's entreaty with a hint of reproach:

Et aprés plusieurs doulce parolle et doulx langaige luy donnait ladite damme a antandre qu'elle l'amoit. Et pour abregiés desiroit sur tout a

---

75 Examples of direct discourse are on pp. 5, 14, 28, 33, 40, 49, and 130. On p. 33, the quotation is limited to the war cries "Le Plesseïs!" and "Bordeaux!"

avoir sa compaignie et de fait ne fut pas cy peu honteuse qu'elle l'en requist. (fol. 223r)

[And after many sweet words and sweet language, the lady gave him to understand that she loved him. And to abbreviate, she desired above all to have his company, and in fact, she was not at all ashamed to ask him for it.]

The distancing mechanism involved in the conversion of direct discourse allows the prose narrator to interpret and judge characters' words. When the traitor Bernard de Naisil announces that he will take revenge on his neighbors, Philippe's translation silences the character's boasting voice and replaces it with the indignant tone of a Lorraine sympathizer:

Prose	Verse
[Bernard] eust moult grant joie en son cuer [...] de la guere aincy esmeute. Car c'estoit tout son desir que de maulx faire et de molester le powre peuple. (fol. 92r)	Or dit Bernart: "Or enforce mis pris, et ma grant joie et mis riches deliz! Or savront bien entor moi mi voisin qui ont les bués et les vaches norriz, qu'an ne peut guerre de neant maintenir; et si savront, ce sachent il de fi, coment je sai de mon tronçon ferir! (*Garin le Loherenc* vv. 3225–31)
[Bernard's heart was overjoyed that the war had been kindled. For it was his fervent desire to do evil and to harm the poor people.]	[Then Bernard says: "Now my reputation, my great joy and abundant happiness have increased! Now my neighbors all around me, who have raised oxen and cows, will know that one cannot wage war with nothing, and they will know also, and let them be sure of it, how well I know how to strike with the stump of my lance!"]

Much of the time, Philippe's prose does reproduce direct discourse as such. In fact, his interest in the art of dialogue is manifest in the *Cent Nouvelles Nouvelles* and his participation in local theater.[76] In the *dérimage*, however, he very often opts for a hybrid solution, translating the first part of a direct speech in the indirect mode, and the remainder in the characters' own words. In the following passage, those assembled at Pepin's court admire the young Begon as he jousts with his companions:

---

[76] See Livingston's introduction to the *Cent Nouvelles Nouvelles*, 48.

Prose

Et fut dit et jugiés de tous et viez
et joune qu'il estoit le plus biaulx
chevalier qui fut en crestienté. "Et
serait" font il "proudon et vaillant c'il
vit." (fol. 71r)

Verse

A lui se tienent li jone et li barbé;
dit l'un a l'autre: "Ce est la verité,
n'a chevalier si gent en la Crestïenté!
Preudom sera, se il vit par aé."
(*Garin le Loherenc* vv. 1074–77)

[And it was said and judged by all,
old and young alike, that he was the
fairest knight in all Christendom.
"And he will be," they say, "a worthy
and valiant man if he lives."]

[Young and old alike are drawn to
him. They say to each other: "Truly,
there is no fairer knight in all Christendom! He will be a worthy man, if
he lives long."]

The mimetic follow-up has an emphatic function, confirming the narrator's account of the court's laudatory remarks and bringing them to a forceful closure.

The mechanisms used to introduce direct discourse are also a function of genre and prose style. Bernard Cerquiglini maintains that the insertion of direct speech reveals fundamental differences in the "grammar" of verse and prose in the later Middle Ages.[77] To signal the shift to direct discourse, both signifying practices prefer the prolepsis, a declarative verb or appellative that precedes and identifies the character's speech. Prose is more apt, however, to insert redundant clauses within or after the utterance.[78] In derhyming the speeches of the *chansons de geste*, Philippe practices this sort of overdeter-mination far more than any other prosifier that I have examined. Redundant signals punctuate not only extended monologues, but also short pronounce-ments:

Prose

Et le duc de ce le remerciait et dit
"Grant mercy sire" ait dit le duc, "car
au besoing voit on l'amis" (fol. 68r)

Verse

"Granz merciz, sire!" ce dit li dux
   Hervis,
"q'au grant besoing voit on bien son
   ami!"
(*Garin le Loherenc* vv. 852–3)

[and the duke thanked him for it and
said "thank you, sire," said the duke,
"for one knows his friend in time of
need']

["Thank you, sire!"says Duke Hervis,
"for one knows a friend in time of
need!"]

In this case, the speaker (the duke), the function of his speech (thanking), and the declarative verb ("dit") are all doubly marked within a single line

[77] Cerquiglini, *La Parole médiévale*, 13. See also Godzich and Kittay, *Emergence of Prose*, 37.
[78] Cerquiglini, *La Parole médiévale*, 38–54.

of prose. One might well attribute this reiteration to a lack of artistry, a clumsy build-up to the friendship proverb. It is nonetheless revealing in light of Philippe's overall interest in establishing a clear framework for acts of speech. Perhaps to compensate for the redundancy of performance, in which the deictic "dit" might be reinforced by a shift in the jongleur's voice, the prosifier substitutes his own system of pleonastic markers to differentiate narration and citation.

Despite this almost obsessive drive to identify the speaker in the text, Philippe's prose occasionally confuses the voices of narrator and character. Jean-Charles Herbin finds seven occurrences of the error, which is most striking when a character's quoted speech inserts the narrator's stock phrase "comme cy dessus avez oÿ" (as you heard above) even though this information was previously told to the reader, not the fictional interlocutor.[79] Less conspicuous, but in the same vein, is a point of information intended for the reader, but embedded into a character's invitation to his cousin:

Prose

Alors Lowis le filz Hernault ait appelleis Yonnet son cousin: "Mon cousin," dit il, "antandés sçay! Montons nous deux a chevaulx et nous allons esbaitre sus la rivier ou dessus une yawe *c'on appelloit* Sorclin." (fol. 308r, my emphasis)

[Then Louis, Hernaut's son, called his cousin Yonnet: "Cousin," he said, "listen! Let us both mount our horses and desport ourselves by the river or along the water that *used to be called* Sorclin."]

Verse

"Cosins," dist il, "entendez a mes dis. Montons es seles des destriers arrabis S'irons jouer sor l'yave de Seclin."[80] (*Anseÿs de Mes* vv. 167–69)

["Cousin," he said, "listen to what I say. Let us mount on the saddles of our Arabian horses and go disport ourselves by the Seclin river."]

Philippe commonly inserts such explanations when he does not recognize a toponym or when he deems it unfamiliar to his readers. Curiously, however, the name "Sorclin" is elucidated here in the imperfect tense by a character speaking in the present about a body of water familiar to him! Thus the translator's mediating voice reveals its presence and intrudes upon the character's speech. As Herbin notes with some amusement, such lapses are most likely due to inattentiveness.[81] Pierre Demarolle, in studying Philippe's overall

79 Herbin, "Approches," 501. The passage in question is from the first book (fol. 40v).
80 The edition gives the toponym as "Torin," as it appears in MS N (Arsenal 3143). This is clearly an error, as subsequent lines refer to the body of water as Seclin (see Index of Proper Names 453).
81 Herbin, "Approches," 501.

approach to the Lorraine material, finds that the translator is often unable to distance himself from diegetic events, lacking the detachment required of a skilled writer.[82]

This breakdown of enunciative coherence, however, points to more than simple carelessness or naiveté. In his other works, Philippe both thematizes and grapples with shifts in narrative voice. It is ironic, for example, that he should be guilty of the sort of blunder that underlies one of his own comic tales. In Novella 64, a young lady seeks to amuse her companions by telling her own tale of misfortune as though it were that of another. As she concludes her third-person narrative, in which a married woman is found naked in bed with her lover, she unwittingly slips into the first person and betrays the identity of the protagonist: "je me trouva toute nue et ne fut jamais plus esbahie ne apoventée que adoncques je fus" (268; I found myself completely naked, and I had never been as astounded or as horrified as I was at that moment). In glossing the tale, the narrator chides the woman for talking too much ("trop parler"), adding: "elle avoit mal parlez de soy avoir nommez, par quoy les auditeurs et escoustans congneurent son cas, qui par avant estoit secret et celez" (268; she misspoke in naming herself, so that her listeners learned of her situation, which had been secret and hidden before this).[83]

If Philippe's own momentary lapses in narrative voice are less blatant (and admittedly less entertaining), they raise similar questions about the enunciating subject – questions not limited to the prose translation. It is useful to turn once again to his autobiographical and lyrical works, which reveal an ongoing search for the discursive mode best suited to a given text or episode. In the early chapters of the *Journal*, for example, Philippe's narrator appears to be struggling with the dual subjectivity inherent in autobiographical writing. Whereas he begins and ends his life story in the first person, the voyage to Italy triggers an abrupt shift from first to third person narration. The change occurs when the young man has arrived in Naples and found work as a valet. Just after referring to lodgings secured by "moy et mon maistre" (myself and my master), the narrator disconnects himself linguistically from the protagonist: "Or demouroit Phelippe avec son maistre" (21; now Philippe stayed with his master). In the following account of his adolescence and early adulthood, the first-person narrator generally distinguishes his authorial persona from the youthful hero "Philippe," but there are occasional slippages between first and third person as the most dramatic of his early life experiences unfold.[84] The abduction of Philippe and his father is recounted in the third person in the *Journal*, but rewritten in the

[82] Demarolle, "De la narratologie," 255.

[83] Livingston notes the similarity between this tale and Novella 62 of the *Heptaméron* (*Cent Nouvelles Nouvelles* 265).

[84] See pp. 134–36 for slippages. 134: "moy Phelippe" and 135: "je estois" but 136: "En ceste année avoit Phelippe délibéré."

first person for the *Chronique*.[85] Clearly, Philippe was testing the parameters of an autobiographical genre whose conventions tended to constrain subjective expression. In most bourgeois journals of the period, the first person is used only sparingly if at all, and entries are typically articulated by the impersonal "Item."[86] Philippe's narrative of the self oscillates between this form and the more introspective (and retrospective) memoir.[87] Surprisingly, lyric seems to have posed similar problems of expression for him. The poems of captivity inserted into the *Journal* bear the traces of self-conscious writing and rewriting. The first poem, "Mauldicte soit trayson," is fraught with corrections in the manuscript, including consistent changes from third to first person.[88]

Like the *Journal*, the *dérimage* as it appears in extant versions is a work in progress that occasionally exposes an unstable enunciating subject. Lapses and emendations document an unschooled writer's experiments and failings with respect to the modulations of voice. If the translator does at times forget who is speaking in the text, this is but a telling stage in the redaction of a work whose final revisions never materialized, or are lost to us today. Philippe was singularly preoccupied with speech – how it is framed, what it reveals, and what risks are involved in speaking. In the various stages of rewriting, he surely was mindful of the cascade of proverbs and admonitions he used to introduce his Novella 64: talking too much is harmful, hold your tongue behind your teeth, and above all: "on doit premier trois fois penser la chose avant que la dire ou aultrement bien souvent on s'en repent" (266; one must first think three times before saying something, or else very often one is sorry for it).

Jane H. M. Taylor has demonstrated that even the least sophisticated translations have underlying transformational strategies, whether or not they are products of a conscious set of translational principles.[89] Philippe's compositional and stylistic choices attest to a moderate level of intervention in the received material. In derhyming the old *chansons de geste*, he does not significantly alter the course of events related in the original, but he does adjust them to the conventions of prose and his own set of authorial preoccupations:

---

[85] *Journal* 45–114, *Chronique* III: 194–255.

[86] See, for example, the *Journal de Jehan Aubrion, bourgeois de Metz*, ed. Lorédan Larchey (Metz: F. Blanc, 1967); the *Journal de Nicolas de Baye, greffier du Parlement de Paris*, *1400–1470*, ed. Alexandre Tuetey (Paris: Renouard, 1885–88); and the *Journal d'un bourgeois de Paris*, *1405–1449*, ed. Alexandre Tuetey (1881; Geneva: Slatkine Reprints, 1975).

[87] Michel Zink finds a similar hesitation in the works of Philippe de Novare and Joinville. See *La Subjectivité littéraire autour du siècle de Saint Louis* (Paris: PUF, 1985), 219–20.

[88] See *Journal* 70–71 and BnF nouv. acq. fr. 6720, pp. 103–06.

[89] Taylor, "Translation as Reception," 492–93.

the careful linking of narrative segments, temporal and spatial precision, clarity, (relative) brevity, and dramatic intensity. While his *dérimage* lacks the rhetorical polish of works commissioned by courtly patrons, it is perhaps even more valuable as a record of the trials and errors of an autodidact who was fully engaged in his daunting task.

5

Conclusion

> La littérature d'un moment est faite, sans doute, des ouvrages écrits et
> publiés à cette époque, mais aussi des livres réédités, des oeuvres étudiées
> dans les écoles, et de tout ce qui est lu à ce moment. Or ces textes "main-
> tenus en usage" peuvent-ils avoir exactement le sens qu'ils avaient lors de
> leur création? Je ne le crois pas [...] les faits, certes, demeurent les mêmes;
> mais leur signification peut s'être modifiée, leur résonance a évolué.[1]

The corpus of Middle French prose has typically been reduced to the works
of its most gifted practitioners. Alongside authors such as Jehan Froissart,
Christine de Pizan, Antoine de la Sale and Philippe de Commynes, however,
prosifiers from diverse backgrounds were producing a substantial body of
literature in translation, intended for the edification and amusement of a
growing reading public.[2] In these pages, I have argued first that the *mises en
prose* ought to be recognized as an integral part of the literary and cultural
history of the period, and second, that Philippe de Vigneulles merits special
attention for his unique contribution to the genre. As V.-L. Saulnier declares,
"Ce n'est pas un inconnu, mais c'est un curieux homme, qu'il faudrait mieux
honorer."[3] Though he possessed neither the erudition nor the rhetorical
training of clerkly translators, Philippe clearly had literary ambitions as well
as a political and cultural agenda. Declaring himself unfit to undertake the
lofty task of rewriting the Lorraine cycle, he nonetheless acquitted himself
admirably, proving to be an astute reader and lively storyteller.

The prosaics of *translatio* reveals itself through an intertextual network
extending beyond the relationship between source and adaptation. Philippe's
derhyming is unparalleled as a document of the versatility of epic material
during this period. Positioning himself as a guardian of urban renewal, this
self-taught storyteller integrates his translation into a coherent corpus that
enlists chronicle, clothmaking, autobiography, comic tale and *chanson de
geste* in the shaping of Metz's cultural identity. His approach to the craft of
prosification involves subtle but distinctive modifications of the source texts.

---

1 Guiette, "Chanson de geste, chronique et mise en prose," 148.
2 See Bérier, "La Traduction en français," 232–35.
3 Saulnier, "Philippe de Vigneulles rimeur de fêtes, de saints et de prisons," 966.

Adapting the old songs to the readerly space of prose, Philippe constructs an authorial voice that blends jongleuresque verve with the authority of a chronicler. He faithfully transmits the events recounted in the verse, but frames them in a new textual system that accomodates both abridgement and redundancy. Like other forms of translation into Middle French, the *mise en prose* is at once a work of literature and a piece of literary criticism.[4] This is nowhere more evident than in Philippe's oeuvre, with its rich testimony of authorial intervention and reflection.

This version of the Lorraine epic was long preserved as part of the cultural patrimony of Metz. Evidence suggests that the manuscripts of Philippe's works were passed down through several generations of family members before their acquisition by public and private libraries.[5] The illustrated version, MS *h*, was acquired in 1644 by the Protestant pastor Paul Ferry of Metz, who exchanged it with the Bibliothèque de Sedan for a copy of the *Champion des Dames* by Martin Le Franc. Ferry, who was married to Philippe's great-granddaughter, also possessed manuscripts of the *Chronique* and the *Cent Nouvelles Nouvelles*. While MS *v* was eventually acquired by the Bibliothèque Municipale de Metz, the more ornate *h* entered into the collection of Count Emmery of Metz and was purchased by the Count of Hunolstein in 1849.

Philippe's derhyming continued to rekindle interest in the Lorraine cycle even after the verse epics began to be edited and translated into modern French.[6] Théodore de Puymaigre and Maurice de Pange, who both published books on regional history and literature, exemplify the reception of the *mise en prose* among aristocratic antiquarians in the early days of medieval studies.[7] They look with condescension upon the translator's belief that the characters and events of the old epic were historically authentic, but recognize his

---

  [4] See Bérier, "La Traduction en français," 265.

  [5] Since both known manuscripts of the *mise en prose* appear to be drafts, it is possible that a final and more polished copy was produced and subsequently lost. See Herbin, "Notice du manuscrit *h*," 224. On the history of manuscript transmission, see Livingston, *Cent Nouvelles Nouvelles*, Introduction, 21–22; Bonnardot, "Essai de classement des manuscrits des *Loherains*, 198–99; Herbin, "Notice du manuscrit *h*," 219–22.

  [6] Paulin Paris was the first modern editor of *Garin le Lorrain*. See *Li Romans de Garin le Loherain, publié pour la première fois, et précédé de l'examen du système de M. Fauriel sur les romans carlovingiens*, 2 vols. (1832–1848; Geneva: Slatkine Reprints, 1969). Édward Le Glay translated the episode of Begon's death into modern French: *La Mort de Bégon de Belin, épisode extrait et traduit du roman de* Garin de Loherain, in *Fragments d'épopées romanes*. Some thirty years after editing *Garin*, Paris produced a modern French translation, *Garin le Loherain, chanson de geste composée au XIIe siècle par Jehan de Flagy, mise en nouveau langage* (Paris: Hetzel, 1862).

  [7] Dom Augustin Calmet, Auguste Prost, Théodore de Puymaigre and Maurice de Pange all provide accounts of Philippe's rendering, though Calmet seems to have known only the abridged version contained in the *Chronique*. See Calmet, *Bibliothèque lorraine*,1012; Prost, *Études sur l'histoire de Metz: les Légendes*, 400; de Puymaigre, *Poètes et romanciers de la Lorraine*, 341–42; de Pange, *Les Lorrains et la France au moyen âge* (Paris: Champion, 1914), 105–21.

contribution to local tradition. De Pange, who reproduced the miniatures and titles of MS *h* in a deluxe edition dated 1901, cringes at Philippe's unabashed use of the Metz dialect, but admires the author's sincerity and seriousness of purpose.[8] It is surely no coincidence that de Pange opted to revive a Francophone literary artifact during the German occupation of Lorraine (1871–1919). The French defeat in the Franco-Prussian war spurred a strong interest in medieval studies on both sides of the border.[9] Indeed, during the same period, Philippe's prose attracted the attention of German scholars. Under the direction of Edmund Stengel, two students undertook comparative analyses between Philippe's prose and extant verse manuscripts.[10] The Belgian scholar Georges Doutrepont, in his 1939 study of the *mises en prose*, devotes several pages to the "brave bourgeois de Metz," noting with some amusement the author's fierce attachment to the Lorraine epic heroes.[11] Due to the loss of MS *v* in 1944, and the inaccessibility of *h* for most of the last century, subsequent scholarship was long limited to Philippe's other books, which were available in modern critical editions. I have sought here to restore the prose translation to its proper place in the works of Philippe de Vigneulles and in the history of Romance epic.[12]

Philippe's prose marks the end of the first wave of intralingual translations designed to popularize the *geste des Loherains*. His successors in the modern period would display varying attitudes toward the material and even the validity of modern translation. After three centuries of relative neglect, the cycle became a vital part of nineteenth-century medievalism, owing largely to the efforts of Paulin Paris. Early in his career, this fervent admirer of the Old French epic scoffed at his compatriots' reluctance to master the language of their forebears:

> On répond que leur langage est devenu pénible, et que la lecture de leurs manuscrits fatigue. Fort bien! il vaut mieux consumer les plus belles années de votre vie à étudier les prosodies grecques ou latines que deux ou trois mois à apprendre les anciennes tournures de votre langue, et les expressions énergiques dont elle a été dépossédée par les siècles classiques![13]

---

8 De Pange, *Les Lorrains et la France au moyen âge*, 119.

9 On the importance of the Franco-Prussian War in the history of medieval studies, see R. Howard Bloch and Stephen G. Nichols, ed., *Medievalism and the Modernist Temper* (Baltimore & London: The Johns Hopkins UP, 1996), particularly the articles by David Hult and Per Nykrog.

10 Otto Böckel, *Phillipp de Vigneulles Bearbeitung des Hervis de Mes*, and Karl Jahn, *Philipp de Vigneulle's Yonnet de Mes und sein Verhältnis zu Redaction N des Romans Anseïs de Mes*.

11 Doutrepont, *Les Mises en prose*, esp. 152–58.

12 Jean-Charles Herbin's forthcoming edition will contribute significantly to the accessibility of Philippe's prose. Unless MS *h* becomes available in digital form or on microfilm, it is likely that he will be obliged to rely heavily on the microfilm of *v*, which is often illegible, and a transcription by Edmund Stengel.

13 Paulin Paris, *Apologie de l'école romantique* (Paris: Dentu, 1824), 27.

Determined to initiate his public, Paris first produced an edition of *Garin le Lorrain*, but was disappointed by its reception among nonacademic readers. Thirty years later, he reconsidered his fundamentalist strategy: "J'ai publié, il y a trente ans, le texte de *Garin le loherain*: j'aurais peut-être mieux fait de commencer par le traduire."[14] Translate it he did, into modern French prose, in the hope of whetting readers' appetites for a literary monument he declared to be more audacious and astonishing than any found in classical literature.[15] Paris appropriated the matter of Lorraine to the interests of French nationalism, framing the story as a foundational myth.[16] Another nineteenth-century translator, Édward Le Glay, also sought to replace the mythology of the ancients with tales rooted in the French-speaking tradition. Le Glay, however, was motivated by regional interests. Limiting his modern translation to the episode of Begon's death, localized in northeast France and Belgium, he sought to revive the "belles rapsodies" that his Romantic imagination located in the ancient hearths of Flanders, Hainaut, Artois, and Cambrésis. Unlike Paris, he sympathized with the modern audience, recognizing that ordinary people read for the pleasure of reading, not for the effort of translating a language only half understood.[17]

The most recent *translatio* of the Lorraine material dates from the 1980s, when modern French prose translations of *Hervis de Metz, Garin le Lorrain* and *Gerbert de Metz* were published by the Presses Universitaires de Nancy.[18] Prefaces and afterwords valorize not only the excellence of the narrative, but also the geopolitical value of a prestigious epic corpus associated with Metz and Lorraine. In the afterword to his translation of *Hervis de Metz*, Philippe Walter wryly questions the motives of Edmund Stengel, who edited the text in 1903. Suggesting that the earlier scholar secretly hoped to claim Metz for Germany, Walter triumphantly points to the privileged relation between Metz and France already evident in the Old French verse.[19] In his preface to the 1986 version of *Garin le Lorrain*, Jean Lanher praises Bernard Guidot's masterful translation, which will inspire readers to take new pleasure in

[14] Paulin Paris, "Étude sur les chansons de geste et sur *Garin le Loherain*," *Le Correspondant* 58 (1863): 721–50, at p. 721.

[15] Paris, *Li Romans de Garin* 239, note 3 and *Garin le Loherain, chanson de geste ... mise en nouveau langage*, 2.

[16] Paris, *Li Romans de Garin*, préface, xv.

[17] Le Glay, *Fragments d'épopées romanes*, 18–19. On the nineteenth-century reception of the Lorraine cycle, see Jones, "The Death of Begon Revisited" and "Autour du 'nouveau langage': La geste des Loherains aux XVIe et XIXe siècles," *L'Épopée romane au Moyen Age et aux temps modernes*, ed. Salvatore Luongo (Naples: Consorzio Editoriale Fridericiana, 2001), II, 693–705.

[18] See Philippe Walter's modern translation of *Hervis de Metz*, as well as *Garin le Lorrain, chanson de geste traduite en français moderne par Bernard Guidot* (Nancy: PU de Nancy, Éditions Serpenoise, 1986) and *Gerbert de Metz, chanson de geste traduite en français moderne par Bernard Guidot* (Nancy: PU de Nancy, 1988).

[19] Walter, *Hervis de Metz*, postface, 201.

works of the "terroir" and even increase their affection for Lorraine.[20] Thus, Philippe de Vigneulles was the first of many prosifiers to readjust the tale to the exigencies of new textual communities. Since the Middle French period, the Lorraine cycle's potential for the advancement of local, regional and national interests has relied on the power of prose.

[20] Lanher, *Garin le Lorrain*, préface, 10.

BIBLIOGRAPHY

Primary Works

Anseÿs de Mes According to Ms. N (Bibliothèque de l'Arsenal 3143): Text, published for the first time in its entirety, with an Introduction. Ed. Herman J. Green. Paris: Les Presses modernes, 1939.

Aubert, David. *Guerin le Loherain: Édition critique et commentaire par Valérie Naudet de la prose de David Aubert extraite des Histoires de Charles Martel (manuscrit 7 de la Bibliothèque Royale de Belgique)*. Aix-en-Provence: Publications de l'U de Provence, 2005.

———. *L'Histoire de Charles Martel et de ses successeurs*. Koninklijke Bibliotheek van België (KBR) MSS 6, 7, 8, 9.

Aubrion, Jehan. *Journal de Jehan Aubrion, bourgeois de Metz, avec sa continuation par Pierre Aubrion, 1465–1512*. Ed. Lorédan Larchey. Metz: F. Blanc, 1857.

Bouchet, Jean. *Le Jugement poetic de l'honneur femenin. Oeuvres complètes* I. Ed. Adrian Armstrong. Paris: Champion, 2006.

Collection Emmery sur l'histoire de Metz. II: 1451–1500. BnF nouv. acq. fr. 22660.

Fierabras: roman en prose de la fin du XIVe siècle. Ed. Jean Miquet. Ottawa: Éditions de l'Université d'Ottawa, 1983.

Garin le Loherain, chanson de geste composée au XIIe siècle par Jehan de Flagy, mise en nouveau langage. Trans. Paulin Paris. Paris: Hetzel, 1862.

Garin le Loheren, According to Manuscript A (Bibliothèque de l'Arsenal 2983) with Text, Introduction, and Linguistic Study. Ed. Josephine Elvira Vallerie. Diss. Columbia U, 1947. Ann Arbor: Edwards Bros., 1947.

Garin le Loherenc. Ed. Anne Iker-Gittleman. 3 vols. Paris: Champion, 1996.

Garin le Lorrain, chanson de geste traduite en français moderne par Bernard Guidot. Préface de Jean Lanher. Nancy: PU de Nancy, Éditions Serpenoise, 1986.

Gerbert de Metz, chanson de geste traduite en français moderne par Bernard Guidot. Nancy: PU de Nancy, 1988.

Gerbert de Mez: chanson de geste du XIIe siècle. Ed. Pauline Taylor. Bibliothèque de la Faculté de Philosophie et de Lettres de Namur 11. Namur, Lille, Louvain: Nauwelaerts, 1953.

Girart de Roussillon: chanson de geste traduite pour la première fois par Paul Meyer. 1884; Geneva: Slatkine Reprints, 1970.

Hervis de Mes. Ed. Jean-Charles Herbin. Geneva: Droz, 1992.

Hervis de Metz: roman du moyen âge adapté par Philippe Walter. Metz: Editions Serpenoise; Nancy: PU de Nancy, 1984.

L'Histoire d'Erec en prose: roman du XVe siècle. Ed. Maria Colombo Timelli. Geneva: Droz, 2000.

Histoire de la Reine Berthe et du Roy Pepin: *mise en prose d'une chanson de geste*. Ed. Piotr Tylus. Geneva: Droz, 2001.

Le Huon de Bordeaux en prose du XVème siècle. Ed. Michel J. Raby. New York: Peter Lang, 1998.

Jean Lemaire de Belges. *Epistre du Roy à Hector et autres pièces de circonstances (1511–1513)*. Ed. Adrian Armstrong and Jennifer Britnell. Paris: Société des Textes Français Modernes, 2000.

Journal d'un bourgeois de Paris, 1405–1449. Ed. Alexandre Tuetey. 1881. Geneva: Slatkine Reprints, 1975.

Mabrien: roman de chevalerie en prose du XVe siècle. Ed. Philippe Verelst. Romanica Gandensia XXVIII. Geneva: Droz, 1998.

La Mise en prose de la geste des Loherains dans le manuscrit Arsenal 3346. Ed. Jean-Charles Herbin. Valenciennes: PU de Valenciennes, 1995.

Nicolas de Baye. *Journal de Nicolas de Baye, greffier du Parlement de Paris, 1400–1417*. Ed. Alexandre Tuetey. 2 vols. Paris: Renouard, 1885–88.

Philippe de Vigneulles. *Cent Nouvelles Nouvelles*. Ed. Charles H. Livingston. Travaux d'Humanisme et Renaissance 120. Geneva: Droz, 1972.

———. *La Chanson de Garin le Loherain mise en prose par Philippe de Vigneulles de Metz. Table des chapitres avec les reproductions des miniatures d'après le manuscrit appartenant à M. le comte d'Hunolstein*. Ed. Maurice de Pange. Paris: Leclerc, 1901.

———. *La Chronique de Philippe de Vigneulles*. Ed. Charles Bruneau. 4 vols. Metz: Société d'histoire et d'archéologie de la Lorraine, 1927.

———. *Gedenkbuch des Metzer Bürgers Philippe von Vigneulles aus den Jahren 1471 bis 1522*. Ed. Heinrich Michelant. 1852. Amsterdam: Rodopi, 1968.

———. *Das Journal des Philippe de Vigneulles: Aufzeichnungen eines Metzer Bürgers (1471–1522)*. Trans. Waltraud and Eduard Schuh. Saarbrücken: Conte Verlag, 2005.

———. *Prose des Loherains* (provisional title). Metz 847 (*v*), preserved on MLA Microfilm 430F. Ferrell MS 6 (*h*).

Rabelais, François. *Pantagruel*. Ed. Floyd Gray. Édition critique basée sur l'édition publiée à Lyon en 1542 par François Juste. Paris: Champion; diffusion Geneva: Slatkine, 1997.

Li Romans de Garin le Loherain, publié pour la première fois, et précédé de l'examen du système de M. Fauriel sur les romans carlovingiens. Ed. Paulin Paris. 2 vols. 1832–1848. Geneva: Slatkine Reprints, 1969.

Le Roman de Guillaume d'Orange. Ed. Madeleine Tyssens, Nadine Henrard, et Louis Gemenne. Tome I. Paris: Champion, 2000.

La Vengeance Fromondin. Ed. Jean-Charles Herbin. Paris: S.A.T.F.; Abbeville: Paillart, 2005.

Villon, François. *Oeuvres*. Ed. and trans. André Lanly. Paris: Champion, 1993.

Wauquelin, Jehan. *La Belle Hélène de Constantinople*: *Mise en prose d'une chanson de geste*. Ed. Marie-Claude de Crécy. Textes littéraires français 547. Geneva: Droz, 2002.

———. *Cronicques des faiz de feurent monseigneur Girart de Rossillon*. Ed. Léonce de Montille. Paris: Champion, 1880.

Yon or la Venjance Fromondin: A Thirteenth-Century Chanson de Geste of the Loherain Cycle. Ed. Simon Mitchneck. New York: Publications of the Institute of French Studies, Columbia University, 1935.

Secondary Works

Abramowicz, Maciej. *Réécrire au moyen âge: Mises en prose des romans en Bourgogne au XVe siècle.* Lublin: Uniwersytetu Marii Curie, 1996.

Adler, Alfred. "*Hervis de Mes* and the Matrilineal Nobility of Champagne." *Romanic Review* 37 (1946): 150–61.

Andersen, Peter, ed. *Pratiques de traduction au moyen âge / Medieval Translation Practices.* Papers from the Symposium at the University of Copenhagen, 25th and 26th October 2002. Copenhagen: Museum Tusculanum Press, U of Copenhagen, 2004.

Auclair, Mathias. "Le Preux et le saint: Garin le Lorrain et Saint Gengoult, ancêtre des ducs de Lorraine." *Romania* 117 (1999): 245–57.

Baker, Mary J. "Narrative Communication in Philippe de Vigneulles' *Cent Nouvelles nouvelles.*" *Orbis litterarum: International Review of Literary Studies* 53 (1998): 73–82.

Bautier, Robert Henri. *Sur l'histoire économique de la France médiévale: la route, le fleuve, la foire.* Aldershot, Hampshire, Great Britain: Variorum; Brookfield, Vermont: Gower, 1991.

Bedos-Rezak, Brigitte. "Civic Liturgies and Urban Records in Northern France, 1100–1400." *City and Spectacle in Medieval Europe.* Ed. Barbara A. Hanawalt and Kathryn L. Reyerson. Medieval Studies at Minnesota 6. Minneapolis & London: U of Minnesota Press, 1994. 34–55.

Beer, Jeanette M.A. *Early Prose in France: Contexts of Bilingualism and Authority.* Kalamazoo, Mich.: Medieval Institute Publications, Western Michigan U, 1992.

——— and Kenneth Lloyd-Jones, ed. *Translation and the Transmission of Culture between 1300 and 1600.* Kalamazoo, Mich.: Medieval Institute Publications, Western Michigan U, 1995.

———. *Translation Theory and Practice in the Middle Ages.* Kalamazoo, Mich.: Medieval Institute Publications, Western Michigan U, 1997.

Benjamin, Walter. "The Task of the Translator." Trans. Harry Zohn. *Illuminations.* New York: Harcourt, Brace, & World, 1968. 69–82.

Bergeron, David M. "Stuart Civic Pageants and Textual Performance." *Renaissance Quarterly* 51 (1998): 163–83.

Bérier, François. "La Traduction en français." *Grundriss der romanischen Literaturen des Mittelalters.* VIII/1: *La Littérature française aux XIVe et XVe siècles.* Heidelberg: Winter, 1988. 219–65.

Blanchard, J. "Compilation et légitimation au XVIème siècle." *Poétique* 74 (1988): 139–57.

Bloch, R. Howard and Stephen G. Nichols, ed. *Medievalism and the Modernist Temper.* Baltimore & London: The Johns Hopkins UP, 1996.

Blumenfeld-Kosinski, Renate, Luise von Flotwo, and Daniel Russell, ed. *The Politics of Translation in the Middle Ages and the Renaissance.* Medieval and Renaissance Texts and Studies 233. Ottawa: U of Ottawa Press, 2001.

Böckel, Otto. *Phillipp de Vigneulles Bearbeitung des Hervis de Mes.* Dissertation. Marburg: C. L. Pfeil, 1883.

Bonnardot, François. "Essai de classement des manuscrits des *Loherains* suivi d'un nouveau fragment de *Girbert de Metz.*" *Romania* 3 (1874): 195–262.

Boulton, Maureen Barry McCann. *The Song in the Story: Lyric Insertions in French Narrative Fiction.* Philadelphia: U of Pennsylvania Press, 1993.

Brucker, Charles. "Mises en prose et genres littéraires à la fin du Moyen Âge: la quête du vraisemblable." *Travaux de littérature* 13 (2000): 29–47.

———. "Théâtralité et rhétorique dans les mises en prose de la fin du moyen âge." *Texte et théâtralité.* Mélanges offerts à Jean Claude. Ed. Raymonde Robert. Nancy: PU de Nancy, 2000. 105–118.

Buridant, Claude. "Blaise de Vigenère traducteur de *La Conquête de Constantinople* de Geoffroy de Villehardouin." *Revue des sciences humaines* 180 (1980): 95–118.

———. "*Translatio medievalis*: Théorie et pratique de la traduction médiévale." *Travaux de linguistique et de littérature* 21 (1983): 81–136.

Busby, Keith. *Codex and Context: Reading Old French Verse Narrative in Manuscript.* 2 vols. Amsterdam & New York: Rodopi, 2002.

Cailly, M. C. *Le Bourgeois de Metz au quinzième siècle: Philippe de Vigneulles.* Metz: Rousseau-Pallez, 1867.

Calmet, Augustin. *Bibliothèque lorraine; ou Histoire des hommes illustres qui ont fleuri en Lorraine, dans les trois Évêchés, dans l'archevêché de Trèves, dans le duché de Luxembourg,* etc. 1751. Geneva: Slatkine Reprints, 1971.

Campbell, Kimberlee A. "The Reiterated Self: Cyclical Temporality and Ritual Renewal in *Hervis de Metz.*" *Transtextualities: Of Cycles and Cyclicity in Medieval French Literature.* Ed. Sara Sturm-Maddox and Donald Maddox. Medieval & Renaissance Texts & Studies 149. Binghamton, NY: Center for Medieval and Early Renaissance Studies, State University of New York at Binghamton, 1996. 157–77.

Catalogue général des manuscrits des bibliothèques publiques des départements. Volume 5: Metz-Verdun-Charleville. Paris: Imprimerie Nationale, 1879.

Cavalli, Marisa. "Boccaccio e Philippe de Vigneulles." *La Nouvelle française à la Renaissance.* Ed. Lionello Sozzi and V.-L. Saulnier. Geneva: Slatkine, 1981. 167–70.

Cerquiglini, Bernard. *La Parole médiévale: Discours, syntaxe, texte.* Paris: Éditions de Minuit, 1981.

Cerquiglini-Toulet, Jacqueline. *La Couleur de la mélancolie: La fréquentation des livres au XIVe siècle 1300–1415.* Paris: Hatier, 1993.

Cigada, Sergio and Anna Slerca, ed. *Rhétorique et mises en prose au XVe siècle.* Actes du VIe colloque international sur le moyen français. Milan: Vita e Pensiero, 1991.

Clercx, M. *Catalogue des manuscrits relatifs à l'histoire de Metz et de la Lorraine.* Metz: F. Blanc, 1856.

Coleman, Joyce. *Public Reading and the Reading Public in Late Medieval England and France.* Cambridge: Cambridge UP, 1996.

Contamine, Geneviève, ed. *Traduction et traducteurs au moyen âge.* Actes du colloque international du CNRS 26–28 mai 1986. Paris: Editions du CNRS, 1989.

Contamine, Philippe. "Autobiographie d'un prisonnier-otage: Philippe de Vigneulles au Château de Chauvency." *Les Prisonniers de guerre dans l'Histoire: Contacts entre peuples et cultures.* Ed. Sylvie Caucanas, Rémy Cazals and Pascal Payen. Toulouse: Privat, 2003. 39–46.

Cook, Robert Francis. "Unity and Esthetics of the Late Chansons de geste." *Olifant* 11 (1986): 103–14.

de la Rue, Gervais (Abbé). *Essais historiques sur les bardes, les jongleurs et les trouvères normands et anglo-normands.* Caen: Mancel, 1834.

Demarolle, Pierre. "À la recherche des sources de Philippe de Vigneulles. À propos d'un passage de sa *Chronique*: La découverte de Terre-Neuve." *Le Moyen Âge* 100 (1994): 263–69.

———. "À propos d'annotations de Philippe de Vigneulles: Comment travaillait le chroniqueur messin?" *Cahiers lorrains* 1 (1989): 3–10.

———. *La Chronique de Philippe de Vigneulles et la mémoire de Metz.* Caen: Paradigme, 1993.

———. "De la narratologie à la syntaxe: les titres des chapitres de la mise en prose de *Garin le Lorrain* par Philippe de Vigneulles." *Rhétorique et mise en prose au XVe siècle.* Actes du VIe Colloque International sur le moyen français. Ed. Sergio Cigada and Anne Slerca. Milan: Vita e Pensiero, 1991. 245–55.

———. "La Mort dans l'univers mental de Philippe de Vigneulles d'après le livre V de la *Chronique* (1500–1526)." Actes du Colloque organisé par le Département de Littérature comparée de l'Université de Nancy II. *La Mort en toutes lettres.* Ed. Gilles Ernst and Louis-Vincent Thomas. Nancy: PU de Nancy, 1983. 25–32.

———. "La Place des apprentissages dans la littérature et dans la vie d'après l'oeuvre de Philippe de Vigneulles." *La Transmission du savoir dans l'Europe des XVIe et XVIIe siècles.* Ed. Marie Roig Miranda. Paris: Champion, 2000. 13–26.

———. "Philippe de Vigneulles chroniqueur: Une manière d'écrire l'histoire." *Revue des langues romanes* 97 (1993): 57–73.

———. "Philippe de Vigneulles et les tombeaux de la cathédrale de Metz." *Regards sur le passé dans l'Europe des XVIe et XVIIe siècles.* Ed. Francine Wild. Berlin: Peter Lang, 1997. 173–81.

———. "Philippe de Vigneulles et le terroir messin." *Provinces, régions, terroirs au moyen âge: De la réalité à l'imaginaire.* Actes du colloque international des Rencontres européennes de Strasbourg. Ed. Bernard Guidot. Nancy: PU de Nancy, 1993. 143–51.

———. "Tourments et inquiétudes dans le dernier livre de la Chronique de Philippe de Vigneulles (1500–1526)." *Tourments, doutes et ruptures dans l'Europe des XVIe et XVIIe siècles.* Actes du Colloque organisé par l'U de Nancy II, 25–27 novembre 1993. Ed. Claude Arnould and Pierre Demarolle. Paris: Champion: 1995. 21–30.

———. "Un Villon messin? La figure de Jehan Mangin chez Philippe de Vigneulles." *Patrimoine et culture en Lorraine.* Ed. F.-Yves Le Moigne. Metz: Editions. Serpenoise, Société d'Histoire et d'Archéologie de la Lorraine, 1980. 451–64.

Dictionnaire du Moyen Français (DMF). *Base de Lexiques de Moyen Français*

(DMF1). ATILF/Équipe "Moyen français et français préclassique" 2003–2005. <http://www.atilf.fr/blmf>.

Dorner, Marie. "Philippe de Vigneulles: un chroniqueur messin des XVe et XVIe siècles." *Mémoires de l'Académie de Metz* (1913–1914): 45–110.

Doutrepont, Georges. *La Littérature française à la cour des ducs de Bourgogne: Philippe le Hardi, Jean sans Peur, Philippe le Bon, Charles le Téméraire.* 1909. Geneva: Slatkine Reprints, 1970.

————. *Les Mises en prose des épopées et des romans chevaleresques du XIVe au XVIe siècle.* 1939. Geneva: Slatkine Reprints, 1969.

Encyclopédie illustrée de la Lorraine. Publiée sous la direction de Guy Cabourdin. II: *L'époque médiévale* par Michel Parisse. Metz: Editions Serpenoise; Nancy: PU de Nancy, 1990.

Enders, Jody. "Theater Makes History: Ritual Murder by Proxy in the *Mistere de la Sainte Hostie.*" *Speculum* 79 (2004): 991–1016.

Feist, Alfred. *Die Geste des Loherains in der Prosearbeitung der Arsenal-Handschrift.* Marburg: N. G. Elwert, 1884.

Fleischman, Suzanne. "Discourse as Space / Discourse as Time. Reflections on the Metalanguage of Spoken and Written Discourse." *Journal of Pragmatics* 16 (1991): 291–306.

Gantelet, Martial. "Entre France et Empire, Metz, une conscience municipale en crise à l'aube des Temps modernes (1500–1526)." *Revue Historique* 301, alt. 617 (2001): 5–45.

Gaudet, Minnette. "Temporal Patterns in the Twelfth Century chanson de geste and the Fifteenth-Century Prose Epic." *Romance Languages Annual* 3 (1992): 50–55.

Gautier, Léon. *Les Épopées françaises. Étude sur les origines et l'histoire de la littérature nationale.* 4 vols. 1878–97. Osnabrück: Zeller, 1966.

Germain, Léon. "Le Culte de Garin le Loherain." *Journal de la société archéologique du Musée Lorrain* 42–43 (1893–94): 275–78.

Gittleman, Anne Iker. *Le Style épique dans Garin le Loherain.* Geneva: Droz, 1967.

Godzich, Wlad and Jeffrey Kittay. *The Emergence of Prose: An Essay in Prosaics.* Minneapolis: U of Minnesota Press, 1987.

Greimas, Algirdas Julien and Teresa Mary Keane. *Dictionnaire du moyen français.* Paris: Larousse, 1992.

Grisward, Joël. Review of *Rückzug in epischer Parade* by Alfred Adler. *Cahiers de civilisation médiévale* 7 (1964): 497–504.

Gros, Gérard. "'Congnoistre et aprendre': Le voyage en Italie de Philippe (Philippe de Vigneulles, *Gedenkbuch*, p. 12–34) ou le mémorial de la chose vue." *Nouvelle Revue du XVIe siècle* 22 (2004): 5–22.

————. "En passant par le Forez (1489): Sur quelques pages des *Mémoires* de Philippe de Vigneulles." *Études sur Etienne Dolet, le théâtre au XVIe siècle, le Forez, le Lyonnais et l'histoire du livre, publiées à la mémoire de Claude Longeon.* Ed. Gabriel-André Pérouse. Geneva: Droz, 1993. 229–38.

Guidot, Bernard. "Formes tardives de l'épopée médiévale." *L'Épopée romane au moyen âge et aux temps modernes.* Actes du XIVe Congrès International de la Société Rencesvals pour l'Étude des Épopées Romanes. Ed. Salvatore Luongo. Naples: Fridericiana Editrice Universitaria, 2001. II: 579–610.

————. "Mesure du temps et flou chronologique dans quelques chansons de geste du XIIIe siècle." *Le Temps et la durée dans la littérature au Moyen Age et à la Renaissance*. Paris: Nizet, 1986. 55–70.

Guiette, Robert. "Chanson de geste, chronique et mise en prose." *Forme et Senefiance*. Etudes médiévales recueillies par Jean Dufournet, Marcel De Grève, and Herman Braet. Geneva: Droz, 1978. 135–62. Orig. in *Cahiers de civilisation médiévale* 6 (1963): 423–40.

Guilbert, Sylvette. "Temps et saisons dans la *Chronique* de Philippe de Vigneulles." *Le temps et la durée dans la littérature du moyen âge et à la Renaissance*. Actes du Colloque organisé par le Centre de Recherche sur la littérature du moyen âge et de la Renaissance de l'Université de Reims. Ed. Yvonne Bellenger. Paris: Nizet, 1986. 125–38.

Guillerm, Luce. "L'Auteur, les modèles, et le pouvoir ou la topique de la traduction au XVIe siècle en France." *Revue des sciences humaines* 180 (1980): 5–31.

————. "L'Intertextualité démontée: Le Discours sur la traduction." *Littérature* 55 (1984): 54–63.

Haidu, Peter. *The Subject of Violence: The Song of Roland and the Birth of the State*. Bloomington & Indianapolis: Indiana UP, 1993.

Hanawalt, Barbara A., and Kathryn L. Reyerson, ed., *City and Spectacle in Medieval Europe*. Medieval Studies at Minnesota 6. Minneapolis & London: U of Minnesota Press, 1994.

Hasselmann, Maryse. "Ademise et non adevise: Note sur un terme technique du droit messin présent dans la *Chronique* de Philippe de Vigneulles." *Études de langue et de littérature françaises offertes à André Lanly*. Ed. Bernard Guidot. Nancy: U de Nancy, 1980. 155–64.

Heinemann, Edward A. *L'Art métrique de la chanson de geste: Essai sur la musicalité du récit*. Geneva: Droz, 1993.

Herbin, Jean-Charles. "*Anseÿs de Gascogne* et la Flandre." *Picard d'hier et aujourd'hui*. Bien Dire et Bien Aprandre 21. Lille: Centre de Gestion et de l'Édition Scientifique, 2003. 207–228.

————. "Approches de la mise en prose de la geste *des Loherains* par Philippe de Vigneulles." *Romania* 113 (1992–95): 466–504.

————. "Géographie des chansons de geste; itinéraires de *Garin le Loherain*." *La Géographie dans les textes narratifs médiévaux*. Actes du Colloque du Centre d'Etudes Médiévales de l'U de Picardie Jules Verne. Ed. Danielle Buschinger and Wolfgang Spiewok. Greifswald: Etudes médiévales de Greifswald 62, Series 3, vol. 38: Reineke-Verlag, 1996. 59–79.

————. "L'Histoire otage des chansons de geste ou l'inverse – Le cas d'*Anseÿs de Gascogne* et de la *Vengeance Fromondin*." *Le Nord de la France entre épopée et chronique*. Arras: Artois Presses U, 2005. 239–65.

————. "Une Mise en prose de la *Geste des Loherains*: le manuscrit Arsenal 3346." *Traduction, transcription, adaptation au moyen âge*. Actes du Colloque du Centre d'études médiévales et dialectales de Lille III, septembre 1994. *Bien dire et bien aprandre* 13–14. 237–56.

————. "Notice du manuscrit *h* de la Prose des Loherains par Philippe de Vigneulles." *Romania* 117 (1999): 218–244.

————. "La 'Translation en prose' de la Geste des Loherains, par Philippe de Vigneulles: Une (Re)trouvaille." *Romania* 109 (1988): 562–65.

————. "*Yonnet de Metz.*" *Les mises en prose.* Ateliers 35. UL3 année 2006. Lille: CEGES, 2006. 31–45.

Hirchbühler, Paul. "L'Omission du sujet dans les subordonnées V1: *Les Cent Nouvelles Nouvelles* de Vigneulles et les *Cent nouvelles nouvelles* anonymes." *Travaux de linguistique*: *Revue internationale de linguistique française* 25 (1992): 25–46.

Huguet, Edmond. *Dictionnaire de la langue française du seizième siècle.* 7 vols. Paris: Champion, 1925–73.

Jakobson, Roman. "On Linguistic Aspects of Translation." *Selected Writings* II: *Word and Language.* The Hague and Paris: Mouton, 1971. 260–66.

Jahn, Karl. *Philipp de Vigneulle's Yonnet de Mes und sein Verhältnis zu Redaction N des Romans Anseïs de Mes.* Dissertation. Greifswald: H. Adler, 1903.

Janniere, Janine. "Filling in Quilt History: A Sixteenth-Century French Patchwork Banner." *Quilt Journal* 3 (1994): 1–6.

Jones, Catherine M. "Autour du 'nouveau langage': La geste des Loherains aux XVIe et XIXe siècles." *L'Épopée romane au Moyen Age et aux temps modernes.* Actes du XIVe Congrès International de la Société Rencesvals pour l'Étude des Épopées Romanes. Ed. Salvatore Luongo. Naples: Consorzio Editoriale Fridericiana, 2001. II: 693–705.

————. "The Death of Bégon Revisited." "*Por la soie amisté*": *Essays in Honor of Norris J. Lacy.* Ed. Keith Busby and Catherine M. Jones. Amsterdam: Rodopi, 2000. 235–46.

————. "Espace, temps, réécriture: La mise en prose des *Loherains* par Philippe de Vigneulles." *Les Chansons de geste.* Actes du XVIe Congrès International de la Société Rencesvals. Ed. Carlos Alvar and Juan Paredes. Granada: U de Granada, 2005. 325–35.

————. "Modernizing the Epic: Philippe de Vigneulles." *Echoes of the Epic.* Ed. David and Mary Jane Schenck. Birmingham: Summa, 1998. 115–32.

————. *The Noble Merchant: Problems of Genre and Lineage in Hervis de Mes.* North Carolina Studies in the Romance Languages and Literatures 241. Chapel Hill: U.N.C. Dept. of Romance Languages, 1993.

————. "Polyglots in the *chansons de geste.*" "*De sens rassis*": *Essays in Honor of Rupert T. Pickens.* Ed. Keith Busby, Bernard Guidot, and Logan Whalen. Amsterdam & Atlanta: Rodopi, 2005. 297–307.

————. Rev. of *Gerbert: Chanson de geste du XIIIe siècle,* Bernard Guidot, trans. Olifant 14 (1989): 212–16.

Jonin, Pierre. *Pages épiques du moyen âge français.* Paris: Société d'Édition d'Enseignement Supérieur, 1970.

Kay, Sarah. *The Chansons de geste in the Age of Romance: Political Fictions.* Oxford: Clarendon, 1995.

————. "La Représentation de la féminité dans les chansons de geste." *Charlemagne in the North: Proceedings of the Twelfth International Conference of the Société Rencesvals.* Ed. Philip E. Bennett, Anne Elizabeth Cobby, and Graham A. Runnells. London: Grant & Cutler, 1993. 223–240.

Keller, Hans-Erich. *Autour de Roland*: *Recherches sur la chanson de geste.* Paris, Geneva: Champion-Slatkine, 1989.

————. "La Chanson de geste au XVe siècle: Bilan." *Le Moyen Français* 44–45 (1999): 297–307.

————. "Facture d'une mise en prose." *Si a parlé par moult ruiste vertu: Mélanges de littérature médiévale offerts à Jean Subrenat*. Ed. Jean Dufournet. Paris: Champion, 2000. 299–311.

————. "Jehan Bagnyon, pseudo-chroniqueur du XVe siècle." *Et c'est la fin pour quoy sommes ensemble: Hommage à Jean Dufournet, professeur à la Sorbonne Nouvelle: Littérature, histoire et langue du moyen âge*. Ed. Jean-Claude Aubailly, Emmanuele Baumgartner, Francis Dubost, Liliane Dulac, Marcel Fauré, René Martin. Paris: Champion, 1993. II: 783–92.

————. "La *Mise en prose* de *Fierabras* par Jehan Bagnyon." *Romance Languages Annual* 2 (1990): 118–22.

————. "The *Mises en prose* and the Court of Burgundy." *Fifteenth-Century Studies* 10 (1984): 91–105.

————. "La Technique des mises en prose des chansons de geste." *Olifant* 17 (1992): 5–28.

Kelly, Douglas. *The Art of Medieval French Romance*. Madison: U of Wisconsin Press, 1992.

————, ed. *The Medieval Opus: Imitation, Rewriting, and Transmission in the French Tradition*. Amsterdam & Atlanta: Rodopi, 1996.

Kelly, L. G. *The True Interpreter: A History of Translation Theory and Practice in the West*. New York: St. Martin's Press, 1979.

Kotin, Armine Avakian. "Le Comique et les moralités dans les Nouvelles de Philippe de Vigneulles: Leur sens ultime." *La Nouvelle française à la Renaissance*. Ed. Lionello Sozzi and V. L. Saulnier. Geneva and Paris: Slatkine, 1981. 171–82.

————. *The Narrative Imagination: Comic Tales by Philippe de Vigneulles*. Lexington: UP of Kentucky, 1977.

Krause, Kathy M., ed. *Reassessing the Heroine in Medieval French Literature*. Gainesville: UP of Florida, 2001.

Labbé, Alain. "Itinéraire et territoire dans les chansons de geste." *Terres médiévales*. Ed. Bernard Ribémont. Paris: Klincksieck, 1993. 159–201.

————. "Sous le signe de saint Jacques: chemins et routes dans la représentation épique de l'espace." *L'Épopée romane*. Actes du XVe Congrès international Rencesvals. Civilisation médiévale 13. Poitiers: Université de Poitiers, Centre d'études supérieures de civilisation médiévale, 2002. 99–116.

Lacy, Norris J. Rev. of *Hervis de Metz*, trans. Philippe Walter. *Olifant* 11 (1986): 260–63.

LaGuardia, David. *The Iconography of Power: The French Nouvelle at the End of the Middle Ages*. Newark: U of Delaware Press; London: Associated UP, 1999.

Larsen, Anne R. "The Claim to Veracity in the Early Sixteenth-Century French *Nouvelle*: Philippe de Vigneulles and Nicolas de Troyes." *The South Central Bulletin* 40 (1980): 152–54.

————. "Comedy and Morality in Philippe de Vigneulles' Tales: The Husband as Victim and Victor." *The Language Quarterly* 20 (1982): 11–14.

Le Gentil, Pierre. "Jean Wauquelin et la légende de Girard de Roussillon." *Studi in onore di Italo Siciliano*. Biblioteca dell'Archivum Romanicum 86. Florence: Leo S. Olschki, 1966. I: 623–35.

————. "Réflexions sur la mort dans les chansons de geste." *Mélanges offerts à Rita Lejeune*. Gembloux: J. Duculot, 1969. II: 801–09.

Le Glay, Édward. *Fragments d'épopées romanes*. Paris: Techener, 1838.

Le Goff, Jacques. "Au Moyen Age: temps de l'Église et temps du marchand." *Pour un autre Moyen Age: Temps, travail, et culture en Occident*. Paris: Gallimard, 1977. 46–65.

————. "Le Temps du travail dans la 'crise' du XIVe siècle: du temps médiéval au temps moderne." *Pour un autre Moyen Age*. 66–79.

Le Moigne, François-Yves, ed. *Histoire de Metz*. Univers de la France et des pays francophones. Toulouse: Privat, 1986.

Logan, Sandra. "Making History: The Rhetorical and Historical Occasion of Elizabeth Tudor's Coronation Entry." *Journal of Medieval and Early Modern Studies* 31 (2001): 251–82.

Lorian, Alexandre. "Maniérisme et genres littéraires: À propos du style formulaire de Philippe de Vigneulles." *Revue roumaine de linguistique* 24 (1979): 83–91.

Lusignan, Serge. *Parler vulgairement: Les intellectuels et la langue française aux XIIIe et XIVe siècles*. 2nd ed. Paris: Vrin; Montréal: PU de Montréal, 1987.

Malkiel, Yakov. "Studies in Irreversible Binomials." *Lingua* 8 (1959): 113–60.

Marchello-Nizia, Christiane. *La Langue française aux XIVe et XVe siècles*. Paris: Nathan, 1997.

Marnette, Sophie. "Du décasyllabe à la prose: narrateur et point de vue dans la mise en roman du cycle épique de Guillaume." *L'Épopée romane au moyen âge et aux temps modernes*. Actes du XIVe Congrès International de la Société Rencesvals pour l'Étude des Épopées Romanes. Ed. Salvatore Luongo. Naples: Fridericiana Editrice Universitaria, 2001. II: 753–81.

————. *Narrateur et points de vue dans la littérature française médiévale: Une approche linguistique*. Bern & New York: Peter Lang, 1998.

Martin, Jean-Pierre. *Les Motifs dans la chanson de geste: Définition et utilisation*. Lille: Centre d'études médiévales et dialectales, Université de Lille III, 1992.

————. "Sur les prologues des chansons de geste: Structures rhétoriques et fonctions discursives." *Le Moyen âge* 93 (1987): 185–201.

Martineau, France. *La Montée du clitique en moyen français. Une étude de la syntaxe des constructions infinitives*. Diss. U of Ottawa 1992.

————. "Le Placement des pronoms objets dans les constructions infinitives chez Philippe de Vigneulles." *Revue québécoise de linguistique théorique et appliquée* 7 (1988): 157–73.

Mas, Jean-Pierre. "Une Étude de l'oeuvre de Vigneulles: *Journal*, tomes III et IV de la *Chronique* et *recueil de contes*." Diss. Université Blaise Pascal Clermont II, 1989.

Monfrin, Jacques. "Les Traducteurs et leur public en France au moyen âge." *Journal des Savants* (Jan.–Mar. 1964): 5–20.

Naudet, Valérie. "Une Compilation de David Aubert: *Les Histoires de Charles Martel*." *Les Manuscrits de David Aubert*. Ed. Danielle Quéruel. Cultures et civilisations médiévales 18. Paris: CNRS-Paris IV, 1999. 69–79.

Nichols, Stephen G. Jr. *Romanesque Signs: Early Medieval Narrative and Iconography*. New Haven and London: Yale UP, 1983.

Noiset, Marie-Thérèse. "La Fonction parodique des *Cent Nouvelles Nouvelles* de Philippe de Vigneulles." *Études françaises* 27 (1992): 107–16.

———. "Les Nouvelles populaires de la Renaissance: Réalisme de quelle réalité?" *Selected Proceedings of the Thirty-Ninth Annual Mountain Interstate Foreign Language Conference*. Ed. Sixto E. Torrence and Carl S. King. Clemson: Clemson UP, 1991. 147–54.

Nouvelle histoire de la langue française. Collectif dirigé par Jacques Chaurand. Paris: Seuil, 1999.

Pange, Maurice, comte de. *Les Lorrains et la France au moyen-âge*. Paris: Champion, 1914.

Paris, Paulin. *Apologie de l'école romantique*. Paris: Dentu, 1824.

———. "Étude sur les chansons de geste et sur *Garin le Loherain*." *Le Correspondant* 58 (1863): 721–50.

Parisse, Michel. "Garin le Loherain dans l'histoire de son temps." *La Geste des Lorrains*. Ed. François Suard. Littérales 10. Paris: Centre de Recherche des Littératures, Université Paris X, Branche française de la Société Rencesvals, 1992. 51–64.

Perouse, Gabriel A. "Quelques remarques sur les gens et l'argent d'après les conteurs français du XVIe siècle." *Lyon et l'Europe, hommes et sociétés: Mélanges d'histoire offerts à Richard Gascon*. Ed. Jean-Pierre Gutton. Lyon: PU de Lyon, 1980. 131–45.

Perret, Michèle. "De l'espace romanesque à la matérialité du livre. L'espace énonciatif des premiers romans en prose." *Poétique* 50 (1982): 173–82.

Pickens, Rupert T. "Marie de France Translatrix." *Le Cygne* n.s.1 (2002): 7–24.

Prost, Auguste. *Notice sur la collection des manuscrits de la Bibliothèque de Metz*. Paris: Imprimerie Nationale, 1877.

———. *Études sur l'histoire de Metz: les légendes*. 1865. Brionne: G. Monfort, diffusion le Portulan, 1972.

Puymaigre, Théodore Joseph Boudet, comte de. *Poètes et romanciers de la Lorraine*. Metz: Pallez et Rousseau, 1848.

Quéruel, Danielle. "L'Art des réécritures: de *Maugis* à *Mabrien*." *Si a parlé par moult ruiste vertu: Mélanges de littérature médiévale offerts à Jean Subrenat*. Ed. Jean Dufournet. Paris: Champion, 2000. 455–65.

———. "Des mises en prose aux romans de chevalerie dans les collections bourguignonnes." *Rhétorique et mise en prose au XVe siècle*. Actes du VIe Colloque International sur le moyen français. Ed. Sergio Cigada and Anne Slerca. Milan: Vita e Pensiero, 1991. 173–93.

———, ed. *Les manuscrits de David Aubert*. Paris: Presses de l'U de Paris-Sorbonne, 1999.

Raby, Michel. "Huon de Bordeaux: Les écarts entre la version épique (1216?) et la version en prose du quinzième siècle." *Olifant* 18 (1993): 21–83.

Rasmussen, Jens. *La Prose narrative française du XVe siècle. Étude esthétique et stylistique*. Copenhagen: Munksgaard, 1958.

Rhode, August. "Die Beziehungen zwischen des Chansons de geste *Hervis de Mes* und *Garin le Loherain*." *Ausgaben und Abhandlungen* 3 (1881): 123–76.

Ruelle, Pierre. "Le Temps, la vie, la mort dans la conception médiévale." *Bulletin de l'Académie Royale de Langue et de Littérature Françaises* 43.2 (1985): 103–21.

Rychner, Jean. *La Chanson de geste: Essai sur l'art épique des jongleurs*. Geneva: Droz, 1955.

Saulnier, V.-L. "Philippe de Vigneulles rimeur de fêtes, de saints et de prisons (avec ses poésies inédites, 1491)." *Mélanges d'histoire littéraire, de linguistique et de philologie romanes offertes à Charles Rostaing*. Ed. Jacques de Caluwe et al. Liège: Association des Romanistes de l'U de Liège, 1974. II: 965–91.

Schneider, Jean. *Lorraine et Bourgogne: 1473–1478*. Nancy: PU de Nancy, 1982.

———. *La Ville de Metz aux XIIIe et XIVe siècles*. Nancy: Imprimerie Georges Thomas, 1950.

Sneddon, Clive R. "Introduction: Translation as a Branch of Writing." *Forum for Modern Language Studies* 35 (1999): 337–38.

Somerset, Fiona and Nicholas Watson, ed. *The Vulgar Tongue: Medieval and Postmedieval Vernacularity*. University Park: The Pennsylvania State UP, 2003.

Spiegel, Gabrielle. *Romancing the Past: The Rise of Vernacular Prose Historiography in Thirteenth-Century France*. Berkeley, Los Angeles, Oxford: U of California P, 1993.

Stefenelli, Arnulf. *Der Synonymenreichtum der altfranzösischen Dichtersprache*. Vienna: H. Böhlaus, Kommissionsverlag der Österreichischen Akademie der Wissenschaften, 1967.

Straub, Richard E. F. *David Aubert, escripvain et clerc*. Faux Titre 96. Amsterdam & Atlanta: Rodopi, 1996.

Suard, François. "L'Épopée." *Grundriss der romanischen Literaturen des Mittelalters*. VIII/1: *La Littérature française aux XIVe et XVe siècles*. Heidelberg: Winter, 1988. 161–77.

———. *Guillaume d'Orange: Étude du roman en prose*. Paris: Champion, 1979.

Taylor, Andrew. "Was There a Song of Roland?" *Speculum* 76 (2001): 28–65.

Taylor, Jane H. M. "Translation as Reception: Boccaccio's *De Mulieribus Claris* and *Des cleres et nobles femmes*." *Por le soie amisté: Essays in Honor of Norris J. Lacy*. Ed. Keith Busby and Catherine M. Jones. Amsterdam & Atlanta: Rodopi, 2000. 491–507.

Tyssens, Madeleine. "Le Roman de Guillaume d'Orange: Étude d'une mise en prose." *Société Rencesvals: Proceedings of the Fifth International Conference, Oxford 1970*. Ed. G. Robertson-Mellor. Salford, Eng.: U of Salford, 1977. 45–63.

Vance, Barbara. "Null Subjects in Middle French Discourse." *Aspects of Romance Linguistics*. Ed. Claudia Parodi, Carlos Quicoli, Mario Saltarelli, and María Luisa Zubizarreta. Washington D.C.: Georgetown UP, 1996. 457–74.

Vance, Eugene. *Mervelous Signals: Poetics and Sign Theory in the Middle Ages*. Lincoln and London: U of Nebraska Press, 1986.

Venuti, Lawrence. *The Translator's Invisibility: A History of Translation*. London & New York: Routledge, 1995.

Venuti, Lawrence, ed.. *Rethinking Translation: Discourse, Subjectivity, Ideology*. London & New York: Routledge, 1992.

Woledge, Brian. *Bibliographie des romans et nouvelles en prose française antérieurs à 1500*. Publications romanes et françaises 42. Geneva: Droz, 1954.

———. *Bibliographie des romans et nouvelles en prose française antérieurs à 1500. Supplément, 1954–1973*. Publications romanes et françaises 130. Geneva: Droz, 1975.

Zink, Michel. "Le Roman." *Grundriss der romanischen Literaturen des Mittelalters*. VIII/1: *La Littérature française aux XIVe et XVe siècles*. Heidelberg: Winter, 1988. 197–218.

———. *La Subjectivité littéraire autour du siècle de Saint Louis*. Paris: PUF, 1985.

INDEX